In Darkest London

The Gothic Cityscape in Victorian Literature

Jamieson Ridenhour

THE SCARECROW PRESS, INC.
Lanham • Toronto • Plymouth, UK
2013

Published by Scarecrow Press, Inc.
A wholly owned subsidiary of The Rowman & Littlefield Publishing Group, Inc.
4501 Forbes Boulevard, Suite 200, Lanham, Maryland 20706
www.rowman.com

10 Thornbury Road, Plymouth PL6 7PP, United Kingdom

British Library Cataloguing in Publication Information Available

Library of Congress Cataloging-in-Publication Data

Ridenhour, Jamieson.
In darkest London : the gothic cityscape in Victorian literature / Jamieson Ridenhour.
p. cm.
Includes bibliographical references and index.
ISBN 978-0-8108-8777-0 (cloth : alk. paper) — ISBN 978-0-8108-8778-7 (ebook) 1. London (England)—In literature. 2. English fiction—19th century—History and criticism. 3. City and town life—England—London—History—19th century. 4. London (England)—Intellectual life. I. Title.
PR468.L65R53 2013
820.9'32421—dc23
2012041173

The paper used in this publication meets the minimum requirements of American National Standard for Information Sciences Permanence of Paper for Printed Library Materials, ANSI/NISO Z39.48-1992.

Printed in the United States of America

Contents

Acknowledgments

Portions of chapters 1 and 5 appeared in a slightly different form as "'In That Boney Light': The Bakhtinian Gothic of *Our Mutual Friend*" in the September 2005 issue of *Dickens Quarterly*. My thanks to the Dickens Society for permission to reprint those passages here.

Many people afforded me assistance in the writing of this book, both in its life as a dissertation project and later as I revised and expanded it into its present form. At the University of Mary, I want to express my deep gratitude to Peggy Zimmerman and the staff at Welder Library for transporting so many important books, newspapers, and periodicals across the frozen North Dakota plains from various points around the country. Their efforts meant I had to travel much less than I would have otherwise expected to consult the texts I needed. Thanks also to the Humanities Division's administrative assistant, Hazel Hoger, for scanning documents and being generally helpful. Especial appreciation goes to Rebecca Schneider, who provided substantial support during the final stages in the form of correspondence and proofreading.

At the University of South Carolina, I am grateful to Patrick Scott, curator of the Rare Books room at Thomas Cooper Library, for his help in searching through their collection for maps of London, and to Zella Hilton for digitizing *Bacon's Gem Map of London and Its Suburbs* for use in generating the maps in chapter 3. Also at USC, I want to thank William Thesing for encouragement in this project's beginning stages (and directing the dissertation), Frank Hardisty for advice on cartography, and Thomas Rice for inspiring the theoretical portions of chapter 4 and for talking through their implications with me. Rebecca Stern offered thoughtful feedback and advice on much of the original draft, particularly sections of chapter 5, and served as an important mentor for the project in its entirety, a relationship from which I continue to draw immeasurable benefit.

My thanks to Florian Schweitzer at the Dickens House Museum in London for his assistance in the museum's photographic archives, and to Gregory Guiliano and Elizabeth Fuller at the Rosenbach Museum and Library in Philadelphia for their help with Bram Stoker's original notes for *Dracula*. I received helpful feedback on portions of the project from attendees at the 2006 NeMLA conference in Philadelphia (especially Bill Misticelli and Jamie Jordan), the 2006 Urban Underworlds conference in Cambridge, UK (especially David Pike and Haewon Hwang), and the 2004–2005 Dickens Universe (especially Dan Shea, Sunie Fletcher, and John Jordan). The University of Indiana's Victoria listserv was invaluable for questions that needed quick answers; the collective wisdom and generosity of that group of scholars is always humbling.

I have been blessed at both UMary and USC with colleagues who are by turns generous, funny, smart, and knowledgeable. My incessant nattering about London and the Gothic was not only suffered through but aided and abetted by my fellow scholars and teachers who offered important insights and listened as I talked my way through problems of research and composition. Thanks are due to Wes Jones, Rebecca Chalmers, Wes Hellman, and Nita Ritzke at UMary and to Ed Madden, Brian Henderson, Amy Reeves, and Celeste Pottier at USC. A larger thanks is extended to Margee Husemann for providing substantive support at all stages of this project across two institutions and half the continental United States.

Most importantly, thank you to my wife, Gwyn, for repeatedly proofreading hundreds of pages of manuscript, but more importantly for living with my obsession with Gothic London for the past twelve years and remaining always intellectually and emotionally supportive.

Introduction

The City is of Night; perchance of Death,
But certainly of night; for never there
Can come the lucid morning's fragrant breath
After the dewy dawning's cold grey air;
The moon and stars may shine with scorn or pity;
The sun has never visited that city,
For it dissolveth in the daylight fair.
—James Thomson, *The City of Dreadful Night*, 1874

It is a dark, foggy night. You are alone in a narrow, cobblestoned alleyway, walking home through an unfamiliar part of the city. The gaslight streetlamps do little to cut through the fog, a London particular that burns your throat and stings your eyes. You had thought you were alone, but now you hear the echoing tap of footsteps. Who else would be out so late? You walk faster, but the footsteps seem to speed up to match your pace. Beginning to panic, you look over your shoulder and see a dark shape dimly outlined in the mist, coming closer. You stop, suddenly mesmerized. The shape behind you comes forward, stepping out of the fog. In terror, you recognize the nighttime stalker. You've seen that maniacal face, had nightmares about what he would say to you, what he would do. The thing in the fog is . . .

Well, it could be any number of things. Images of the gaslit, fog-enshrouded streets of Victorian London, and the killers and demons which haunt them, have become iconic, if not clichéd, in the signification of Gothic fiction. I began studying the urban Gothic in 2001, while beginning work on my doctoral dissertation at the University of South Carolina. But I had been fascinated by Gothic novels as a reader for years, since elementary school, in fact. As a child, I learned a love of the old Universal horror films from my mother during our weekly ritual of late-Friday night TV double features, hosted on our local television station for a time by a badly accented vampire whose stage name I've forgotten, and then later by Elvira, Mistress of the Dark. These double features usually consisted of an episode of the short-lived supernatural thriller series *Kolchak: The Night-Stalker*, followed by a full-length horror movie, more often than not one of Universal's films from the 1930s (although the occasional Val Lewton/Jacques Tourneur RKO film found its way onto the schedule). If we were lucky, the feature film would include Bela Lugosi or Boris Karloff, or both, as I found when I happily discovered *The Body-Snatcher* during one of these late-night moviefests. At eleven or twelve, I eagerly soaked in the standard details that denoted the Universal horror film—dramatic music scores, exquisite overacting, atmospheric lighting, and above all the crumbling castles and houses, the cobwebbed staircases, the deserted cobblestone streets that signified a particular type of creep factor. I still love to watch Bela Lugosi ham his way through Tod Browning's *Dracula*, even though I can now see the film for what it is: a clunker.[1]

As an avid reader, I soon learned that most of the old Universal films had origins in nineteenth-century novels. Of the standard movie monsters, only the Wolf Man had no direct fictional antecedent.[2] And so I became enamored of the source novels. At least two of these, *The Strange Case of Dr. Jekyll and Mr. Hyde* (1886) and *Dracula* (1897), were set in London and moreover depended on London for much of their narrative force. This sort of reading (and, again, old movies starring Basil Rathbone and Nigel Bruce) led me to Arthur Conan Doyle's Sherlock Holmes stories. Although Holmes and Watson spent much of their time in the English countryside, there were plenty of stories that plumbed the bowels of the city, and the detectives' home base at 221B Baker Street always featured prominently in at least the opening scene of each case.

It isn't surprising, or even particularly unusual, that I grew to understand a version of Victorian London as the mysterious fog-bound arena of fear that I describe in the opening paragraph of this introduction. Much later, when I discovered Charles Dickens, I saw a city that I recognized. Dickens's London is a clear antecedent to the city of Stevenson and Stoker, just as his Inspector Bucket is a literary precursor to Sherlock Holmes. Dickens, of course, explores a wider range of human experience than Stoker or Stevenson, but the Dickensian city is certainly the same metropolis that Edward Hyde and Count Dracula haunt.

Further exploration proved that this was not a coincidence. Dickens was simply the best-known purveyor of a response to the Victorian city that was widespread during the nineteenth century. By the time James Thomson wrote his 1874 poem *The City of Dreadful Night*, a long and dark paean to London that imagines the city as a Dantean Hell, the idea of London as a Gothic cityscape was a well-established formula familiar to contemporary readers through novels, plays, poetry, and journalism. By the end of the nineteenth century, London was both a dominant metropolis and a standard locus for narratives of terror. The Gothic novel's shift from pastoral to urban settings, which began in the late 1830s, had a profound effect on fiction throughout the rest of the century, and even in the twenty-first century Gothic novels continue to make use of the tropes established during the Victorian era. The urban Gothic is often referred to in surveys of the Gothic form, but, despite its pervasiveness few critics have focused on its distinctive characteristics, functions, and limitations, and few have provided an in-depth study.

In Darkest London is an attempt to rectify this situation. My purpose here is to define the British urban Gothic and investigate its function and practice. A cursory glance at the dates of the first urban Gothic writings, analogous to Victoria's ascension to the throne in 1837, shows us that the rise of this form parallels the rise of London as the most powerful and populous city in the world. The Victorian Gothic, a form reflective of societal anxieties of all kinds, responds to the emerging urban experience in striking and unique ways. This book will explore the reasons why mid-to-late-century writers found Victorian London such a good fit for Gothic narratives and also look at the specific ways in which the city functions in those narratives.

Of course, London during the nineteenth century was a complex, vibrant, and multifaceted city, the first true metropolis, and as such it contained within it a widely disparate array of worlds and cultures. Representations of London varied just as widely, and the Gothic cityscape is but one of the ways in which contemporary writers and commentators attempted to wrap their minds around the totality of Victorian London. But it is an important one, and one which highlights pervasive anxieties that do much to elucidate the nineteenth-century populace's relationship to the city, the empire, and one another. By focusing on the urban Gothic, I am necessarily ignoring a host of corollary urban representations. It should be remembered that urban novels by William Makepeace Thackeray, Elizabeth Gaskell, George Gissing, Amy Levy, and many others were offering differing and sometimes opposing interpretations of London concurrently with the gruesome crew here considered. The dialogue produced by these variable portraits of Victorian London is the closest we can come to a true understanding of the city. My purpose is to plumb the darker side of these representations.

In Darkest London is arranged to move from broad considerations of the Gothic as a historical mode, through the development of London and the concurrent rise of the urban Gothic, to very specific aspects of London's representation in these urban Gothic works, using recent and then-contemporary theories, close readings of relevant texts, and cartography to support and expand my ideas.

I begin by considering the definition of "Gothic" as a literary form. Critics have put forth a variety of definitions for the word during the past forty years, usually falling back on a list of conventions or recurring devices of setting and narrative. I identify, in the first chapter, a historical thematic that forms the underlying structure of the Gothic novel from its inception and then demonstrate how that idea—the tension between the past and the present—shifted through time to maintain the Gothic novel's relevance. While doing this, I will give a brief overview of the history of the Gothic novel from the 1760s to the Victorian fin de siécle, in particular focusing on London's intrusion into the standard Gothic narrative.

Chapter 2 begins a consideration of the urban Gothic proper by looking at London itself; the growth of London during the nineteenth century and its attendant ills are crucial to any understanding of why the empire's great city became an object of terror in so many late-century novels. I use a variety of eyewitness reports on conditions of the working classes in the East End and elsewhere, including those of Henry Mayhew and Frederick Engels. Additionally I look at more generalized contemporary writings about London, from tourist guides to *Punch* to sensational journalism surrounding the 1888 Whitechapel murders. This last is used to examine the connection or crossover between journalistic representations of the city and the urban Gothic novel by highlighting the furor around actor Richard Mansfield's London stage production of *Dr. Jekyll and Mr. Hyde*, which coincided with the 1888 Whitechapel murders. Mansfield's play and its attendant societal impact provide a convenient means by which to tie nonfiction accounts of the Victorian city into a general overview of the urban Gothic novel, using representative works by Robert Louis Stevenson, G. W. M. Reynolds, and Charles Dickens, the latter of whom maintained an enthrallment to London that I take a brief digression to examine more closely.

In chapter 3 I draw on Robert Mighall's idea of criminal districts of London as "vestigial stains on modernity," demonstrating these as primary manifestations of the historical Gothic. On a concrete level, London in the urban Gothic mode is perceived and represented as a city demarcated by areas of poverty and crime. Contemporary observers often relegated these "dark" areas to the East and South, offering a reassuring topography for criminal activity. The reality was much more complex, and even Gothic novels that seem to draw on this East/West dichotomy belie the simplicity of such a view. I examine how the "light" and "dark" areas of London function literally and metaphorically in *Our Mutual Friend, Little Dorrit, Picture of Dorian Gray, The Strange Case of Dr. Jekyll and Mr. Hyde, The Beetle,* and *Dracula* and then map out the narrative and character placement of those novels in an attempt to create a Gothic cartography of nineteenth-century London. The resultant maps graphically depict the overlapping of contemporary fears with literary practice, while demonstrating the fundamental instability of the West End/East End split.

Chapter 4 examines one of the most common representations of London in literature from the mid-nineteenth century onward, that of the city as a labyrinth. I explain the historical reasons (rapid growth coupled with a marked lack of urban planning and no municipal government to oversee expansion) why London is so frequently described as such, before turning to cultural theorist Michel de Certeau's essay "Walking in the City" and to the French concept of the *flâneur* as espoused by Charles Baudelaire and Walter Benjamin. I consider two ideas: the applicability of the *flâneur* (traditionally strongly connected to Paris) to Victorian London, and the ways in which the function and experience of the *flâneur* alter when placed in a Gothic milieu. As examples of Gothic *flânerie* in London, I highlight passages from Dickens's *Dombey and Son*, Arthur Machen's *The Three Impostors*, Richard Marsh's *The Beetle*, Edgar Poe's "The Man in the Crowd" (demonstrating the trans-Atlantic nature of London's Gothic image), James Thomson's *The City of Dreadful Night*, Stevenson's *Dr. Jekyll and Mr. Hyde*, and G. K. Chesterton's *The Man Who Was Thursday*. De Certeau's distinction between a cartographer or planner who has a complete understanding of a city's layout and a walker who experiences the urban landscape as he negotiates its windings is crucial to my conception of the Gothic *flâneur*.

Moving from the level of the walker on the streets down to the level of language, chapter 5 focuses on the historicity of Mikhail Bakhtin's theory of dialogism and heteroglossia and its function in understanding Victorian Gothic writing. Heteroglossia occurs in a number of ways in the Gothic mode, being most easily recognized in the epistolary elements of many of the better-known Gothic works. I expand upon Jacqueline Howard's ideas on Bakhtinian Gothic to suggest that the heteroglossia of Gothic fiction is actually constitutive of its Gothic modality. The various discourses in urban Gothic fiction utilize established Gothic set pieces and language, but more importantly they draw on the contemporary ideas about London and its dangers set out in chapter 1. After outlining the urban Gothic's Bakhtinian pedigree, I close-read passages from Dickens's *Our Mutual Friend* and Marsh's *The Beetle*, looking at both authorial narrative discourse and the speech of specific characters to underscore the ways in which language reinforces London's role as Gothic milieu.

Finally, I look into the twentieth century to briefly demonstrate the ways in which the two elements of the historical Gothic (teleological anxiety and historical specificity) continue to emerge in post-Victorian urban Gothic fiction. In the twentieth (and indeed in the twenty-first) century, the past/present tension is still very much alive in urban Gothic novels, but now it is Victorian London that has become the haunting past. I begin chapter 6 by considering the life-after-death of the Victorian city as it is played out in museums and the heritage industry. Using the knowledge of Victorian London's spectrality thus exposed, I closely examine the Gothic mode in two works from either end of the twentieth century which are steeped in the London experience: Marie Belloc Lowndes's *The Lodger* and Neil Gaiman's *Neverwhere*.

Let us begin, however, by considering the question of what defines the Gothic as a recognizable form. Before we delve any deeper, it will be helpful to clarify what constitutes the Gothic as a form, and specifically how I'll be using the term in this book. What exactly does the term mean when applied to literature?

NOTES

1. Old horror movies are not the focus of this book, and so I force myself not to wax poetic. For readers interested in a fascinating cultural reading of the twentieth-century horror film, with a particular focus on the Universal films of the 1930s, there is the well-researched and eminently readable *The Monster Show: A Cultural History of Horror*, by David Skal (New York: Norton, 1993).

2. Boris Karloff's Mummy contains elements of both Arthur Conan Doyle's short story "The Ring of Thoth" (1890) and Bram Stoker's 1903 novel *The Jewel of the Seven Stars*. Although the werewolf legend had cultural currency during the nineteenth century, there were relatively few fictional representations (with the notable exception of G. W. M. Reynolds's *Wagner the Wehr-Wolf* in 1846–1847). A case could be made that *The Wolf-Man* was influenced by Sabine Baring-Gould's *Book of Werewolves* (1865), a "nonfiction" account of eastern European superstitions, but more likely screenwriter Curt Siodmak cobbled the story together from a collective public knowledge of the werewolf tradition.

Chapter One

The Gothic Is History

And yet, unless my senses deceive me, the old centuries had, and have, powers of their own which mere "modernity" cannot kill.—Bram Stoker, *Dracula*, 1897

THE GOTHIC NOVEL

London determines the form of the nineteenth-century urban Gothic because of its cultural, financial, and physical presence on the world stage. More importantly, the conflicting aspects of the British capital—wealth, culture, and industry interwoven with filth, poverty, and crime—serve as a ready-made symbol for the tension between perceptions of the modern and the primitive.

But the journey to London took nearly a hundred years. The earliest examples of the Gothic mode in British literature—the eighteenth-century works of Hugh Walpole, Ann Radcliffe, Matthew Lewis, and others—followed what appeared to be fairly rigid rules, what twentieth-century critics would later call "Gothic conventions." One of the most reliable of these conventions was setting: first-wave Gothics occur as a rule in southern Europe, in predominantly Catholic countries such as Italy or Spain, which were far enough removed from England to house horrors that could be shuddered over with relative impunity. Added to this geographic location was the specific physical setting: a crumbling monastery, castle, or mansion, equipped with hidden passages, shadowy alcoves, and subterranean catacombs in which hapless protagonists were often lost for days. This sort of setting holds sway throughout the second half of the eighteenth century and well into the nineteenth. These stock settings and characters became vehicles for wild tales of horrific acts; Lewis's *The Monk* (1796), standing as the pinnacle of

1790s Gothic excess, contains murder, rape, and incest, and deals with the Devil, all performed in the cells and catacombs of a monastery in Madrid by Brother Ambrosio, the monk of the title. The settings and characters, however, were calculated to be removed from the British reader's life. As Howard Anderson says in his introduction to the Oxford World Classics edition of *The Monk*, "Inquisitional Spain seems too remote to be taken seriously as a setting for anything touching actual experience, whether in the eighteenth century or the twentieth."[1]

If the Gothic had remained static, if the novels of Walpole, Radcliffe, and Lewis had remained the point of departure for all subsequent practitioners of the form, it would most likely have gone the way of the powdered wig—a late eighteenth-century museum piece. But as the early popularity of the Radcliffian novel faded and the merely derivative degenerated into unintentional parody (or outright ridicule as in Jane Austen's *Northanger Abbey*, written in 1809), the Gothic began to transform. One of the most notable aspects of this transformation is a shift in geography. This geographic shift occurred in two stages: first a move from the Catholic south to England, retaining the isolated edifice and wild landscapes, and second an urbanization, lifting the mode from the rural and placing it in London.

The first half of this geographic relocation, the homegrown non-urban or pastoral Gothic, manifested itself primarily as romance and sensation fiction. Relying heavily on the Radcliffian concept of familial transgression and the isolated edifice, these novels usually presented some variation of the familiar dark, brooding, Byronic hero opposed with the young, virginal, and resourceful heroine. This form of the Gothic was perfected by Charlotte and Emily Brontë, whose mid-century work typified this use of the Gothic mode; both *Jane Eyre* (1847) and *Wuthering Heights* (also 1847) feature brooding anti-heroes Rochester and Heathcliff, wild expanses of moorland, and the imposing, haunted castle-like manor houses Thornfield and Wuthering Heights itself. Thornfield, for example, is described in Gothic terms by Jane Eyre:

> It was three stories high, of proportions not vast, though considerable: a gentleman's manor-house, not a noble-man's seat: battlements round the top gave it a picturesque look. Its grey front stood out well from the background of a rookery, whose cawing tenants were now on the wing: they flew over the lawn and grounds to alight in a great meadow, from which these were separated by a sunken fence, and where an array of mighty old thorn trees, strong, knotty, and broad as oaks, at once explained the etymology of the mansion's designation. [2]

Jane goes on to describe the nearby mountains that seem to "embrace Thornfield with a seclusion" remarkable in consideration of the house's proximity to the town of Millcote.[3]

The exterior similarities to the castles of Walpole and Radcliffe are obvious, and the interior provides more of the same—Jane finds the secluded third story of Thornfield furnished with old furniture no longer used on the lower floors: ancient chairs, bedsteads carved with cherubs, and "half-effaced embroideries, wrought by fingers that for two generations had been coffin-dust." The third story feels to Jane as if it were "a home of the past: a shrine of memory." She tells us that though the place is pleasant enough during the day she "by no means covet[s] a night's repose on one of those wide and heavy beds."[4]

Thornfield is obviously a haunted house. There is no actual ghost—*Jane Eyre* is for the most part a nonsupernatural novel—but Thornfield is no less haunted for that. The house is haunted by Rochester's past and by his hidden wife, whose low, guttural laugh can be heard echoing through the halls of the third story. Occasionally the madwoman ventures forth and attempts to burn Rochester in his bed or thrusts her hideous visage into Jane's astonished face. And these things seem at home here; Thornfield is a classic Gothic edifice. Normalcy and happiness cannot occur for Jane and Rochester until Thornfield and its cackling inmate are destroyed by fire and the action is removed to the less Radcliffian Ferndean.

This domestication of the Gothic by the Brontë sisters and others helped imbue the mode with new relevance by familiarizing its horrors; examples of this pastoral Gothic continued throughout the nineteenth century in the works of sensationalist writers such as Wilkie Collins and Mary Elizabeth Braddon (and lived on in the twentieth century in works like Daphne du Maurier's *Rebecca* and thousands of Harlequin romance novels). But the mid-nineteenth century presented new issues and anxieties that called for a further change in Gothic geography.

In the late 1830s and early 1840s novels begin appearing that bear all the hallmarks of what we now call Gothic fiction but that feature settings more immediately recognizable to the increasingly urban-dwelling nineteenth-century British readership: the streets and back alleys of London. The specific physical settings now become abandoned houses, moldering buildings, tenements, and rookeries. Charles Dickens's *Oliver Twist* (1838) and G. W. M Reynolds's interminably serialized *The Mysteries of London* (1844–1948) both use the landscape of London to tell tales not too far removed from those of Ann Radcliffe. By the end of the century, this urban Gothic had become a standard of the horror novel; indeed, the Gothic novels from 1880 onward that remain as classic or definitive in present-day minds are nearly all set in London: *The Strange Case of Dr. Jekyll and Mr. Hyde*, *The Picture of Dorian Gray*, *Dracula*. This book explores this form of the Gothic, describing its attributes and offering possible readings of its meaning and function.

GOTHIC AS HISTORY/HISTORY AS GOTHIC

But what is a "Gothic" novel? We have talked about setting, and we have alluded to fear and anxiety as elements. But beyond that, how do we define this dark fiction? In his introduction to the Blackwell *Companion to the Gothic*, David Punter says, "the notion of what constitutes Gothic writing is a contested site,"[5] and indeed the definition of the Gothic often seems as murky and unstable as many of the form's plot outlines. But for all the various and varying definitions offered by critics during the past hundred years, I believe there is a fairly straightforward answer.

The Gothic's primary characteristic is a tension between the present (i.e., the culture that produces a given work) and the past. This tension is grounded in a teleological view of history: the progressive present is haunted by the primitive past, whose presence threatens the stability of the modern situation. The reemergence of this past is the principal fear expressed by Gothic fiction, a fear that encompasses the myriad psychological, political, and other symbolic readings espoused by twentieth-century critics. Additionally, Gothic fictions, like all works of literature, are subject to reinvention by both authors and readers at different historical moments, because the various cultural forces, anxieties, and forms of discourse present in a novel are historically determined. The shifting of the form over time, coupled with the teleological anxiety of the haunting past, are the keys to the Gothic in all its forms.

The debate over Gothic fiction's definition and its place in the literary canon is nearly exclusively a product of the twentieth century. Markham Ellis reminds us that "literary criticism first located the gothic novel as a separate and discrete entity in the 1920s."[6] Ellis cites critical studies by Edith Birkhead and Montague Summers and asserts that the "rise" of the Gothic in the eighteenth century is a relatively recent invention, saying "the notion of the gothic novel (and its history) . . . was almost unknown to writers in the late eighteenth century."[7] By the late twentieth century, however, critics were expending much energy in attempts to pin down the boundaries of this nebulous form.

As stated above, a standard line of critical discourse on the Gothic concerns itself with the cataloging of "conventions," a static set of physical accoutrements, stock characters, and interchangeable plot devices that define the Gothic as a generic form. In 1939, the American writer of weird tales H. P. Lovecraft describes these conventions as

> consist[ing] first of all of the Gothic castle, with its awesome antiquity, vast distances and ramblings, deserted or ruined wings, damp corridors, unwholesome hidden catacombs, and a galaxy of ghosts and appalling legends, as a nucleus of suspense and daemonaic fright. In addition, it included the tyrannical and malevolent nobleman as villain; the saintly, long-persecuted, and generally insipid heroine who undergoes the major terrors and serves as a point of

> view and focus for the reader's sympathies; the valorous and immaculate hero; . . . and the infinite array of stage properties which includes strange lights, damp trap doors, extinguished lamps, mouldy hidden manuscripts, creaking hinges, shaking arras, and the like.[8]

Lovecraft is speaking of the early, Radcliffian Gothic, but later works also find themselves categorized in this superficial way. Jerrold Hogle, in his introduction to the *Cambridge Companion to the Gothic* written sixty years after Lovecraft's death, makes allowances for the sizable number of permutations the form has taken since Radcliffe (and indeed since Lovecraft), but he still finds it necessary to define the Gothic as a set of conventions:

> A Gothic tale usually takes place (at least some of the time) in an antiquated or seemingly antiquated space—be it a castle, a foreign palace, an abbey, a vast prison, a subterranean crypt, a graveyard, a primeval frontier or island, a large old house or theatre, an aging city or urban underworld, a decaying storehouse, factory, laboratory, public building, or some new recreation of an older venue, such as an office with old filing cabinets, an overworked spaceship, or a computer memory. Within the space, or a combination of such spaces, are hidden some secrets from the past (sometimes the recent past) that haunt the characters, psychologically, physically, or otherwise at the main time of the story.[9]

Hogle risks invalidating the idea of a Gothic defined by conventions by his broad inclusiveness. In particular, it is interesting to note Hogle's parenthetical "at least some of the time" to qualify his list, in case some Gothic work is written that completely flies in the face of his definition. He also adds an important element missing from Lovecraft's definition: the idea of the hidden secret, which is less convention than controlling narrative device, as another way of phrasing the teleological basis of the form. The secret becomes the past, threatening the here and now.

Gothic fiction absolutely uses these conventions, and critics are correct to point them out. Standard conventions are usually the first indication a reader has that the book she is reading is a Gothic novel. But, as Hogle and others have discovered in the new light cast by the increase of critical assessment of the Gothic during the twentieth century, there are deeper issues buried beneath the cobwebs and crumbling masonry. Although it is still customary to make such lists as Lovecraft and Hogle do when attempting to define the Gothic, and most discussions of the form include a consideration of its "trappings," critics of the last thirty years or so have turned to thematics and metaphors, acknowledging that the Gothic may be more than a collection of interchangeable set pieces. Let us now consider a few of these approaches.

The majority of attempts to define the Gothic during the latter half of the twentieth century have been psychological. There were earlier, nonpsychological critical considerations of the Gothic (e.g., Edith Birkhead's *The Tale of Terror* [1921], and Lovecraft, quoted above), but these often still placed the Gothic in the realm of "mere" popular fiction and denied a deeper function. Serious critical assessments, such as Devendra Varma's *The Gothic Flame* (1957), were comparatively few and did not exert a wide influence. The Gothic-as-repressed-psychosis critical tack began in 1969 with Robert Hume's "Gothic versus Romantic" in *PMLA*. Hume's article offered a "positive revaluation of the Gothic novel"[10] that stressed the "psychological interest" of the form. It was this article that opened the gates for the deluge of psychological theories during the 1970s and 1980s.

Freud is the commonly invoked deity of psychological Gothic readings. In particular, his 1919 essay "The Uncanny" has attained status as a foundational text for Gothic criticism. There are strong arguments for psychological readings of the Gothic, and the preponderance of these readings produced not a few beneficial effects. Markham Ellis writes that "the effect of psychoanalysis was to universalize the lessons of the gothic novel, oddly increasing its cultural significance and prestige by explicating its relevance and importance."[11] There are also reasons to include Freud's theories in the historicist Gothic: his own place in history and the way it haunts psychological theory are as important as the past/present dichotomy inherent in the act of psychoanalysis.

Post-Hume, a plethora of writers have offered various psychological lenses through which to read the Gothic novel, readings that privilege sexual repression, familial dysfunction, or the divided self. Writers such as Anne Williams and Alison Milbank have placed great emphasis on the division between "male Gothic" and "female Gothic," and the various characteristics and effects of each. Valdine Clements's *Return of the Repressed* (1999) offers a Jungian approach, and the various articles in the Blackwell *Companion to the Gothic* (2000) focus almost exclusively on psychological readings. Among the strongest and most flexible of these psychological theorists is Eve Kosofsky Sedgwick, who lays out her psycho-spatial model of the Gothic in this way:

> It is the position of the self to be massively blocked off from something to which it ought normally to have access. This something can be its own past, the details of its family history; it can be the free air, when the self has been literally buried alive; it can be a lover; it can be just all the circumambient life. . . . Typically, however, there is both something going on inside the isolation (the present, the continuous consciousness, the dream, the sensation itself) and something intensely relevant going on impossibly out of reach. . . . And the lengths there are to go to reintegrate the sundered elements . . . are the most characteristic energies of the Gothic.[12]

Sedgwick is typical of other critics here; the physical spaces of the Gothic function for her as metaphors for the psychologies of its protagonists. This is a useful approach, especially the emphasis on the spatial aspects of the form, but Sedgwick doesn't carry it quite far enough. Her references to the past, family histories, and the like indicate a historical characteristic to the Gothic, and the physical forms of the spatial isolation she bases her theories on are determined by specific temporal moments. Victorian London, southern Europe, Thornfield Hall—while all these settings serve as apt metaphors for the psychologies of various literary characters, their existence in the first place is determined by the particular time periods in which they occur.

All of these readings, then, point to important elements of the Gothic mode, while not completely expressing the totality of the form's function. The very fact of the Gothic's mutability indicates a historically specific determinant at work—Gothic novels change in setting, theme, and structure depending on the temporal moment that produces them. As Robert Mighall writes, "the Gothic cannot be an essence, for what is Gothicized constantly changes. This depends on how each culture chooses to represent itself, and where it locates progress and its necessary antithesis."[13] In spite of the sometimes shared concordances of Gothic conventions, it is clear that the contemporary Gothic novel (by Joyce Carol Oates or Peter Straub, for example) is clearly not the same sort of book as *The Castle of Otranto*. Anne Rice is not Ann Radcliffe, and even the late Victorian Gothics were markedly different than the eighteenth-century originators of the form, no matter how many haunted castles they had in common. The only true commonality among these disparate works is a sense of the past as threatening.

Horace Walpole—author of *The Castle of Otranto* (1764), universally recognized as the first Gothic novel—wrote in his introduction to the second edition of that book that he intended *Castle of Otranto* to "blend the two kinds of romance, the ancient and the modern."[14] Walpole defined the ancient romance as all "imagination and improbability" and the modern as works in which "nature is always intended to be . . . copied with success,"[15] effectively outlining in advance nineteenth-century debates over realism and idealism in literature. Walpole goes on to say that while the modern romance is stifled in its imaginative faculties, the older tales suffer from having "totally excluded" nature. That his novel became the model and inspiration for the first wave of Gothic horror novels in the 1790s implies a common thread among these works—they marry the fantastic and the realistic, which Walpole associates with the past and the present.

During the last decade or so, critics have increasingly given attention to historicist readings of the Gothic.[16] As an example, Robert Mighall's 1999 study, *A Geography of Victorian Gothic Fiction*, places the Gothic mode firmly in a historical context, demonstrating the origins of the term "Gothic" and then setting up the Victorian Gothic in particular as a form mediated by its relationship with the past. Mighall describes Gothic criticism as having a "pull to interiority" which has ignored the mode's fundamental grounding in the historical past,[17] in the external cultural forces that shape literature and life. "The Gothic," Mighall tells us, "dwells in the historical past, or identifies 'pastness' in the present, to reinforce a distance between the enlightened now and the repressive or misguided then."[18]

As Mighall suggests, the Gothic's emphasis on ancient curses, usurped family titles, and medieval architecture are all manifestations of a preoccupation with history as something to be frightened of, even if the fright is often tempered with fascination. The physical settings, whether in Spain or Italy in the eighteenth-century novels or in the decayed criminal precincts of the city in late nineteenth-century works, are evocative of what has been—of national, individual, and cultural histories. The Gothic edifice, always huge and crumbling, is the physical metaphor of both the rotten inner self of the villain and a decayed and imposing history. Anxiety over the past and its often terrifying eruption into the present are the true hallmarks of the Gothic as a literary form, and the various psychological themes explored by earlier critics are merely manifestations of this fear, metaphors for this dichotomy. In a Gothic novel, the threatening past is used as a foil for the more enlightened present, reassuring modern readers of a historical telos of which they are the ultimate beneficiaries while simultaneously threatening the overthrow of that progressive paradigm.

Reading the Gothic through this historicist lens opens up both interpretive possibilities and the applicability of the form to a wider variety of experiences. In Victorian Gothic fiction particularly, repressed sexuality may be productively read as a marker of a deeper fear of the primitive (or the uncivilized past). Contemporary anxiety over degeneration (codified in Max Nordau's famous treatise) and the Gothics inspired by it (such as *The Strange Case of Dr. Jekyll and Mr. Hyde* and *The Island of Dr. Moreau*) are another form of this fear. If Darwin teaches that we have evolved from a primitive time in which we were, as a species, Other, then the re-emergence of that past is most certainly something to be dreaded. Indeed, all "Otherings" are subsumed under this teleological heading; the society which produces a work of Gothic fiction sees itself as the positive end of a trajectory of enlightenment and modernity, and anything that differs from that society (or nationality or ethnicity, etc.) as the primitive Other.

Even readings that foreground familial dysfunction (such as Margot Backus's work on the Anglo-Irish Gothic) function within this model; repressed and/or overcome traumas within the past of a single lifetime are metaphorized into the specters and castles of the Gothic. The resulting narrative of trauma is itself a microcosmic teleology of history—the healthy present is created through the healing/exorcising of the damaging and damaged past. By foregrounding the historical sources of political and sexual anxieties, historicist readings do not preclude or supersede earlier psychological readings, but rather encompass them.

One of the side effects of this controlling historicism on traditional attitudes toward the Gothic is an expansion of the Gothic canon. The implications of a historicist reading are such that supernatural elements, for instance, are no longer prerequisites for the Gothic mode to occur, nor are old castles or corrupt noblemen. Importantly, we find that the Gothic is not a genre, in the sense of requiring conformity to a pre-existing set of conventions or formulae, but rather a mode or thematic concern. The Gothic, as Mighall states, "is a process, not an essence. . . . Epochs, institutions, places, and people are gothicized, have the Gothic thrust upon them."[19] Thus preoccupation with the past's effects on the present reveal a work like Iris Murdoch's *A Word Child* to be as much a Gothic novel as *The Monk* (albeit better written), and some critical work has been done toward planting a Gothic flag even in works firmly within the nineteenth-century realist movement.[20] Conversely, some novels accepted as cornerstones of the Gothic canon are excluded in an historicist revision of the mode: Mary Shelley's *Frankenstein* springs to mind as a novel that, because of its evocation of fear of the *future* and its critique of modernity, is more closely allied to science fiction than to the Gothic.[21]

The Urban Gothic

A brief look at any of the established examples of the mode demonstrates the Gothic's primary narrative as the story of the ignorant, violent past being subdued and banished by modernity. In *Dracula*, as many critics have commented, Bram Stoker goes to great lengths to include every modern convenience the late nineteenth century has to offer: shorthand, typewriters, phonograph diaries, cameras, telegraphs.[22] As Jonathan Harker, the novel's nominal protagonist, says, these technologies represent the "nineteenth century up-to-date with a vengeance." What matters more to the story, however, is the sentence that follows Harker's often-quoted line: "And yet, unless my senses deceive me, the old centuries had, and have, powers of their own which mere 'modernity' cannot kill."[23] Or, as Cannon Schmitt tells us,

> even as Britain appears to move further away from the feudal and the feral along the path toward modernity and rationality, *Dracula* insists (the Gothic insists) such otherness remains or returns: in out-of-the-way corners of London, in legacies, in the blood.[24]

Dracula himself is, of course, the manifestation of these "old centuries" in the novel—he is the past that requires the combined force of all the modern philosophy, science, and gadgets of Van Helsing's crew to be repressed. His slim, black figure may encompass myriad elements—Irish rebellion, Anglo-Irish anxieties, British imperialist guilt, repressed sexuality, and deviance of all kinds[25] —but he is most terrifying because he chooses to erupt in London, the pinnacle of modernity in the 1890s. That is the crux of this study. The middle-class reader in the Victorian era had learned through experience and training to find elements of fear in the great metropolis, and this fear informed Victorian representations of the city.

The British urban Gothic novel was sixty years old by the time Stoker published *Dracula* in 1897. At least, the main elements that seem recurrent in the form were all in place in Charles Dickens's second novel, *Oliver Twist*, which was serialized from February 1837 until April 1839. If, as some critics argue, *Oliver Twist* could be considered the first Victorian novel,[26] then we see that the city as a source of fear is inherent in Victorian literature from its very beginnings.

Oliver Twist is in the Gothic mode for several reasons. The past haunts the narrative in the form of Monks and his secret, for example, but, as we will see in chapter 2, it is in the setting, the evocation of a particular vision of London, that *Oliver Twist* truly finds ties to earlier terror literature. This distinction is important, yet the urban Gothic consists of more than just the transplanting of eighteenth-century Gothicisms into nineteenth-century London. As Robert Mighall points out, urban Gothic is "not just a Gothic in the city, it is a Gothic *of* the city. Its terrors derive from situations peculiar to, and firmly located within, the urban experience."[27] In these novels, the cityscape replaces the classic Gothic edifice, or rather multiplies it—London is the home of innumerable edifices, each capable of evoking the atmosphere of isolation and decay required for a true haunted castle. This point is explicit in a later Dickens novel, the highly Gothic *Little Dorrit* (1857), a novel that can be viewed as representative of the ways in which earlier Gothic tropes are translated in the urban Gothic form.

Little Dorrit's credibility as a Gothic work has been documented by David Jarrett in his 1977 article "The Fall of the House of Clennam." Jarrett focuses his observations on the novel's Clennam/Flintwich/Rigaud plot and the conventions it employs: the "dream" sequences of Affery Flintwinch, the imposing edifice of Mrs. Clennam's house, the actual doubling of Flintwinch and his brother, and most importantly the secret of Arthur Clennam's parentage and the codicil involving Little Dorrit, all of which are revealed by the document in the iron box. The lurid tale of Arthur's true mother and the suppression of the codicil contains deceit, a child born out of wedlock, a usurped fortune, insanity, and death—a true Gothic plot.

The Clennam house is a classic Gothic edifice which, as Jarrett points out, collapses into itself at the end of the novel much as Poe's House of Usher does at the end of its story and the Castle of Otranto at the end of Walpole's novel. We see the Clennam House for the first time when Arthur returns to his boyhood home after twenty years in China:

> An old brick house, so dingy as to be all but black, standing by itself within a gateway. Before it, a square courtyard where a shrub or two and a patch of grass were as rank (which is saying much) as the iron railings enclosing them were rusty; behind it, a jumble of roots. . . . Many years ago, it had had it in its mind to slide down sideways; it had been propped up, however, and was leaning on some half-dozen gigantic crutches: which gymnasium for the neighbouring cats, weather-stained, smoke-blackened, and overgrown with weeds, appeared in these latter days to be no very sure reliance.[28]

Once inside the Clennam house, we find it to be always darkened and possessed of enough sets of winding stairs, dusty and disused rooms, and haunted and haunting inmates to make one of Ann Radcliffe's mad clerics feel at home. Arthur can only spend one night here, where his austere and crippled mother sits on a "black bier-like sofa" propped on a "black bolster like a block at a state execution"[29] before he understandably decamps to lodgings in Covent Garden.

Little Dorrit also contains a second edifice, the Marshalsea Debtor's Prison where Edward Dorrit lives, attended by his daughter. The Marshalsea's role as a Gothic castle is reflected in its claustrophobic description at the beginning of chapter 6: "it was an oblong pile of barrack building, partitioned into squalid houses standing back to back, so that that there were no back rooms; environed by a narrow paved yard, hemmed in by high walls duly spiked at the top."[30] It is out of this confined greystone dungeon that Little Dorrit travels each day to work in the confined wooden dungeon of the Clennam house. In between she is in London.

Nancy Aycock Metz points out that the London of *Little Dorrit* is different from the London of Dickens's other novels because of its focus on the past. "*Little Dorrit*," she says, "lingers over the traces of a London that seems at times more ruin than real."[31] This extensive focus on the city as ruin, emphasized repeatedly throughout the novel, suggests another reading of London—the city itself as a vast Gothic edifice, encompassing within its environs millions of secrets, millions of decayed and dangerous pasts waiting to blossom into story.

The isolation and decay associated with the classic edifice is present even within the crowded streets of London. In contrast to Dickens's other novels, Metz explains, where the insistent crowd is the hallmark of the city, *Little Dorrit* features repeated instances of empty streets and deserted areas, and each instance reinforces the image of London as a ruin. A case in point is Arthur's return to London in chapter 3, where we find him walking toward his mother's house on a Sunday evening, "passing silent warehouses and wharves, and here and there a narrow alley leading to the river, where a wretched little bill FOUND DROWNED, was weeping on the wet wall."[32] Or, later, when Little Dorrit and Maggy are locked out of the Marshalsea and spend the night walking the streets:

> Three o'clock, and half-past three, and they had passed over London Bridge. They had heard the rush of the tide against obstacles; and looked down, awed, through the dark vapor on the river; had seen little spots of lighted water where the bridge lamps were reflected, shining like demon eyes, with a terrible fascination in them for guilt and misery. They had shrunk past homeless people, lying coiled up in nooks. They had run from drunkards. They had started from slinking men, whistling and signing to one another at bye corners, or running away at full speed.[33]

Other scenes drive the idea home: Arthur looking out of his window at the forest-like rows of chimney stacks; Little Dorrit's meetings on the Iron Bridge with Chivery and Clennam; Arthur's eavesdropping on Tattycoram, Miss Wade, and Rigaud in the Adelphi; Affery and Jeremiah coming upon Rigaud outside Mrs. Clennam's house—each of these incidents gives the reader an image of isolation within a great ruin of a city, and many describe a sense of anxiety in the characters wandering through these deserted streets.

In these scenes, London does more than provide a backdrop for plot development. The events of *Little Dorrit*, especially the first book, could no more take place outside of London than could *The Strange Case of Dr. Jekyll and Mr. Hyde*. The city is integral to the situations played out within it. This is true on the literal level—the Marshalsea is a distinctly urban phenomenon—and on the metaphorical. Just as the traditional Gothic edifice is a projection of the ruined inner self of the villain, so London in its urban Gothic mode is a projection of all manner of societal and personal ills, not the least of which is the familial wrong that Arthur Clennam feels must be righted. The secrets upon which many Gothic plots hinge are, in the urban Gothic, analogous to the hidden areas of London society—the prostitute encountered by Little Dorrit and Maggy, the inhabitants of Bleeding Heart Yard who are squeezed dry by Casby's greed, the debtors who live in the Marshalsea. All of these are encompassed and reflected in the deserted churches, crumbling houses, and labyrinthine streets of *Little Dorrit*'s London.

Of course, this brief analysis only prods at the surface of a deep metropolitan tarn, pointing out superficial similarities between the crumbling edifices of eighteenth-century Gothic novels and the dusty houses and prisons of Dickens's London. In the urban Gothic novel, London becomes more than just a convenient stage set; the topography of the city, the experience of walking its streets, even the language various writers used to represent these events contribute to the creation of a Gothic identity that became one of the dominant images of nineteenth-century London. The rest of this book unpacks the urban Gothic, diagramming the various ways London and its representations informed Victorian terror literature and (in some instances) vice versa.

We begin, however, with the question "why London?" as any understanding of the reasons and function of the urban Gothic must be founded on a knowledge of the city itself. Let us now turn our attention to that "infernal wen" and discover how the reality of Victorian London lent itself to the tale of horror.

NOTES

1. Howard Anderson, introduction to *The Monk*, by Matthew Lewis (Oxford: Oxford University Press, 1980), vii.
2. Charlotte Brontë, *Jane Eyre*, ed. Richard Dunn, Norton Critical Edition (1847; New York: Norton, 2001), 84.
3. Brontë, *Jane Eyre,* 84.
4. Brontë, *Jane Eyre,* 90.
5. David Punter, ed., *A Companion to the Gothic* (Oxford: Blackwell, 2000), vii.
6. Markham Ellis, *The History of Gothic Fiction* (Edinburgh: Edinburgh University Press, 2000), 12.
7. Ellis, *The History of Gothic Fiction,* 12.
8. H. P. Lovecraft, *Supernatural Horror in Literature* (1939; New York: Dover, 1973), 24–25.
9. Jerrold E. Hogle, ed., *The Cambridge Companion to Gothic Fiction* (Cambridge: Cambridge University Press, 2002), 2.
10. Jacqueline Howard, *Reading Gothic Fiction: A Bakhtinian Approach* (Oxford: Clarendon Press, 1994), 18.
11. Ellis, *The History of Gothic Fiction,* 13.
12. Eve Kosofsky Sedgwick, *The Coherence of Gothic Conventions* (New York: Methuen, 1986), 12–13.
13. Robert Mighall, *A Geography of Victorian Gothic Fiction: Mapping History's Nightmares* (Oxford: Oxford University Press, 1999), 286.
14. Horace Walpole, *The Castle of Otranto* (1764; New York: Collier Books, 1963), 19.
15. Walpole, *The Castle of Otranto,* 19.
16. Most critics also consider the historical context of *their own writings*. Much as I've done here, it is customary for Gothic theorists to begin by recounting preceding ideas (see also note 17 below).
17. Mighall turns this idea to clever use by demonstrating how the Gothic fear of the past is manifested in Gothic criticism itself, a critical body he maintains is governed by an anxiety over what has come before and a need to prove its own enlightenment. Thus every Gothic critic becomes a Gothic writer as well.
18. Mighall, *A Geography of Victorian Gothic Fiction,* xviii.
19. Mighall, *A Geography of Victorian Gothic Fiction,* xviii.
20. A recent example is Peter K. Garrett, *Gothic Reflections: Narrative Force in Nineteenth-Century Fiction* (Ithaca, NY: Cornell University Press, 2003). Garrett spends a chapter apiece exploring the Gothic impulse in George Eliot and Henry James, among others. Using works not usually considered Gothic (*Daniel Deronda* and "The Beast in the Jungle"), Garrett demonstrates affinities between these writers and the aesthetics of Edgar Allan Poe.
21. This focus necessitates another critical adjustment in regard to the often-made assumption that the Gothic is at heart a "subversive" form. As some critics have realized, the usual re-establishment of paradigmatical order at the end of a Gothic novel (at least in those prior to the second half of the twentieth century) indicates not only that the Gothic mode is not subversive but also that it could actually be described as reactionary. But even this easy definition is complicated by Bakhtinian dialogics, which foreground ongoing conversations between discourses and therefore a lack of resolution. See chapter 5.

22. Kathleen Spencer defines the urban Gothic by this focus on scientific and technological advances. In two articles ("Purity and Danger: *Dracula*, the Urban Gothic, and the Late Victorian Degeneracy Crisis," *ELH* 59, no. 1 [Spring 1992]: 197–225, and "Victorian Urban Gothic: The First Modern Fantastic Literature," *Intersections: Fantasy and Science Fiction,* ed. George E. Slusser and Eric S. Rabkin [Carbondale: Southern Illinois University Press, 1987], 87–96), Spencer locates the urban Gothic within Zgorzelski's theory of the fantastic; a fantastic element enters into a real world model and produces terror, wonder, or awe in the characters who experience it. She identifies "thematization of the mystery plot" ("Urban Gothic," 92) and a "concern with contemporary science" (93) as markers for the urban Gothic as a form, going on to cite "mad scientist" narratives such as Jekyll and Hyde as examples.

23. Bram Stoker, *Dracula*, ed. Nina Auerbach and David J. Skal, Norton Critical Edition (1897; New York: Norton, 1997), 40–41.

24. Cannon Schmitt, "The Gothic Romance in the Victorian Period," *The Blackwell Companion to the Victorian Novel*, ed. Patrick Brantlinger and William Thesing (Villston, VT: Blackwell, 2002).

25. Dracula also represents the contemporary fears of degeneracy mentioned above. For a complete discussion of this particular anxiety in Stoker's novel, see Kathleen Spencer, "Purity and Danger: *Dracula*, the Urban Gothic, and the Late Victorian Degeneracy Crisis," *ELH* 59, no. 1 (Spring 1992): 197–225.

26. For example, Paul Schlike in his entry on *Oliver Twist* in the *Oxford Reader's Companion to Dickens*. Victoria took the throne on June 20, 1837, the month that chapter 8 of *Oliver Twist* appeared in *Bentley's*. The novel's temporal placement combined with its social reform agenda and self-professed attempt at gritty realism herald the great Victorian novels to come.

27. Mighall, *A Geography of Victorian Gothic Fiction,* 30.

28. Charles Dickens, *Little Dorrit*, ed. John Holloway (1857; Harmondsworth, England: Penguin, 1967), 78.

29. Dickens, *Little Dorrit*, 78.

30. Dickens, *Little Dorrit*, 97.

31. Nancy Aycock Metz, "*Little Dorrit*'s London: Babylon Revisited," *Victorian Studies* 33, no. 3 (Spring 1990): 465.

32. Dickens, *Little Dorrit,* 70.

33. Dickens, *Little Dorrit,* 217.

Chapter Two

"Darkness Enough"

The Gothicity of Victorian London

Then the vision of an enormous town presented itself, of a monstrous town more populous than some continents and in its man-made might as if indifferent to heaven's frowns and smiles; a cruel devourer of the world's light. There was room enough there to place any story, depth enough for any passion, variety enough there for any setting, darkness enough to bury five millions of lives.—Joseph Conrad, Author's Note to *The Secret Agent*, 1920

During the reign of Queen Victoria, London was the greatest city in the world. This statement is hyperbolic only so far as the city itself was hyperbole—London was the wealthiest, most populous, and physically largest urban center, as well as being arguably the most influential commercially and culturally. The British empire was the most extensive and powerful in existence, and London was the jewel in its crown. The city's centrality to nineteenth-century civilization can be gauged by considering the creation of the prime meridian in 1884, placing London (specifically Greenwich) as the principal reference point of time and space worldwide. London was truly the center of the empire—commerce, culture, industry, society, and government all had their place of origin there; as a hub for innovations in science, industry, and social welfare, London sat on the cutting edge of technology and progress. And as with any city of such expansiveness, London also had its problems: poverty, disease, and crime were as evident in the capital as prosperity, growth, and progressivism.

This dichotomy, and the extremes to which each side could rise or sink, made London a source of anxiety and ambivalence for its residents, as well as for journalists, poets, and writers of fiction. Victorian Londoners, Anne Humpherys tells us, "were fascinated and intermittently horrified by their developing urbanization,"[1] and the urban Gothic novel arose partially as an acknowledgement of the disquiet caused by attempts to reconcile the two responses.

MODERN BABYLON

Joseph Conrad, explaining his decision to use London as the setting for his 1907 novel *The Secret Agent*, instinctively felt the darker side of the great city. Writing at the far end of the long Victorian period, Conrad calls the city a "cruel devourer" and feels it has "darkness enough to bury five millions of lives."[2] But he also chooses other adjectives for it: London is "enormous," "monstrous," with "room enough" for any sort of narrative imaginable. There is, he says, "depth" and "variety" in this city "more populous than some continents."

Conrad's observations are obvious, perhaps. But, especially during the Victorian era and the city's meteoric ascendancy, simply saying London is large, even huge, does not completely encompass the reality of the "infernal wen," as William Cobbett dubbed the metropolis, or the impression it made on visitors and residents alike. Writers of all types working in every genre felt compelled to comment on the impact of the city's size and diversity. London's expansion during the 1800s was unequaled, even in an era when urban growth was escalating exponentially around the globe.

Charting the population increase alone is suggestive: London had just over 900,000 inhabitants at the turn of the nineteenth century; one hundred years later, that number was closer to seven million. None of the other large industrial towns in England could boast even one million (Manchester, the next largest urban center in England, had only a little over 700,000). In his *British Novelists and Their Styles* (1859), David Masson writes of the growing city:

> As the greatest aggregate of human beings on the face of the earth, a population of several millions crushed together in one dense mass on a space of a few square miles—this mass consisting, for the most part of Englishmen, but containing also as many Scotchmen as there are in Edinburgh, as many Irishmen as there are in Dublin, and a perfect Polyglot of other nations in addition—London is as good an epitome of the world as anywhere exists, presenting all those phenomena of interest, whether serious or humorous, which result from great numbers, heterogeneousness of composition, and close social packing; besides which, as metropolis of the British Empire, it is the centre whither all the sensations of the Empire tend, and whence the motive currents issue that thrill to the extremities. If any city could generate and sustain a species of Novel entirely out of its own resources, it might surely be London; nor would ten thousand novels exhaust it.[3]

Historian Roy Porter provides the startling information that London's population "far exceeded Switzerland and Australia; it had twice the numbers of Norway or Greece."[4] By 1870, "every eight minutes, of every day of every year, someone died in London; every five minutes, someone was born."[5] These numbers were substantially augmented by the influx of immigrants from all corners of the vast British empire, many of whom were drawn by the hopeful glimmer of prosperity in the metropolis.

In response to the increase in population, London itself expanded. Outlying areas and smaller townships were absorbed into the spreading mass of greater London, which extended around the square mile of the original City for miles (see fig. 2.1). Bacon's 1888 Ordnance Map of London shows the city encompassing an area roughly 12 by 16 miles. Baedeker's *London and its Environs* for the year 1900, stricter in what it considers to be within the bounds of the city, gives these figures:

Figure 2.1. "Bird's-eye View of London As Seen From a Balloon, 1884" by W. L. Wylie and W. H. Brewer. Looking roughly east across the Houses of Parliament in the foreground, we can see London stretching away to the horizon. The amount of smoke and fog is especially notable, both floating up in single wisps from houses and factories and also hanging in huge clouds over the city. Guildhall Library, City of London.

> [London] has doubled in size within the last half-century, being now, from Stratford and Blackwall on the E. to Kew Bridge and Acton on the W., 14 M. in length, and, from Clapham and Herne Hill on the S. to Hornsey and Highgate on the N., 8 M. in breadth, while it covers an area of 122 square miles. This area is, at a rough estimate, occupied by 8000 streets, which if laid end to end would form a line of 3000 M. long. The 600,000 buildings of this gigantic city include 1500 churches of various denominations, 7500 public houses, 1700 coffeehouses, and 500 hotels and inns. The Metropolitan and City Police District, which extends 12-15 M. in every direction from Charing Cross, embraces an area of 690 sq. M., with 7000 miles of streets and roads and 900,000 inhabited houses.[6]

Henry Mayhew, journalist and social writer, went up in a balloon to take it all in. Writing in the *Illustrated London News* on September 18, 1852, he admitted that

> it was impossible to tell where the monster city began or ended, for the buildings stretched not only to the horizon on either side, but far away into the distance, where, owing to the coming shades of evening and the dense fumes from the million chimneys, the town seemed to blend into the sky, so that there was no distinguishing earth from heaven.[7]

Similarly, Frederick Engels writes in *The Condition of the Working Class in England* (1845) that a place like London, "where a man may wander for hours together without reaching the beginning of the end, without meeting the slightest hint which could lead to the inference that there is open country within reach, is a strange thing."[8]

Other commentators felt the "strange thing" as well—anxiety was a common response. W. Cooke Taylor, writing about the large industrial cities of the north of England, expressed the feeling that he could not "contemplate these 'crowded hives' without feelings of anxiety and apprehension almost amounting to dismay,"[9] and London contained several times the numbers of inhabitants as Blackpool or Manchester. Henry James wrote to his sister in 1869 that he had "been crushed under a sense of the sheer magnitude of London—its inconceivable immensity—in such a way as to paralyse my mind."[10] London had become a staggering phenomenon—not just the largest city in the world but the largest city in history, or, as Peter Ackroyd calls it, "the climax, or the epitome, of all previous imperialist cities"[11]

The advent of the railway (the first station in the capital was London Bridge, which opened in 1836) helped tie the jumble together, although the building of tracks and terminals disrupted life and demolished housing in many areas. Dickens famously described the effect of the coming of the railway to a London suburb in *Dombey and Son* (1848):

> The first shock of a great earthquake had, just at that period, rent the whole neighborhood to its centre. Traces of its course were visible on every side. Houses were knocked down; streets broken through and stopped; deep pits and trenches dug in the ground; enormous heaps of earth and clay thrown up; buildings that were undermined and shaking, propped up by great beams of wood.[12]

Here "progress" causes as much destruction and chaos as it is supposed to create convenience and order. Five years later, however, Dickens writes of a train journey from London Bridge station to Paris in an article in *Household Words* entitled "A Flight":

> What has the South Eastern done with all the horrible little villages we used to pass through in the *Diligence*? What have they done with all the summer dust, with all the winter mud . . . with all the beggars?[13]

Dickens here imagines that the railway has somehow magically erased all the inconveniences and ugliness of the older methods of travel, leaving only the pleasant accoutrements of the trip, the "dreamy pleasure in this flying."[14] This indecisive attitude toward railway travel, astonishment at the marvellous innovation and concern over the cultural cost, is typical of Dickens, but it is also a fair summation of the ambivalence inspired by Victorian London in residents and commentators alike.

The railway also assisted in the rise of a commuter class, which in turn affected conditions in the city. Prosperous Londoners moving to the growing suburbs left behind aging buildings that were quickly taken over by the needy houseless; the resultant "rookeries" became notorious for housing tens of thousands of London's poor in conditions that Andrew Mearns, writing in *The Bitter Cry of Outcast London* (1883), likened to those of the hold of a slave ship;[15] there are reports of as many as seventeen living in a single room,[16] though the average number was between five and seven.[17] Fredrick Engels describes one of the most notorious of these rookeries, St. Giles near New Oxford Street:

> The houses are occupied cellar to garrett, filthy within and without, and their appearance is such that no human being could possibly wish to live in them. But all this is nothing in comparison with the dwellings in the narrow courts and alleys between the streets, entered by covered passages between the houses, in which the filth and tottering ruin surpass all description. Scarcely a whole window-pane can be found, the walls are crumbling, doorposts and window-frames loose and broken, doors of old boards nailed together, or altogether wanting in this thieves' quarter, where no doors are needed, there being nothing to steal. Heaps of garbage and ashes lie in all directions, and the foul liquids emptied before the doors gather in stinking pools. Here live the poorest of the poor. . . . Nor is St. Giles the only London slum.[18]

St. Giles was "penetrated by a couple of broad streets"[19] soon after this 1845 description was written, but, as Engels says, it was only the most infamous of a widespread phenomenon. In 1847, twenty-seven houses on Church Lane in Westminster housed 1,095 people. Fifty-four people, most likely all inhabitants of the same house, signed an open letter to the *Times* in July 1849:

> Sur,
> May we beg and beseech your proteckshion and power. We are Sur, as it may be, living in a Wilderniss, so far as the rest of London knows anything of us, or as rich and great people care about. We live in muck and filthe. We aint got no privez, no dust bins, no drains, no water splies, and no drain or suer in the whole place. The Suer Company, in Greek Street, Soho Square, all great, rich and powerfool men, take no notice watsomedever of our complaints. The Stenche of a Gully-hole is disgustin. We al of us suffer, and numbers are ill, and if the Colera comes Lord help us.[20]

It is more than possible that this letter is itself a social commentary, a fictional construct meant to raise awareness of urban social issues—the too convenient misspelling "powerfool" seems to suggest this possibility. But it speaks of reality, and whether its author is a clever crusader for reform or the deprived collective the document claims, the conditions described certainly existed.

And the cholera did come—major outbreaks of the deadly disease occurred four times during the nineteenth century: in 1831, 1848–1849, 1854, and 1866. During the 1866 epidemic, over 5,000 people died in a period of three weeks; a 50 percent mortality rate was the norm.

Disease was partially caused by pollution, which was the natural byproduct of the industrialization that helped make London prosperous and the rapid growth that resulted from that prosperity. Due to the lack of proper sanitary conditions, or of any reliable method of waste removal or containment, disease in the poorer areas was widespread and deadly. The crowded conditions spawned epidemics whenever contagious disease occurred, so naturally the poor suffered from communicable disease on a much greater scale than the middle and upper classes—not only the terrifying scourge of cholera but the more common and ongoing scarlet fever, smallpox, whooping cough, and a host of other contagions, venereal and otherwise. In economically depressed areas of the city, "over a third of institutionalized paupers became infirmary patients"[21]

Cholera, brought in from India through trade routes, was spread through the water supply, itself contaminated by the huge amounts of garbage and raw sewage being dumped directly into the Thames, from which most of the private water companies pulled their supply. In addition to the direct spread of disease in this manner through public water pumps and so on, the miasma around the river was at times intolerable. The pollution of the Thames reached critical mass during the summer of 1858, when extremely hot and dry weather combined with the sewage in the river to produce what came to be known as the "Great Stink." The smell was so bad that the windows of the Houses of Parliament were hung with sheets soaked in chloride of lime. It was, in fact, this inconveniencing of Parliament that led to improvements—Joseph Bazalgette was charged with reforming the sewer system after the Great Stink, a task he completed in 1869.

Another side effect of pollution was the fog. The smoke from coal-burning factories and chimneys combined with London's natural propensity for mist to create the famous "London particulars" (see fig. 2.2), fogs that often turned mid-day into twilight. These fogs caused chronic health problems and not a few deaths, some through asphyxiation and some through travelers losing their way and unwittingly walking into the Thames. The fog could vary in color from yellow to brown to black (Thomas Carlyle described it as "fluid ink"); it got into houses, required gaslights to be lit at all hours of the day, and provided a cover of darkness for cut-purses, murderers, and rapists. One of the worst fogs began in November 1879 and lasted well into March 1880, and though this duration is unusually protracted, more days than not seem to have been affected by this oppressive atmosphere. In his *Saunterings in and around London* (1858), Max Schlesinger describes the London particulars:

> The winter-fogs of London are, indeed, awful. They surpass all imagining; he who never saw them, can form no idea of what they are. He who knows how powerfully they affect the minds and tempers of men, can understand the prevalence of that national disease—the spleen. In a fog, the air is hardly fit for breathing; it is grey-yellow, of a deep orange, and even black at the same time, it is moist, thick, full of bad smells, and choking. The fog appears, now and then, slowly, like a melodramatic ghost, and sometimes it sweeps over the town as the simoom over the desert. At times, it is spread with equal density over the whole of that ocean of houses; on other occasions, it meets with some invisible obstacle, and rolls itself into intensely dense masses, from which the passengers come forth in the manner of the student who came out of the cloud to astonish Dr. Faust. It is hardly necessary to mention, that the fog is worst in those parts of the town which are near the Thames.[22]

The fog, pollution, overcrowding, and cramped topography made London a dark city—dark in the physical sense, as a sensory phenomenon. Peter Ackroyd even postulates that the darkness of the city was exacerbated by the clothing of the "male Londoner, [whose garments] switched from variegated and bright colours to the solemn black of the frock coat and stove-pipe hat" as the century progressed.[23] For whatever reasons, London was a city "packed to blackness."[24]

Figure 2.2. "A Thoroughbred November and London Particular." This 1827 aquatint shows a well-dressed Londoner attempting to stave off the poisonous fog. In the background upper-class men and women are paying men with rush-lights to light their way across the street. Guildhall Library, City of London.

Attempts were made to cut through the darkness; gaslight was commonplace by the time Victoria took the throne, the last oil-lighted street moving to gas in 1842. An 1845 article in *Punch* satirically describes a group of thieves deciding to change location after gaslight is introduced into the "road they had been in the habit of frequenting." The short sketch states that the thieves find no problem getting business "the other side of Hammersmith gate," which was as yet unlighted. Though satirical, the implication is that gaslight deters crime and that universal lighting would go a long way toward eradicating thievery. But even though it was widely thought that gas lighting helped to dissuade crime, the fact is that gaslight, which "created patches of light interspersed with pools of darkness," had "the power equally to create illumination and to cast shadows."[25] And even gaslight was hard pressed to cut through a full-on London particular.

It is unsurprising that crime of all kinds flourished under these conditions: we can see that much of Victorian London consisted of crowded and inadequate housing, poverty, disease, pollution, and darkness. The rookeries housed large groups of thieves numbering into the hundreds, many of them children, who preyed upon victims in the crowded streets. These thieves were estimated by James Greenwood in his 1869 *The Seven Curses of London* to number twenty thousand. Traffic in opium occurred in Limehouse and other areas, and fraud, both financial and in the form of adulterated food and other products, was a common occurrence throughout the capital. Public concern and general need led to the creation of the Metropolitan Police Force in 1829 (housed in Whitehall Street but entered through Scotland Yard), and in 1839 the city formed its own police force to patrol the square mile of its jurisdiction. A detective department was created in 1842.

Prostitution was another widespread problem that concerned, shocked, and fascinated Victorian London. By mid-century there were an estimated 80,000 prostitutes in London, many of whom were supplementing incomes earned through work as milliners, seamstresses, laundresses, and so forth. Prostitutes were said to stand in rows like hackney cabs near the Bank of England and were even more in evidence in Haymarket and Soho. There was also a flourishing trade in child prostitutes, a business that was sensationally exposéd in 1885 as the "Maiden Tribute of Modern Babylon" by W. T. Stead in the pages of *Pall Mall* magazine. Books and articles discussed, reviled, and lamented the plague of prostitution, seen by many as a symbol of all that was wrong with society. Among these, William Acton's "Prostitution, Considered in its Moral, Social, and Sanitary Aspects" (1870) was influential, and notable for its insistence (not unique to Acton) that the male sexual urge created a need for the profession. Acton maintains that prostitution is "an inevitable attendant upon civilized, and especially closely-packed, population." This popularly held belief—that "civilized" society naturally carries with it an immoral or "uncivilized" corollary and that this savage self is exacerbated by a "closely-packed population"—dovetails neatly with the concerns of Gothic fiction.

Although London also contained areas of prosperity and wealth, cultural, spiritual, and scientific vanguards that assisted in solidifying the metropolis's status as first among cities, the public's concern with (and fear of) the depressed conditions of impoverished districts and their negative by-products spawned the urban Gothic novel as well as the Gothic-styled journalism practiced by W. T. Stead and writers like him. As Tina Choi points out, "Victorian representations of the city are almost interchangeable with, and nearly always collapse into, Victorian representations of lower-class space."[26] It is these "lower-class spaces" that form the foundation of the urban settings found in Victorian Gothic novels.

LONDON AS GOTHIC SETTING

As we can see, the tension between the past and the present is evident everywhere in London. Peter Ackroyd, perhaps the most persistent celebrant of London to emerge during the latter half of the twentieth century, reminds us in his sprawling *London: The Biography* (2001) that the nineteenth century saw a revival of Gothic architecture in the city and that, by referencing the past, this neo-Gothic movement "possessed the consolation of supposed antiquity; in a city which seemed to be careering beyond all familiar or predictable bounds, it offered the reassurance of some theoretical or presumed permanence."[27] Ackroyd also points out that the sacred imagery invoked by these neo-Gothic buildings (the Houses of Parliament, the Law Courts, and St. Pancras station among them; see fig. 2.3) contained as well an implicit reference to the historical origins of the word "Gothic"—the Goths and their barbarism. Thus, Ackroyd tells us, "the city of empire was also known as a city of savages."[28] The very architecture of the nineteenth-century city, Ackroyd implies, reflects the light/dark dichotomy of Gothic literature. It is unsurprising then that authors began to use the city as much for Gothic effect as for setting.

Although, as I suggest in chapter 1, true urban Gothic novels arose with the advent of the Victorian era, London had begun its life as a setting for dark fiction as far back as the early eighteenth century. The first-wave Gothic novels of the mid- to late 1700s consistently used southern European settings, but London featured as a dangerous place in novels like Samuel Richardson's *Clarissa* (1748), where the city becomes the site of the heroine's imprisonment and loss of innocence. Likewise, in the world of visual art, William Hogarth depicted a vice-ridden London waiting to seduce naïve young girls (as in his 1732 series *The Harlot's Progress*) or spendthrift young noblemen (as in the 1734 series *The Rake's Progress*). In his narrative series and in single works like *Southwark Fair* (1733), Hogarth presents a London peopled with crowds of grotesques and ne'er-do-wells, exerting an

Figure 2.3. St. Pancras Train Station, one of the most striking examples of nineteenth-century neo-Gothic architecture in London. Photo by Jamieson Ridenhour.

important influence on later artists and writers of the city (particularly Charles Dickens). More importantly, however, is Hogarth's use of London architecture to denote morality (or lack thereof) in his characters (see fig. 2.4). Peter Whitfield has commented that Hogarth uses "London's social topography as symbols in the journeys which his characters make through life,"[29] referring to sequences such as *A Rake's Progress*, where Tom Rakewell's descent into profligacy and madness is marked by his movements within the city. Rakewell's debt is demonstrated by his imprisonment in a debtor's prison (probably the same Marshalsea that would later figure prominently in Dickens's *Little Dorrit*), and Bedlam hospital is the primary signifier of his final madness. In Hogarth's conception, London becomes a Babylon that entraps the innocent—enticing to the uninitiated (such as Moll Hackabout in the first scene of *A Harlot's Progress*) but ultimately a place where "tragedy or retribution waits around the street corner or at the half-open door."[30]

By the early nineteenth century, London's growing size and importance guaranteed the city literary representation. Thomas De Quincey's nominally nonfiction *Confessions of an English Opium-Eater* (1821) includes, among its nightmare recountings of the horrors of opium addiction, scenes that could occur nowhere but in London: De Quincey squatting in an abandoned house, waited on by a ten-year-old homeless girl afraid of ghosts in the rat-infested dwelling; the nighttime wanderings through Soho with Ann, the good-hearted prostitute. De Quincey makes reference to the social conditions of Regency London while explaining how Ann became a streetwalker:

> The stream of London charity flows in a channel which, though deep and mighty, is yet noiseless and underground; not obvious or readily accessible to poor houseless wanderers: and it cannot be denied that the outside air and frame-work of London society is harsh, cruel, and repulsive.[31]

Elsewhere, De Quincey refers to "so mighty a world as London"[32] and calls Oxford Street a "stony hearted step-mother" who "listenest to the sighs of orphans, and drinkest the tears of children."[33]

Other popular precursors of the Victorian urban Gothic were the so-called Newgate novels of the 1830s, which glorified the lives of criminals in melodramatic narratives often derived from the popular Newgate calendars. These novels (such as William Ainsworth's *Jack Shepard* in 1839) relied occasionally on urban settings for effect, but the main image of London in those works is that of Newgate Prison itself, a Gothic edifice casting a long shadow over the lives of the villain-heroes.

There were also novels that depicted the hardships and deprivations of the poorer classes in order to bring about reform. These novels were generally melodramatic portrayals of the increasing gulf between the wealthy and the

Figure 2.4. William Hogarth's "Gin Lane," 1751. Typically for Hogarth, this depiction of a gin-soaked lower class is flush with characters and situations, rewarding careful examination. Of particular note are the brisk business being done by the pawnbroker on the left, the suicide in the upper right, and the baby toppling over the railing as its drunken mother reaches for a pinch of snuff. Guildhall Library, City of London.

indigent, showing how the cycle of poverty replicates itself and advocating the need for social improvement organizations to assuage the problem. One such was Catherine Sinclair's *London Homes* (1853), a work that self-consciously lays out its project in Sinclair's earnest preface:

> The author has received much information in respect to her suffering countrymen from the excellent Secretary to the Mendicity Society, and having also read several recent works on "The Rookeries of London;" she has been induced by that fervent desire of usefulness which is her sole motive in writing . . . her own conception of the contrast which exists at present between the two extremes of luxury and wretchedness. [34]

Sinclair, and similar writers such as Mrs. Sewell and Mrs. Craven, wrote from this sense of "usefulness" to raise consciousness of the conditions of the working poor in London and, as a sideline, to denounce the Catholicism of the Irish who were seen as the worst examples of criminal poverty—"anti-Romish fiction written by militant Protestants."[35]

All of these categories of urban novels participated in the Gothicization of London in the public's consciousness. But true British urban Gothic—fiction that used the topography and conditions of Victorian London to highlight the past/present anxiety and to elicit terror or horror in its readers—can be traced to two very different works, written by the two most popular novelists of the Victorian era: G. W. M. Reynolds's *The Mysteries of London* (1846–1848) and Charles Dickens's *Oliver Twist* (1839).

George William MacArthur Reynolds was an aspiring politician, a pro-Chartist who was elected as representative for Derby. He also edited *Reynolds's Political Instructor* and *Reynolds's Weekly Newspaper*, periodicals that "played an important part in the formation and publicizing of radical thought in England throughout the nineteenth century."[36] He is remembered today, when he is remembered at all, as a publisher and writer of inexpensive weekly serialized fiction that "exploit[ed] the new technologies of steam press, cheap paper, and national distribution through the developing railway network."[37] His works were revampings of earlier Gothics, such as *Faust: A Romance* (1846) and *Wagner the Wehr-Wolf* (1847), and of other writers' work, such as his series of novels featuring Dickens's Mr. Pickwick. But the work that made his name was among the first urban Gothics in English and was additionally the best-selling novel of the nineteenth century.[38] Like Reynolds's other novels, *The Mysteries of London* was not an idea original to the author; the novel is largely inspired by Eugene Sue's *Mysteries of Paris* (1843), an urban Gothic set in Paris.[39]

The Mysteries of London plays heavily on the contrasts of the city. The "Prologue" catalogs the plight of the poor, saying that "there are but two words known in the moral alphabet of this great city; for all virtues are summed up in the one, and all vices in the other: and those words are WEALTH | POVERTY."[40] The narrative opens with an excess of atmosphere: the heroine Eliza (disguised as a youth when we first meet her) is wandering through a dubious district in the city as a horrible storm builds and then bursts. Our heroine takes shelter in an old house that turns out to be the refuge of a band of robbers.[41] The weather, the isolation and dilapidation of both the house and its Smithfield location, and the innocent heroine threatened by banditti paint the entire scene in a Gothic light. Later, in chapter 23, the narrator again holds forth on the expansiveness and contradictions of the city: "Fair and attractive as the mighty metropolis may appear to the superficial observer, it swarms with disgusting, loathsome, and venomous objects, wearing human shapes."[42] In the same passage Reynolds contrasts the sorts of people seen at different times of the day in London, beginning with "morning, when only the industrious and the thrifty are abroad" and concluding with "night, when every lazar-house vomits forth its filth, every den lets loose its horrors, and every foul court and alley echoes to the footsteps of crime!"[43]

The exclamation point at the end of that last sentence indicates the level of melodrama to which Reynolds frequently resorts. *The Mysteries of London* introduces the breathless reader to resurrection men, thieves, murderers, fallen women, indigent girls driven to pose as artist's models,[44] mesmerists, and members of Parliament. Pure women are entrapped, the initially well-meaning poor descend into crime, and more than one character spends time in a dungeon. It is commonly accepted that Reynolds's best-known work is not high art, but it serves as an interesting transitional work between the first-wave Gothics, such as those of Ann Radcliffe, and works that more completely exploit the urban Gothic mode later in the century—Dickens's later novels such as *Bleak House*, *Little Dorrit*, and *Our Mutual Friend* and the fin de siècle Gothics such as *The Picture of Dorian Gray* (1891), *Dracula* (1897), or *The Beetle* (1897).

Mysteries of London, while having elements of the Newgate novel and the social awareness novel of the sort written by Catherine Sinclair, primarily works as an old-school Gothic because of its language and the stock situations and characters it exploits. But it is a Gothic informed by the conditions and settings of the city. Reynolds is concerned with the problems created by the city—poverty, crime, and so on—but his purpose here is to use these issues as sources of sensationalism and terror. Though Reynolds asserts, in a passage detailing the horrors of slum life in the Smithfield district, that the "wealthy classes of society are far too ready to reproach the miserable poor for things which are really misfortunes and not faults,"[45] he immediately thereafter recounts the story of Bill Bolter, whose wife is planning to put their five-year-old daughter's eyes out so she can make more money as a blind beggar. Bill murders his wife, in front of the two children, during a violent argument, and then abandons the children with the corpse of their mother when he realizes what he's done. Here, as in much of *Mysteries of*

London, Reynolds's compulsion to Gothic excess trumps his social commentary in a spectacular manner.

Oliver Twist was serialized seven years earlier than *The Mysteries of London* and as such may be the first British novel fully in the urban Gothic mode. But Dickens's novel does much more than simply transplant the diction and situations of Radcliffe and Lewis to London. As in Reynolds, there is a reformist agenda; in Dickens's preface to the 1841 edition of *Oliver Twist*, the author defends his decision to use characters "chosen from the most criminal and degraded of London's population" by saying that he "ha[s] yet to learn that a lesson of the purest good may not be drawn from the vilest evil."[46] Dickens goes on to advocate a form of urban realism, complaining that thieves and rogues in Newgate novels are always portrayed as dashing and enviable, living lives of daring resourcefulness. He purports his project in *Oliver Twist* to be the depiction of the reality of thieves and murderers, an altogether grimmer and grittier business. Dickens writes that "the stern truth . . . was part of the purpose of this book, [so] I did not . . . abate one hole in the Dodger's coat, or one scrap of curl-paper in Nancy's dishevelled hair."[47] Defending his characterization of the prostitute Nancy later in the same preface, he says:

> It is useless to discuss whether the conduct and character of the girl seems natural or unnatural, probable or improbable, right or wrong. It is *true*. Every man who has watched these melancholy shades of life, must know it to be so. From the first introduction of that poor wretch, to her laying her bloodstained head upon the robber's breast, there is not a word exaggerated or overwrought. . . . It involves the best and worst shades of our nature; much of its ugliest hues, and something of its most beautiful; it is a contradiction, an anomaly, an apparent impossibility; but it is a truth. I am glad to have had it doubted, for in that circumstance I should find it an assurance (if I wanted any) that it needed to be told.[48]

Dickens claims here to be performing a public service—raising awareness of the condition and character of the real thieves and fallen women on which he modeled his characters. By presenting the reality of the criminal world, he would "dim the false glitter surrounding something which really did exist, by showing it in its unattractive and repulsive truth."[49] And there is evidence that this was the effect of *Oliver Twist*; Dickens's popularity meant that many of the social causes he championed in his fiction rose to the forefront of the public consciousness and subsequently were addressed legislatively.

In the process of presenting these issues, however, Dickens dips into the urban Gothic mode, terrifying his readers as surely as little Oliver was terrified by Fagin, Sikes, and the awful surroundings and circumstances that come with them. The city in *Oliver Twist* is a wild landscape of shadows and menace, only slightly mitigated by the bright middle-class world of the

Brownlows. Like Hogarth, whose etchings hung in Dickens's parlor during the writing of *Oliver Twist*, Dickens repeatedly evokes the dirt and squalor of the areas of London where his criminal characters live. Here are Oliver's first impressions on approaching Fagin's den in Saffron Hill:

> A dirtier and more wretched place he had never seen. The street was very narrow and muddy; and the air was impregnated with filthy odours. There were a good many small shops; but the only stock in trade appeared to be heaps of children, who even at that time of night, were crawling in and out at the doors, or screaming from the inside. The sole places that seemed to prosper, amid the general blight of the place, were the public-houses; and in them, the lowest orders of Irish were wrangling with might and main. Covered ways and yards, which here and there diverged from the main street, disclosed little knots of houses, where drunken men and women were positively wallowing in filth; and from several of the door-ways, great ill-looking fellows were cautiously emerging: bound, to all appearance, on no very well-disposed or harmless errands.[50]

As a catalog of the dirt, poverty, and crime of the poorer districts of London, this passage is fairly inclusive. All the senses are assaulted by these squalid surroundings, and the middle-class Londoner's fear of rampant vice is reinforced by documentation of drunkenness, criminal intent, and the all-pervasive filth—a physical and metaphorical patina spread over the whole of London's dark side. The overcrowding is evident, and indeed Oliver is being taken by the Dodger to what amounts to a smallish rookery. These conditions undermine the idea of London as a cosmopolitan light of modernity, exposing a primitive underbelly beneath the light and wealth of prosperous areas.

Later in the novel, when Nancy keeps her midnight appointment with Rose Maylie and Mr. Brownlow, Dickens paints the riverside setting of London Bridge as isolated, fog-enshrouded, and dilapidated:

> A mist hung over the river, deepening the red glare of the fires that burnt upon the small craft moored off the different wharfs, and rendering darker and more indistinct the mirky buildings on the banks. The old smoke-stained storehouses on either side, rose heavy and dull from the dense mass of roofs and gables, and frowned sternly upon water too black to reflect even their lumbering shapes. The tower of old Saint Saviour's Church, and the spire of Saint Magnus, so long the giant-warders of the ancient bridge, were visible in the gloom; but the forest of shipping below bridge, and the thickly scattered spires of churches above, were nearly all hidden from sight.[51]

Again, London is a dark city, where even on an open space like London Bridge visibility is restricted, and what can be seen is "heavy," "dull," and sternly frowning. Dickens repeatedly conjures up images of meanness and darkness, accurately describing areas of London he had seen himself while a reporter writing *Sketches by Boz*.

A corollary to the new urban Gothic novels was the plethora of poems and articles in the press that utilized Gothic imagery to highlight specific urban problems. Just as writers like Dickens and, to a lesser extent, Reynolds used the language of older Gothic novels to highlight social agendas, the popularity of the new urban Gothic novels altered the ways in which the media addressed these same issues. More and more as the nineteenth century progressed, journalists used urban Gothic tropes to sensationalize commentary on disease, crime, sanitation, prostitution, and any other urban concern under consideration.

As an example, what follows are the opening stanzas of a poem bewailing miasmic smells, believed by many to be the source of infectious disease, that emanate from overcrowded city cemeteries like the one depicted in Dickens's *Bleak House* (1853). In addition to using the image of the vampire, well known to contemporary readers from John Polidori's short novel *The Vampyre* (1819) and the hugely popular penny dreadful *Varney the Vampire* (1847), this piece also attributes a creepy Gothic setting to the urban graveyard. The poem, from an 1847 issue of *Punch*, is entitled "The Vampyre (No Superstition)":

> The bloodshot moon glares on the close-crowded graves,
> Through the foul mist that over the sepulchres waves,
> On the tombs where the City, with people o'erspread,
> In the midst of the living hath buried its dead.
>
> A glimmering vapour creeps over the ground,
> You may see whence it issues—yon newly-raised mound;
> Mark what spectre ascends in that horrible light—
> Lo, the Vampyre Infection is rising to-night!
>
> The Vampyre! The Vampyre! Avoid him! His breath
> Is the reek of the charnel, the poison of death:
> He has broken his prison of pestilent clay,
> And the grave yields him up, on the living to prey.[52]

Disease, like crime, was particularly prone to Gothicization because of its invisibility and killing force, and because of the difficulty in preventing or controlling it. If the very air becomes deadly, what recourse do city-dwellers have? Crime, housing, prostitution—all of these urban issues found expression in cartoons, poetic polemic, and editorials that used the language and images of Gothic fiction to raise awareness and of course to scare readers. Eventually the Gothic impulse in London would reach a point where the excesses of these urban horror novels seemed to bleed into reality.

DR. JEKYLL AND JACK THE RIPPER

The year 1886 saw the publication of one of the Victorian era's fundamental urban Gothic narratives. Robert Louis Stevenson wrote *The Strange Case of Dr. Jekyll and Mr. Hyde*, so the famous anecdote goes, over a period of three days after having been inspired by a nightmare. His wife, Fanny, after having the novella read aloud to her, objected to it, and Stevenson burned the manuscript. He then wrote it again in another three days.[53] Published in January of 1886, *Jekyll and Hyde* was immediately successful, selling forty thousand copies by June. The novella tells its story of divided selves and violent crime in the very contemporary setting of the city, in particular evoking the "London particulars" and the light-in-darkness of the gas lamps. In the following passage, the lawyer Utterson is traveling by cab to Edward Hyde's address in Soho following Hyde's murder of Sir Danvers Carew:

> It was by this time about nine in the morning, and the first fog of the season. A great chocolate-coloured pall lowered over heaven, but the wind was continually charging and routing these embattled vapours; so that as the cab crawled from street to street, Mr. Utterson beheld a marvelous number of degrees and hues of twilight; for here it would be dark like the back-end of evening; and there would be a glow of rich, lurid brown, like the light of some strange conflagration; and here, for a moment, the fog would be quite broken up, and a haggard shaft of daylight would glance in between the swirling wreaths. The dismal quarter of Soho seen under these changing glimpses, with its muddy ways, and slatternly passengers, and its lamps, which had never been extinguished or had been kindled afresh to combat this mournful reinvasion of darkness, seemed, in the lawyer's eyes, like a district of some city in a nightmare.[54]

In this passage, Stevenson expresses his fears regarding gaslight—he called the gas lamp "a lamp for a nightmare! Such a light as . . . should shine only on murders and public crime, or along the corridors of lunatic asylums, a horror to heighten horrors."[55] The darkness of the fog is somewhat mitigated by the lights, but the overall effect is like a "city in a nightmare." Earlier in the novel an even starker evocation of gaslit chiaroscuro is given by Mr. Enfield when he describes the night he first saw Hyde:

> I was coming home from some place at the end of the world, about three o'clock of a black winter morning, and my way lay through a part of town where there was literally nothing to be seen but lamps. Street after street and all the folks asleep—street after street, all lighted up as if for a procession and all as empty as a church—till at last I got into that state of mind when a man listens and listens and begins to long for the sight of a policeman.[56]

London at night evokes thoughts of crime. *Jekyll and Hyde* is explicitly concerned with crime and criminal haunts and with a largely implied catalog of vices of which Hyde is guilty: alcohol, opium, illicit sex. The novel takes as a given the fog-bound darkness of the city. It is "the greatest novel of London fog,"[57] but it is also a novel that acknowledges London as dark, dangerous, and threatening. Jekyll's house, fronting a well-to-do square but accessed from behind through a dilapidated alleyway, is one of the most concrete examples of London topography as a metaphor both for a character and for the telos of history; Hyde is associated narratively and geographically with the criminal and poor of London, and his obvious casting as an atavistic throwback makes a strong statement about the evolutionary state of London's lower classes.[58] *The Strange Case of Dr. Jekyll and Mr. Hyde* is thus one of the quintessential urban Gothic novels, perfectly wedding the social and geographical realities of Victorian London with a series of terrifying metaphorical comments on contemporary anxieties.

Two years later, the public's anxieties reached an unprecedented fever pitch. Between August 31 and November 9, a murderer who came to be known as Jack the Ripper killed and mutilated a number of women in the Whitechapel area of East London.[59] A series of violent crimes against prostitutes in the poorest area of the great city, the Whitechapel murders encapsulated middle- and upper-class Londoners' fears of the East End and confirmed for the poorer classes what they already knew—London is a dark and deadly place.

Although murder was commonplace in the East End, and even serial murder not unheard of,[60] the ferocity of the Ripper murders coupled with the police's continuing inability to identify the killer created a terrible sensation among the public. Jack the Ripper was "probably the first [serial killer] to appear in a large metropolis at a time when the general populace had become literate and the press was a force for social change."[61] Guided by the media's presentation of the murders, public response to Jack's activities was immediate and extreme (see fig. 2.5). Letters to the *Times* offered daily advice and criticism for the Metropolitan Police Department; the papers continually ran stories of the "Whitechapel Horrors." Eventually the Ripper panic was such that a "blood lust and . . . lynching mood" prevailed: in October 1888, police chasing a small-time thief called "Squibby" through Whitechapel found themselves in the midst of a full-scale riot after an observer saw the chase and, making assumptions, shouted "Jack the Ripper! Lynch him!"[62] The public, especially East Enders, was terrified.

The *Penny Illustrated Paper*, as usual, played the events for maximum effect, accompanying the stories with lurid drawings of the murder sites and the positions of the victims. The rest of the media followed suit. In an article in the *Times* on October 1, 1888 (the morning after the so-called double event, when the killer murdered both Elizabeth Stride and Catherine Ed-

Figure 2.5. "A Suspicious Character," from the *Illustrated London News*, October 27, 1888. Members of the Vigilance Committee follow a shady-looking man in the East End passing beneath an announcement of one of the Whitechapel murders.

dowes within forty-five minutes of each other), the anonymous writer frequently lapses into melodrama:

> Shortly before 1 o'clock yesterday morning, or about three quarters of an hour after the [murder of Elizabeth Stride], it was discovered that a second woman had been horribly murdered and mutilated, this being in Mitre-square, Aldgate, within the City boundaries, but on the confines of the now notorious district. It appears that Police Constable Watkins (No. 881), of the City Police, was going round his beat when, turning his lantern upon the darkest corner of Mitre-square, he saw the body of a woman, apparently lifeless, in a pool of blood. . . . The scene then disclosed was a most horrible one. The woman, who was apparently about 40 years of age, was lying on her back quite dead, although the body was still warm. Following the plan in the Whitechapel murders, the

> miscreant was not content with merely killing his victim, but had dreadfully mutilated her.[63]

The descriptive modifiers in this article—"horribly," "notorious," "horrible," "dreadfully"—as well as words like "miscreant," display a need to force the issue. Adjectival commentary was standard practice in Victorian journalism, but this writer seems particularly insistent that readers understand that these events push the envelope of normal East End crime.

Other journalists were even less reserved. On October 6, *The East London Advertiser* printed a commentary titled "A Thirst for Blood" that began in this way:

> The two fresh murders which have been committed in Whitechapel have aroused the indignation and excited the imagination of London to a degree without parallel. Men feel that they are face to face with some awful and extraordinary freak of nature. So inexplicable and ghastly are the circumstances surrounding the crimes that people are affected by them in the same way as children are by the recital of a weird and terrible story of the supernatural. It is so impossible to account, on any ordinary hypothesis, for these revolting acts of blood that the mind turns as it were instinctively to some theory of occult force, and the myths of the Dark Ages rise before the imagination. Ghouls, vampires, bloodsuckers, and all the ghastly array of fables which have been accumulated throughout the course of centuries take form, and seize hold of the excited fancy. Yet the most morbid imagination can conceive nothing worse than this terrible reality; for what can be more appalling than the thought that there is a being in human shape stealthily moving about a great city, burning with the thirst for human blood, and endowed with such diabolical astuteness, as to enable him to gratify his fiendish lust with absolute impunity?[64]

Here we see a newspaper report on a factual event become a Gothic narrative, complete with supernatural beings and purple prose. There was even, in final victim Mary Jane Kelly, a Gothic heroine—not virginal, surely (she was pregnant at the time of her murder), but characterized by papers as an "unfortunate woman . . . twenty-four years of age, tall, slim, fair, of fresh complexion, and of attractive appearance."[65]

Other writers used similar supernatural comparisons; werewolves, vampires, monsters, and ogres were repeatedly invoked to describe the killer. "The mind travels back," says an article in the *Times* on September 10, "to the pages of De Quincey for an equal display of scientific delight in the details of butchery; or Edgar Allan Poe's 'Murders in the Rue Morgue' recur."[66] As cultural historian Judith Walkowitz notices, the media could find no historical precedent and so "resorted to horrifying fictional analogues"[67]

The overlapping of fiction and reality reached its apex in the events surrounding the London production of a stage adaptation of Stevenson's *The Strange Case of Dr. Jekyll and Mr. Hyde*, playing in the West End during the first of the Ripper murders. "What adds to the weird effect [the murders] exert on the London mind," wrote the *New York Times*' London correspondent on September 9, "is the fact that they occur while everybody is talking about Mansfield's *Jekyll and Hyde* at the Lyceum."[68]

American actor Richard Mansfield had bought dramatic rights to the novel soon after its 1886 publication and had written an adaptation that played to great success in Boston and New York in 1887 and early 1888. Mansfield took the play across the ocean in late summer and opened in London on August 4, 1888, three weeks before the murder of Polly Nichols. Mansfield's *Jekyll and Hyde* played at Henry Irving's Lyceum Theatre while Irving's company was on sabbatical.[69]

The play was successful, perhaps too much so. Mansfield's production portrayed Edward Hyde as a "sadistic sex criminal"[70] who expresses his insatiable desires in violence. The addition of a female character not present in the novel—Jekyll's fiancé who is murdered by Hyde in a narrative move that echoes Mary Shelley's *Frankenstein*—cemented the idea of Hyde as a sexual killer. This sensational characterization, coupled with Mansfield's (by all accounts remarkable) onstage transformation, tied the play in the public's minds to the Whitechapel murders when they began three weeks after the play opened. The connection was strengthened by W. T. Stead's assertion, in an article entitled "Murder and More to Follow," that the killer was a "Jekyll and Hyde" type. Judith Walkowitz cites Stead's characterization of Jack the Ripper as a "'renewed reminder of the potentialities of revolting barbarity which lie latent in man,' and as a 'plebian Marquis de Sade at large in Whitechapel.'"[71] In later articles, Stead would suggest that authorities look for a respectable man, possibly with a West End address, further underlining the Jekyll/Hyde idea.[72] Soon the media was full of the Jekyll/Hyde theory, and Richard Mansfield himself came under attack.

Mansfield's transformation scene, accomplished through special effect lighting and make-up, and his subsequent portrayal of the murderer Edward Hyde, proved too much for some viewers during the heightened atmosphere surrounding the Ripper murders. Although the *Illustrated London News*, on September 22, remarked that even though "the mere subject of such a drama may startle or shock the sensitive, it is, unquestionably, a remarkable tour de force on the part of the young actor," other reviewers implied that perhaps Mansfield's portrayal could function as an inspirational role model for murderers. There is also evidence that the public's anxiety was heightened by the play. On September 29, the day before the double-event murders of Elizabeth Stride and Catherine Eddowes, *St. Stephen's Review* reported:

> A well-dressed man . . . had bolted out of a 'bus while it was going at a rapid rate, and then fallen down in a fit. It appeared he had been to see Mr. Mansfield as Dr. Jekyll, and on getting into the 'bus found himself beside a most repulsive-looking man, whom he immediately concluded must either be the Doctor himself or the Whitechapel murderer. In a fit of fearful nervousness, he jumped from his seat, and came to grief as mentioned.[73]

Eventually angst around the murders resulted in Mansfield himself becoming suspect. Danahay and Chisholm reproduce a letter sent to the City of London police on October 5 in which the writer claims he:

> went to See Mr Mansfield Take the Part of Dr Jekel & Mr Hyde I felt at once that he was the Man Wanted & I have not been able to get this Feeling out of my Head. . . . I thought of the dritfull manor he Works himself up in his Part that It might be Posable to work himself up So that he would do it in Reality I do not think there is A man Living So well able to disgise Himself in a moment as he does in front of the Public.[74]

Mansfield closed the play in fear on September 29 after a highly successful ten-week run, prompting the *Daily Telegraph* to remark that "there is no taste in London for horrors on the stage. There is quite sufficient to make us shudder out of doors."[75] But this is clearly wrong—there was great taste in London for horrors on stage: the play was by all accounts a huge success while it ran. Indeed, after "continued and great demand"[76] Mansfield re-opened the play to run through much of October. The populace needed something to express the terror of living in London, the pervasive fear caused by the killings. In many ways, London was the perfect venue for Mansfield's play; not only is the play set in London, but in the autumn of 1888 the citizens of London felt they were living in a Gothic narrative.[77]

Victorian London was an overwhelming phenomenon, both to those seeing it for the first time and to those who habitually moved through its streets. The urban Gothic arose due to the many difficulties, adverse conditions, and criminal outrages attendant on a city growing an average of sixty thousand people per year. The city's size, overcrowding, pollution, darkness, and crime all contributed to the Gothicization of London, a process participated in by the media and realized in the increasing number of novels in the Gothic mode that used the city as both setting and muse.

The ways in which London is represented in the Gothic mode make up the rest of the present study. To begin with, we will look closer at what has been hinted at in this chapter—the dividing of London into "safe" and "dangerous" areas by both authors and the general public, a division not as simple or straightforward as it may first appear.

NOTES

1. Anne Humpherys, "Knowing the Victorian City: Writing and Representation," *Victorian Literature and Culture* (2002): 602.

2. Joseph Conrad, *The Secret Agent: A Simple Tale* (1907; New York: Penguin, 1990), 41.

3. David Masson, *British Novelists and Their Styles: Being a Critical Sketch of the History of British Prose Fiction* (Boston: Gould and Lincoln, 1859), 244–45.

4. Roy Porter, *London: A Social History* (Cambridge, MA: Harvard University Press, 1994), 207.

5. Peter Ackroyd, *London: The Biography* (New York: Nan A. Talese, 2001), 565.

6. Karl Baedeker, *London and Its Environs: A Handbook for Travellers*, Facsimile Edition (1900; Moretonhampstead, Devon: Old House Books, 2002), 96.

7. Henry Mayhew, Article on Ballooning in *Illustrated London News*, *The Victorian Dictionary*, http://www.victorianlondon.org/entertainment/ballooning.htm.

8. Frederick Engels, *The Condition of the Working Class in England: From Personal Observation and Authentic Sources* (1845; Chicago: Academy, 1984), 57.

9. W. Cooke Taylor, *Notes of a Tour in the Manufacturing Districts of Lancashire*, Reprints of Economic Classics (1842; New York: Augustus M. Kelley, 1968), 6.

10. Quoted in Peter Ackroyd, *London: The Biography* (New York: Nan A. Talese, 2001), 258.

11. Ackroyd, *London*, 256.

12. Charles Dickens, *Dombey and Son*, ed. Alan Horsman, Oxford World's Classics (1848; Oxford: Oxford University Press, 2001), 68.

13. Charles Dickens, "A Flight," *Household Words,* August 30, 1852, 532.

14. Dickens, "Flight," 530.

15. Quoted in Roy Porter, *London: A Social History* (Cambridge, MA: Harvard University Press, 1994), 275.

16. Porter, *London*, 269.

17. Donald Rumbelow, *The Complete Jack the Ripper* (London: Penguin, 1988), 19.

18. Engels, *Condition of the Working Class*, 61.

19. Engels, *Condition of the Working Class*, 60.

20. Quoted in Porter, *London*, 259.

21. Porter, *London*, 259.

22. Max Schlesinger, *Saunterings in and around London*, 1858, *The Victorian Dictionary*, http://www.victorianlondon.org/ weather/fog.htm.

23. Ackroyd, *London*, 564.

24. Ackroyd, *London*, 564.

25. Lynda Nead, *Victorian Babylon: People, Streets, and Images in Nineteenth-Century* London (New Haven, CT: Yale University Press, 2000), 83.

26. Tina Young Choi, "Writing the Victorian City: Discourses of Risk, Connection, and Inevitability," *Victorian Studies* 43, no. 4 (Summer 2001): 563.

27. Ackroyd, *London*, 570–71.

28. Ackroyd, *London*, 571.

29. Peter Whitfield, *London: A Life in Maps* (London: The British Library, 2006), 85.

30. Whitfield, *London*, 85.

31. Thomas De Quincey, *Confessions of an English Opium-Eater and Other Writings,* Oxford World Classics (1821; Oxford: Oxford University Press, 1985), 21.

32. De Quincey, *Confessions*,23.

33. De Quincey, *Confessions*, 34.

34. Catherine Sinclair, *London Homes: Including The Murder Hole; The Drowning Dragoon; The Priest and the Curate; Lady Mary Pierrepoint; & Frank Vansittart* (London: Richard Bentley, 1853), vi.

35. Michael Moorcock, "Lost London Writers," *London Bone* (London: Scribner, 2002), 239.

36. Trefor Thomas, introduction to *The Mysteries of London,* by G. W. M. Reynolds (Staffordshire, UK: Keele University Press, 1996), xiii.

37. Thomas, introduction, xii.

38. This statistic is due in part to the manner in which *Mysteries of London* was published. The wildly popular novel was brought out in two series of weekly parts from October 1844 through September 1848. The interminable, soap opera–like nature of the publication ensured steady sales and a devoted readership. Additionally, the connected narrative *Mysteries of the Court of London* began soon after the end of the first novel and was serialized until 1856. Sales of the works in English and translation have been estimated at over a million.

39. The French began writing urban Gothics eight or ten years before the British—Sue's novel is only one example of a mode best exemplified by Hugo's *The Hunchback of Notre Dame* (1831). For reasons we will see in chapter 4, London is more effective as a Gothic setting than Paris, though writers like Balzac continued to utilize the Parisian cityscape for similar purposes throughout the nineteenth century.

40. G. W. M. Reynolds, *The Mysteries of London*, ed. Trefor Thomas (1844–1856; Keele, Staffordshire, UK: Keele University Press, 1996), 4.

41. For a detailed analysis of the opening chapter of Reynolds's novel along with a point-by-point comparison with first-wave Gothic novels, see chapter 2 of Robert Mighall's *Geography of Victorian Gothic Fiction* (Oxford: Oxford University Press, 1999).

42. Reynolds, *Mysteries of London*, 46.

43. Reynolds, *Mysteries of London*, 46.

44. Sweet, seventeen-year-old Ellen is driven by poverty and the responsibility of an ailing father to first sell her face's likeness to a sculptor, then to pose topless for a painter, and finally to serve as an "experimental" subject for a photographer who requires to her to disrobe completely and be photographed in "every attitude." Thus, the narrator tells us, Ellen becomes "essentially a foul soul in a chaste and virgin form" (89).

45. Reynolds, *Mysteries of London*, 38.

46. Charles Dickens, *Oliver Twist*, ed. Fred Kaplan, Norton Critical Edition (1838; New York: Norton, 1993), 3.

47. Dickens, *Oliver Twist*, 5.

48. Dickens, *Oliver Twist*, 6.

49. Dickens, *Oliver Twist*, 6.

50. Dickens, *Oliver Twist*, 60.

51. Dickens, *Oliver Twist*, 305.

52. "The Vampyre," *Punch,* July-December 1847, 134.

53. Fanny Stevenson's objections to the original manuscript are unclear. They have been contrastingly documented as both her being terrified by it or conversely feeling that Louis had written a sensational work when he should have written an allegorical one. "Some have suggested," writes Martin Danahay, "that the original manuscript dealt with material, perhaps sexual in nature, that a Victorian readership would have found unacceptable" (introduction to *The Strange Case of Dr. Jekyll and Mr. Hyde,* by Robert Louis Stevenson, ed. Martin A. Danahay [1886; Peterborough: Broadview, 1995], 15). At any rate, Stevenson later maintained that the first manuscript was the best he had ever produced and that "Fanny had ruined his effort."

54. Robert Louis Stevenson, *The Strange Case of Dr. Jekyll and Mr. Hyde*, ed. Martin A. Danahay (1886; Peterborough: Broadview, 1995), 47–48.

55. Quoted in James Krasner, "Crime and Street Lighting in Jekyll and Hyde," *Perspectives on Jekyll and Hyde,* http://mural.uv.es/blasis/crime.html.

56. Stevenson, *The Strange Case of Dr. Jekyll and Mr. Hyde*, 32–33.

57. Ackroyd, *London*, 430.

58. For fuller examinations of various aspects of *Jekyll and Hyde*, see chapters 3 and 4.

59. The actual number is a subject of some debate—there are authorities who say only three and those who advocate as many as seven. Most "ripperologists" agree on what are known as the "canonical five": Mary Ann "Polly" Nichols, Annie Chapman, Elizabeth Stride, Catherine Eddowes, and Mary Ann Kelly. All five of these women were prostitutes at one time or another.

60. Indeed, at the time of the Ripper murders, another series of unsolved atrocities, the "Thames Torso Murders," was continuing in other parts of the city. These crimes were revealed

by the discovery of the dismembered corpses of five women between 1887 and 1902. R. Michael Gordon explores these savage killings in *The Thames Torso Murders of Victorian London* (Jefferson, NC: McFarland, 2002), a book which presents a detailed examination of each of the Torso murders before descending into speculation to connect the Torso and Ripper crimes through a single suspect (Severin Klowsoski, who most likely committed neither).

61. Stephen P. Ryder, "Introduction to the Case," *Casebook: Jack the Ripper*, http://www.casebook.org/intro.html.

62. Rumbelow, *Complete Jack the Ripper*, 73.

63. "More Murders at the East End," *Times*, October 1, 1888, 6.

64. "A Thirst for Blood, " *East London Advertiser*, October 6, 1888, *Casebook: Jack the Ripper*, http://casebook.org/press_reports/ east_london_advertiser/ela881006.html.

65. "East End Tragedies. A Seventh Murder. Another Case of Horrible Murder," *Daily Telegraph*, November 10, 1888, *Casebook: Jack the Ripper*, http://casebook.org/press_reports/daily_telegraph/ dt881110.html.

66. Untitled article, *The Times*, September 10, 1888, in *The Strange Case of Dr. Jekyll and Mr. Hyde*, by Robert Louis Stevenson, ed. Martin A Danahay (Peterborough: Broadview, 1995), 186.

67. Judith R. Walkowitz, *City of Dreadful Delight: Narratives of Sexual Danger in Late-Victorian London*, Women in Culture and Society series (Chicago: University of Chicago Press, 1992), 196. Readers wanting a more detailed account of how contemporary newspaper reports created and fed off the hysteria around the Ripper murders should consult Walkowitz's book, which contains a fascinating analysis of media coverage of the Autumn of Terror. Walkowitz also gives details of W. T. Stead's various sensational exposés in the press (especially his "Maiden Tribute of Modern Babylon," which focused on child prostitution) and other pivotal events in the representations of sexuality and gender during the 1880s. The book culminates in the Ripper story as a logical conclusion to the narratives of sexual violence and male victimization of women already impressed upon the public consciousness during the 1880s.

68. "Whitechapel Startled by a Fourth Murder," *New York Times*, September 9, 1888, in *The Strange Case of Dr. Jekyll and Mr. Hyde*, 185.

69. As a coincidental Gothic footnote, the Lyceum Theatre, where Mansfield's production of *Jekyll and Hyde* played during the Autumn of Terror, was managed from 1878 onward by Bram Stoker, author of the Gothic apotheosis *Dracula* (1897).

70. Walkowitz, *City of Dreadful Delight*, 206.

71. Walkowitz, *City of Dreadful Delight*, 206.

72. Walkowitz, *City of Dreadful Delight*, 207.

73. Quoted in Martin A. Danahay and Alex Chisholm, *Jekyll and Hyde Dramatized: The 1887 Richard Mansfield Script and the Evolution of the Story on Stage* (Jefferson, NC: McFarland, 2005), 175.

74. Quoted in Danahay and Chisholm, *Jekyll and Hyde Dramatized*, 180.

75. Quoted in Danahay and Chisholm, *Jekyll and Hyde Dramatized*, 17.

76. Quoted in Danahay and Chisholm, *Jekyll and Hyde Dramatized*, ix.

77. Martin Danahay and Alex Chisholm have recounted and illuminated the story of Mansfield's *Jekyll and Hyde* in *Jekyll and Hyde Dramatized*. Their book gives details of Mansfield's life and career, the strange overlapping of the play with the Whitechapel murders, and a complete collated script drawn from the several revisions of the play which Mansfield performed.

Chapter Three

London Chiaroscuro

A Gothic Map of Victorian London

> *The East End of London is entirely too awful, and too intricate a neighborhood to be dismissed in a chapter. It is the back yard of the greatest city in the world, into which all the unpleasant and unsightly things are thrown and hidden away from sight, to be dragged out occasionally and shaken before the eyes of the West End as a warning or a menace.*—Richard Harding Davis, "The West and East Ends of London," 1894

In his 1998 *Atlas of the European Novel*, Franco Moretti attempts to make "the connection between geography and literature explicit" by "mapping it: because a map is precisely that, a connection made visible."[1] In mapping the London of Jane Austen, Edward Bulwer-Lytton, Charles Dickens, and Arthur Conan Doyle, Moretti explicates two Londons: the bright and fashionable West End and the dark and dirty East End. He shows us, for example, that events in the silver-fork novels of the early nineteenth century occurred nearly exclusively to the west of Regent Street and that the villains in *Oliver Twist* made their lairs in Whitechapel and Jacob's Island, among other places. In so doing, Moretti is merely replicating a standard reading of London's economic topography that was already well established by the time Victoria took the throne.

In this chapter I will consider the partitioning of London into "light" and "dark" areas and attempt to map out these divisions to see if they hold true in the urban Gothic novel. Additionally, we will look more closely at the map of London, discovering in the process that Gothic London was more complex than this light/dark division, both on the streets and in literature, and consider how from this complex space there often arose the most terrifying of the Gothic's urban manifestations.

Flora Tristan, the Parisian-born social reformer and early feminist, divides London into three parts: the city, the West End, and the suburbs. Writing in her *London Journal* (1840), Tristan explains that the city is inhabited by those of "pure John Bull stock,"[2] merchants and bankers and shopkeepers, while the West End is the home of the "upper aristocracy."[3] The suburbs—and by "suburbs" Tristan refers to the East End and Surrey-side—"contains the workers, prostitutes and the rabble of transients whom lack of work and vice of every kind force to lead a life of vagrancy, or whom poverty and hunger drive to beggary, theft and murder."[4] Tristan goes on to describe and bewail prostitution, the condition of prisons, and other characteristics of what she calls suburban London.

Tristan participates in a tradition well ingrained in nineteenth-century attitudes about London—the sectioning of London into districts of prosperity and deprivation. Tristan's tripartite division allows her to separate the aristocracy from the honest Cockneys of the city, providing a space for her to criticize the upper classes along with the conditions of the poor.

Similarly, Moretti finds a third space in the writings of Dickens—the middle-class London located in the center, the city, which is "indeed a class *in the middle*: encircled by villains, East and West."[5] Moretti feels that *Our Mutual Friend* is the novel that fully establishes Dickens's "third space": the middle-class, central location of Mortimer and Eugene's lodgings in the city. Moretti's chapter "A Tale of Two Cities" makes an effective argument for this "third space," showing how Dickens had hitherto not allowed the upper or lower classes to experience the "other side." The most powerful example of this is Moretti's explication of Oliver Twist's and Bill Sikes's journey across London, which is topographically detailed until they reach Holborn. "Then," Moretti writes, "the novel skips several miles, and starts again when they are well west of Hyde Park."[6] The East and West Ends of London cannot be shown to meet. The third space, the space of the middle class, is ultimately the ground where the upper and lower classes can mingle, because middle-class characters are able to move between them. The city, lying in the center of London, is literally and metaphorically the middle ground. This thematic is especially true for Dickens, who often utilizes the Gothic mode in service of a larger social reform agenda. Moretti's argument, bolstered by comparisons with Balzac's Paris, is compelling. Even so, he makes clear that the East/West dichotomy is firmly in place before this third space is created.

But the urban Gothic mode is more concerned with the perceived threat of the lower classes (and a host of corollary Others) than the establishment of a space for the middle class, although the two concerns can and often do commingle. Characters in the urban Gothic can move between the two spaces, but the crossing of that threshold is evidence not of class mobility but rather of a terrifying threat to the British way of life. I first want to examine the perception of tension between the West and East ends of London, both in nonfiction and in Gothic novels, and then outline how the urban Gothic ups the ante by transgressing those well-established boundaries. To do so, I map out the spaces in several representative novels, demonstrating how the concrete geography of London structurally and thematically reinforces the urban Gothic project. I have based the maps in this chapter on clues and descriptions in the novels themselves. In the few cases where authors are vague about location, I have made (hopefully) educated guesses as to likely areas; I explain these at the appropriate points in the text.

EAST VS. WEST

It is dangerous to assume any sort of homogeneity in a city the size and population of Victorian London. Victorian urban centers were "fragmented, intricate, eclectic, messy,"[7] and so are the individual impressions they created. London certainly was the zenith of modernity during its nineteenth-century ascendancy. But as even a superficial overview of the Victorian city makes clear, there was a darker side to London's role as a city on the cutting edge of science, art, philosophy, and industry. Widespread poverty, crime, and pollution in many areas of the city made London a sinister and often dangerous place. Bright, fashionable areas like Mayfair were reflected in inversion by underprivileged districts such as Limehouse or Whitechapel, where poverty was the norm and crime was often a way of life.

Throughout the nineteenth and early twentieth centuries, most commentators on the city used this simple partitioning: London has safe areas and dangerous areas, wealthy areas and poor areas, areas of lawfulness and lawlessness. Middle- and upper-class Londoners saw these divisions in a simple spatial formula: the West End and the city set against the East End and the areas south of the Thames.

The West End, according to the 1900 edition of Baedeker's, was "that part of London which spends money, makes laws, and regulates the fashions."[8] This region is where the aristocracy, lawmakers, and more fashionable shopkeepers lived, where the well-dressed women and children of the upper classes would display their finery on the Ladies' Mile in Kensington Gardens, described by Blanchard Jerrold in 1872:

> The high-bred, delicate, rose-tinted beauty of women and children; the courage and comeliness of the amazons; the calm, solid air of their cavaliers; the perfect horses; the severe simplicity and perfect appointments of the liveried attendants; the genial air of quiet strength and grace which is upon all the scene.[9]

This London contains Buckingham Palace, the theatre district, and the fashionable shops of Regent and Oxford Streets. Also here are the intellectual and cultural centers: the British Museum, the British Library, and the Natural History Museum, among many others. Most tellingly, Hyde Park in the center of the West End was the original site of the Crystal Palace, home in 1851 of the Great Exhibition. In showcasing achievements from around the world, the Exhibition also effectively demonstrated England's superiority in industry, technology, culture, and science. Equally appealing and accessible to all classes, the Exhibition was also an excellent example of the teleological attitude of the British empire. Even the poorest Londoners compared themselves favorably with Chinese acrobatic troupes or "savages" from New Guinea in native dress, living exhibits akin to the animals in Regent's Park Zoo in the minds of the British citizens filing though the Crystal Palace. Thus, the Great Exhibition was the most visible expression of London as the site of progressiveness, the cutting edge of fashion, finance, and the future, especially as opposed to the uncivilized outer reaches of the empire.

By contrast, the higher crime rates in poorer districts (Whitechapel, for instance) caused many writers to associate the poor with the criminal, and thus economically depressed areas came to be represented as dangerous. In 1872, Jerrold describes visiting the East End: "From low house to low house we go, picking up some fresh scrap of the history of Poverty and Crime—they must go hand in hand hereabouts—at every turn."[10]

In 1882, Walter Besant called the East End a separate city, one intrinsically cut off from the progressive achievements of the city and the West End:

> Probably there is no such spectacle in the whole world as that of this immense, neglected, forgotten great city of East London. It is even neglected by its own citizens, who have never yet perceived their abandoned condition. They are Londoners, it is true, but they have no part or share of London; its wealth, its splendours, its honours exist not for them. They see nothing of any splendours . . . the city lies between them and the greatness of England.[11]

In fact, those familiar with the more "enlightened" areas of London often described the East End and Surrey-side as a different country altogether. The wider ethnic diversity as well as overcrowding, poverty, and dirt gave areas like Spitalfields or Limehouse an air of otherworldliness. Blanchard Jerrold writes that in the East End,

> the German, the Jew, the Frenchman, the Lascar, the swarthy native of Spitalfields, the leering thin-handed thief, the bully of the court . . . with endless swarms of ragged children, fill road and pavement. The Jewish butchers lounge—fat and content, in their doorways; the costermongers drive their barrows slowly by, filling the air with their hoarse voices. The West Ender is as completely in a strange land as any traveller from the Continent. A saunter through the extensive vegetable market of Spitalfields; a turn in Houndsditch, by Bishopsgate Church; a pause where Whitechapel joins Aldgate . . . or a trip in the heavily charged atmosphere of Rosemary Lane, where

> the flat, stale odour of old clothes soon unnerves the too curious observer . . . will reveal a new world of London to many a Cockney who thought he knew the great City well.[12]

And from observations of the population in the East End, it would be excusable for the naïve wanderer to imagine himself in a foreign country. Immigrants from all over the world, drawn by London's reputation for wealth, congregated in the East End after discovering that the great city did not provide an untroubled passage to success. Large populations of Chinese and Germanic Jews represented the East End for many.

In *Wentworth Street, Whitechapel* (fig. 3.1), one of the etchings that accompany Jerrold's text, Gustave Doré shows the commonly presented face of the East End in the Victorian era. The group of figures who are the focus of Doré's etching are sullen and indolent, lounging in the street with no occupation, except perhaps for the man drying the plate, but his sly expression belies any honest business. Several different ethnic groups are evident: the dark-skinned man with the plate, the swarthy man to his left in the cloth cap, the man in the lower right corner with the hook nose and pointed beard of the stereotypical Jew, the kinky hair and/or oriental features of several of the children. The street is narrow and dirty, the aspect of the men loitering against the walls forbidding. This is the foreign country Jerrold refers to, separated from the West End by money, culture, ethnicity, and space.

For all intents and purposes, the East End in these representations becomes a stand-in for the empire—an imperial doppelgänger as mysterious and daunting to explorers as the interior of the Congo. William Booth, who founded the Salvation Army in 1878 in response to conditions in the East End, published *In Darkest England and the Way Out* in 1890. The novel, which became a best-seller, consciously presented the West/East dichotomy as civilized England set in opposition to the savagery of Africa. The title, a reference to Henry Morton Stanley's adventure travelogue *In Darkest Africa*, was the form for the whole book, which deliberately paralleled Stanley's descriptions of equatorial Africa with Booth's equally sensational details of life in Whitechapel and Spitalfields. He extended his metaphor down to the solution offered—colonize the East End just as Africa and India had been colonized. It is a complicated and rather grand method of soliciting funds for the Salvation Army (trying to draw on the sort of "telescopic philanthropy" described by Dickens in *Bleak House*), but it is also part and parcel of the West/East split. Solving the problems of the East End is best done by extending the civilizing influence of Britain into these untamed lands. Booth's novel was a best-seller, however, more likely due to the thrill for middle-class readers of hearing about these savage districts hidden within their own city.

Figure 3.1. Gustave Doré's 1872 etching *Wentworth Street, Whitechapel*, showing the crowded conditions, squalor, and ethnic diversity of the East End.

The dynamic at work in the media coverage of the Ripper murders examined in chapter 2 is the same. The location of the murders had as much to do with the aura of mystery and terror that surrounded them as did the atrocities themselves. "To middle-class observers," writes Judith Walkowitz, "Whitechapel was an alien place, a center of cosmopolitan culture and *entrepôt* foreign immigrants"[13] that seemed as unlike the West End as could possibly be imagined. The use of geographically specific information in articles about the Ripper, Walkowitz goes on to say, constituted an "'argument from geography' about the territorially based nature of crime."[14]

The irony of these two disparate worlds existing in such close proximity was not lost on pundits. In 1902, Jack London visited what he called the "under-world" of the city and reported his experiences in *The People of the Abyss*. It is telling that in his preface London notes that

> it will be readily apparent to the reader that I saw much of what was bad. Yet it must not be forgotten that the time of which I write was considered "good times" in England. The starvation and lack of shelter I encountered constituted a chronic condition of misery which is never wiped out, even in periods of greatest prosperity.[15]

London (the writer) has encapsulated here the main thrust of the sizable number of journalistic representations of London's poverty and crime throughout the second half of the nineteenth century. Through all of the prostitution exposés, all the wide-eyed and whisper-voiced newspaper articles on East End crime, even throughout serious attempts at social commentary like Henry Mayhew's *London Labour and the London Poor*, the message was the same: that London was composed of two parts, East and West, what Walkowitz calls "a class and geographically divided metropolis of hovels and palaces."[16] The eastern part was presented as a sort of Dantean Hell (the first section of *People of the Abyss*, in which Jack London travels to the East End, is called "The Descent"), and Jerrold, Booth, London, Mayhew, and hosts of other writers were explorers of that hell—delving into an unknown territory as awesome and terrifying as any in the "savage" outreaches of the Empire. Jack London reports that "everybody" told him to use a policeman as a guide and refused to even tell him how to get there. "'But we know nothing of the East End,'" London's friends tell him, "'It is over there, somewhere.' And they waved their hands vaguely in the direction where the sun on rare occasions may be seen to rise."[17] Turning, as the explorer might, to the well-known travel firm Thomas Cook and Sons, London is again rebuffed, causing him to narratively berate the company: "unhesitatingly and instantly, with ease and celerity, could you send me to Darkest Africa or Innermost Thibet, but to the East End of London, barely a stone's throw distant from Ludgate Circus, you know not the way!"[18] When he suggests that at least now they will know he's going to the East End, in case he gets into any trouble, the clerk at Cook's understands. "'Ah, I see; should you be murdered, we would be in a position to identify the corpse.'"[19]

As early as Thomas De Quincey's 1821 *Confessions of an English Opium-Eater*, parts of London had been called terra incognita, and by the end of the nineteenth century the metaphor had been codified into literary trope. So it's no wonder that newspaper reports of conditions in the East End sometimes read like adventure travelogues or else like shilling shockers.

THE WORST STREET IN LONDON

On Tuesday, July 16, 1901, the *Daily Mail* ran a feature entitled "The Worst Street in London: Where Our Criminals Are Trained." The street in question is Dorset Street, which ran between Crispin and Commercial Streets near Christ Church, Spitalfields, and the Spitalfields Market (fig. 3.2). Only a single block in length, Dorset Street is, according to the article,

> a place which boasts of an attempt at murder on an average once a month, of a murder in every house, and one house at least a murder in every room. Policemen go down it as a rule in pairs. Hunger walks prowling in its alleyways, and the criminals of to-morrow are being bred there to-day.[20]

Figure 3.2. Dorset Street, Spitalfields, circa 1901. This photo, from Jack London's *People of the Abyss*, seems to show the entire length of "the worst street in London."

Already the article sounds like a Gothic novel. Reynolds's *Mysteries of London* contains many such descriptive passages. Yet, there is independent evidence that this report is true. It was in Miller's Court, an alley off Dorset Street, that Mary Kelly was murdered by Jack the Ripper. In 1901, the same year as the *Daily Mail* article, Mary Ann Austin was stabbed to death at 35 Dorset Street, a house which had been the residence of the Ripper's second victim, Annie Chapman, at the time of her death. In 1909, a woman named Kitty Ronan was killed in the same house as Mary Kelly.

During the late nineteenth and early twentieth century, Dorset Street was composed mainly of cheap dosshouses and "furnished rooms," tiny and extremely cheap rooms that were rented out with no questions asked. Many of these were owned by local slumlord John McCarthy, who ran the "McCarthy's Rents" on Miller's Court where Mary Kelly was killed. A pamphlet circulated in 1901 in rebuttal of the *Daily Mail* article was largely written by McCarthy. Given his financial stake in renters coming to Dorset Street and the violent history of his own buildings in Dorset Street and Miller's Court, he hardly seems a reliable source.[21]

Whether the short length of Dorset Street was qualitatively "worse" than any other backstreet or alley in Spitalfields or Whitechapel is a point open to debate. Certainly police records and eyewitness reports indicate that Dorset Street contained the extremes of poverty and crime that formed the reputation of the East End. What makes the *Daily Mail*'s "Worst Street in London" article interesting in light of our discussion here is the manner in which the writer presents his information. In eleven paragraphs, the *Daily Mail* correspondent evokes urban Gothic novels by name, uses Gothic language to sensationalize the facts, and explicitly points out the differences between the residents of Dorset Street and the readership of the paper.

After admitting that not everyone living on Dorset Street is a murderer ("There are many men . . . who are simply 'down on their luck'"), the writer suggests that even the honest poor cannot help but be seduced into crime as a result of living in such close proximity with the criminal element:

> If they are in want, as they usually are, it is often enough a thief who shares his spoils with them to give them bread. And there are those who are always ready to instruct these newcomers in the simple ways of making a dishonest living. Boy thieves are trained as regularly and systematically around Dorset-street to-day as they were in the days of Oliver Twist.[22]

This is a remarkable example of the ways in which the urban Gothic novel had become conflated in the public's mind with the realities of life in the poorer districts of London. Oliver Twist (who was trained by Fagin in Clerkenwell, incidentally, and not Spitalfields) is invoked as if he were a historical figure. Sixty-three years on from Dickens's novel, the *Daily Mail* needs only to speak the character's name to conjure in its readers' minds ready-made images of squalor and exploitation. And it seems almost a passage from Reynolds or Dickens when readers are told that "the children are trained in the gutter, their first lessons are in oaths and crime. They learn ill as they sip from their mother's gin, and you can see them at six and eight years' old gambling in the gutter-ways."[23]

Furthermore, the writer of the article heightens the sense of literary conflation with this statement: "There must seem, I am well aware, an air of unreality about this to folks who read it in comfortable suburban homes or bright country houses. It seems impossible that in our new century these things should continue."[24] This statement is a fair summation of how the Gothic informed the media's response to the realities of poverty. In these two sentences, the *Daily Mail* reporter invokes both the experience of reading a novel and the teleological underpinning of the Gothic mode. The image of sitting in a "comfortable suburban home" reading about the "unreality" of Dorset Street's crime is perfectly analogous to those same readers curling up with *Jekyll and Hyde* or *Little Dorrit.* In fact, it is most likely readers' familiarity with these sorts of fictions that allows the media's language to interchange so fluidly with that of the Gothic novel. And by pointing out the enlightened progressiveness of "our new century," the conditions on Dorset Street are consigned as mere relics of the past—an uncivilized situation that London should have outgrown by now.

GOTHIC DISTRICTS IN LITERATURE

The most progressive and "modern" city in the world is also, then, a city seen to be demarcated by zones of poverty and crime. Gothic fiction presents these darker areas of London, the Clerkenwell of *Oliver Twist* or Edward Hyde's Soho, as being inherently of the past. Dangerous districts are not represented as the natural by-products of industrialization or progress, but rather as "anachronistic anomalies, vestigial stains on the city's modernity."[25] As the writers of the pleading letter to the *Times* quoted in chapter 1 say, these regions are a "Wilderniss," with all a wilderness's attendant savagery.

The urban Gothic mode is fundamentally concerned with these dangerous spaces; in some ways the Gothic districts of London replace the foreign settings and villains of the Radcliffean Gothic. Peopled by foreigners, separated financially and culturally from the bright thoroughfares of Piccadilly or Oxford Street, the East End allows the teleological narrative of the Gothic to be told in the modern city. Though the urban Gothic complicates the simple East/West split (as we will see below), the mode uses as a basic underpinning both the "darker" areas of London and their status as geographically Other.

As examples, let us look at two urban Gothic novels written twenty-five years apart: Dickens's *Our Mutual Friend* (1865) and Oscar Wilde's *The Picture of Dorian Gray* (1891).

Charles Dickens, both as novelist and as social reform advocate, knew the East/West dichotomy of London well. Dickens uses the traditional light and dark areas of London to demonstrate what F. S. Schwarzbach calls the "hellish nightmare of urban experience"[26] in most of his novels—we've already seen *Oliver Twist*'s descriptions of poverty-stricken districts and read some similar passages in *Little Dorrit*. In *Our Mutual Friend*, we see a continuation of Dickens's preoccupation with the poor areas of London contrasted with the districts of wealth. The stories of Gaffer Hexam and Rogue Riderhood, who make their living scavenging corpses from the Thames, are juxtaposed with the nouveau riche Veneerings and their upper-class dinner guests; various other stages of wealth and poverty are represented by the Boffins, John Harmon, Bella Wilfer, and the Lammles.[27] The indolent lawyers Eugene Wrayburn and Mortimer Lightwood, as representatives of the middle class, form the connection between these two incongruous worlds and are able throughout the novel to travel between them. It is through Eugene and Mortimer's perceptions of these areas of London that the reader is given the fullest sense of their contrast.

Consider the following description of Eugene and Mortimer's journey (during chapter 3) from the prosperous West End of the Veneerings' home across the city to the East End riverside of the Hexam hovel:

> The wheels rolled on, and rolled down by the Monument and by the Tower, and by the Docks; down by Ratcliffe, and by Rotherhithe; down by where accumulated scum of humanity seemed to be washed from higher grounds,

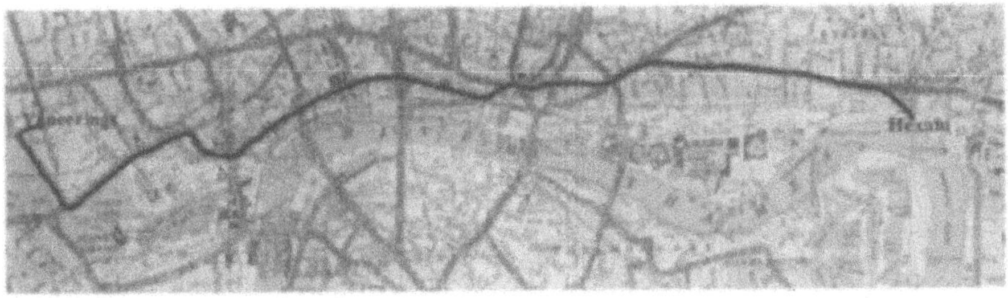

Figure 3.3. Mortimer and Eugene's journey from the Veneerings' mansion to Gaffer Hexam's riverside hovel in chapter 3 of *Our Mutual Friend*. I assume a Mayfair address for the Veneerings (it is assuredly in the West End). Dickens's description of the route seems to indicate they cross the river by way of the Thames Tunnel. Drawn from Bacon's Gem Map of London, 1910; Rare Books Room, University of South Carolina.

> like so much moral sewage, and to be pausing until its own weight forced it over the bank and sunk it in the river . . . the wheels rolled on, until they stopped at a dark corner, river-washed and otherwise not washed at all, where the boy alighted and opened the door. . . .
>
> "This is a confoundedly out-of-the-way place," said Mortimer, slipping over the stones and refuse on the shore.[28]

The Veneerings live in an area removed from the past and its threats; Dickens has gone to great pains to tell us earlier that the Veneerings live in a "bran-new quarter" of the city.[29] Just as in the East End, the environment in this "bran-new house" seems to influence the Veneerings themselves: "what was observable in the furniture, was observable in the Veneerings—the surface smelt a little too much of the workshop and was a trifle stickey."[30] On the map in figure 3.3, I have chosen a Mayfair address for the Veneerings, even though Dickens doesn't give us a definite street address. This choice isn't entirely arbitrary. The Veneerings' social circle primarily live in Mayfair: Miss Tippins and the Podsnaps are in the immediate area, and even the hapless Twemlow resides on the fringes of Mayfair. There were prosperous families living to the north (in Hampstead or Highgate, for example), but Dickens normally uses the outlying suburbs as dwellings for the truly good in his novels—the Carkers in *Dombey and Son* and the Pockets in *Great Expectations* are but two examples. The wealthy families that are often the targets of Dickens's social satire generally live in the West End—the Barnacles in *Little Dorrit*, the Dedlocks in *Bleak House*, the Podsnaps. At any rate, the world of the Veneerings is lavish and wealthy, a portrait that well complements Jarrold's description of "rose-tinted" women and children frolicking in Hyde Park.

But the overwhelming impression of the riverside is one of dirt, darkness, and corruption ("moral sewage"). The Hexam's dwelling is old and unplastered, which gives "a lowering aspect to the chamber; and roof, and walls, and floor, alike abounding in old smears . . . and damp, alike had a look of decomposition."[31] It is, to the middle-class lawyers used to moving among the upper classes, most definitely an "out-of-the-way place." It is also at the other extremity of the city, at the far east away from the Veneerings' western townhouse. To reach Hexam's home, the two lawyers traverse almost the entirety of the city. Geographic distance, Dickens seems to be saying, is necessary for the crossing of class lines into the dangerous areas of London.

Our Mutual Friend is consistent in its spatial deployment—Jenny Wren, Riah, the Riderhoods, the Hexams, and even the Wilfers are all separated by class and geography from the Veneerings, the Boffins, the Lammles, and the Podsnaps. In the urban Gothic mode, as we saw in chapter 2, for the upper and middle classes to venture into the territory of the lower classes (the Others) is to risk infection by their conditions.

We see this "infection" at work when Mortimer and Eugene return to the Hexam place to search for the missing Gaffer in chapter 13:

> Lightwood helped [Eugene] to some more of that stuff, but it had been cooling, and didn't answer now.
>
> "Pooh," said Eugene, spitting it out among the ashes. "Tastes like the wash of the river."
>
> "Are you so familiar with the flavor of the wash of the river?"
>
> "I seem to be tonight. . . . "
>
> "Influence of locality," suggested Lightwood.[32]

A similar movement across social space occurs late in Oscar Wilde's 1891 novel *The Picture of Dorian Gray*, when the eponymous protagonist takes a journey from the prosperous West End to the corrupt East End. In fact, Dorian's midnight ride to the opium den in Limehouse is nearly identical to both Eugene and Mortimer's earlier excursion and a real-world trip to the East End described by Jack London in *People of the Abyss*.

After murdering his friend Basil Halliward and blackmailing Alan Campbell into disposing of the body, Dorian attends a party at Lady Narborough's home. He then returns to his own residence, where, perhaps because of guilty stress, he is overcome with the need to smoke opium. Leaving his Grosvenor Square mansion, Dorian Gray hails a cab in Bond Street and gives the driver an address in the Limehouse district. The hansom driver is initially reluctant to venture into the East End: "the man shook his head. 'It is too far for me,' he muttered."[33]

Compare that scene with Jack London's difficulties in getting a hansom driver to take him to the East End in 1902. Having given no set address (he just wants to see the East End), the driver is resistant but "grumblingly started his horse."[34] After aimlessly driving around Spitalfields for a while, the driver pulls up to Stepney Station and stops. London tells us that

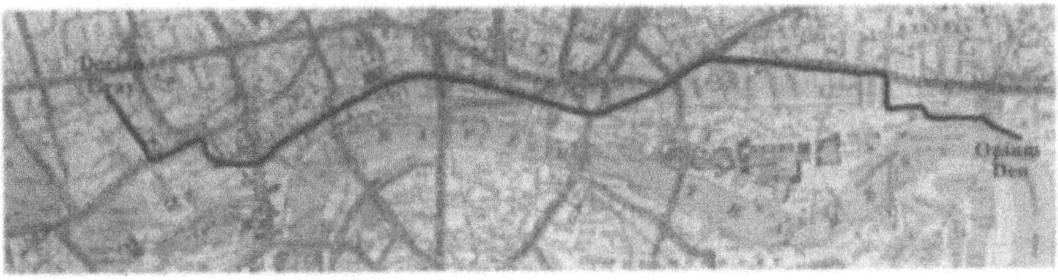

Figure 3.4. Dorian Gray's midnight ride. Although he has an ample supply of opium in his Mayfair home, Dorian travels to Limehouse to indulge in his habit. Gothic behavior demands a Gothic environment? Drawn from Bacon's Gem Map of London, 1910; Rare Books Room, University of South Carolina.

> it really was a railroad station, and he had driven to it as the one familiar spot he had ever heard of in all that wilderness.
>
> "Well?" I said.
>
> He spluttered unintelligibly, shook his head, and looked very miserable. "I'm a strynger 'ere," he managed to articulate. "An' if yer don't want Stepney Station, I'm blessed if I know wotcher do want."[35]

But like Jack London, Dorian Gray eventually does get driven to Limehouse. A promise of two sovereigns changes the cabbie's mind; after being told that they will "be there in an hour," Dorian Gray sets off for the riverside (see fig. 3.4). The two-page trip to Limehouse is interminable and nightmarish. The lumbering pace and feverish intensity is due in part to Dorian's "hideous hunger for opium,"[36] but the experience is narrated through the passing cityscape, which quickly becomes very different from Dorian's Mayfair point of origin:

> Lying back in the hansom, with his hat pulled over his forehead, Dorian Gray watched with listless eyes the sordid shame of the great city. . . . The moon hung low in the sky like a yellow skull. From time to time a huge misshapen cloud stretched a long arm across and hid it. The gaslamps grew fewer, and the streets more narrow and gloomy. Once the man lost his way, and had to drive back half a mile. A steam rose from the horse as it splashed up the puddles. The side-windows of the hansom were clogged with a grey-flannel mist. . . .
>
> Most of the windows were dark, but now and then fantastic shadows were silhouetted against some lamp-lit blind. They moved like monstrous marionettes, and made gestures like live things. . . . As they turned a corner a woman yelled something at them from an open door, and two men ran after the hansom for about a hundred yards. The driver beat at them with his whip. . . .
>
> Suddenly the man drew up with a jerk at the top of a dark lane. Over the low roofs and jagged chimney-stacks of the houses rose black masts of ships. Wreaths of white mist clung like ghostly sails to the yards.
>
> "Somewhere about here, sir, ain't it?" he asked huskily through the trap.[37]

Wilde's Limehouse is a combination of real-life squalor and Gothicized tropes.[38] The otherworldliness of the skull-like moon and the shadows like "monstrous marionettes" is balanced by the very concrete threat of the two men who chase the hansom, presumably because anyone who can afford a cab in that part of London automatically becomes a target for robbery. The mist becomes "ghostly," the streets "like the black web of some sprawling spider."[39] The overall effect is one of an almost hallucinatory intensity. This East End is not the "strange country" of Jerrold and Doré, or even the tropical terra incognita of William Booth, but rather a darkened dream-world completely removed from the bright solidity of Grosvenor Square. Like the social commentators writing in the real world, Dorian Gray has descended into Hell.

Another pause here, as we turn once again to Jack London, who describes his trip to Spitalfields thusly:

> The region my hansom was now penetrating was one unending slum. The streets were filled with a new and different race of people, short of stature, and of wretched or beer-sodden appearance. We rolled along through miles of bricks and squalor, and from each cross street and alley flashed long vistas of bricks and misery. Here and there lurched a drunken man or woman, and the air was obscene with the sounds of jangling and squabbling. . . .
> Not a hansom did I meet with in all my drive, while mine was like an apparition from another and better world, the way the children ran after it and alongside. And as far as I could see were the solid walls of brick, the slimy pavements, and the screaming streets; and for the first time in my life the fear of the crowd smote me. It was like the fear of the sea; and the miserable multitudes, street upon street, seemed so many waves of a vast and malodorous sea, lapping about me and threatening to well up and over me.[40]

Jack London's experience is nearly identical to Dorian Gray's, down to the hansom being chased because of its status as "apparition from another and better world." Both London and the fictional Gray feel thrown into a hellish and alien country.

The most curious aspect of Dorian Gray's journey, however, is revealed in the scene immediately prior. Before Dorian leaves home to hail a hansom, we see him as the opium craving comes upon him. As his breath becomes quicker and his "eyelids droop . . . until the long fringed lashes almost touched his cheek,"[41] he stares at a lapis-inlaid Florentine cabinet standing between the windows of his library. Eventually he goes to the cabinet, opens it, and withdraws "a green paste waxy in lustre, the odour curiously heavy and persistent."[42] Dorian does not partake, however; after hesitating and "shivering, though the atmosphere of the room was terribly hot,"[43] he puts away his private opium stash, dresses, and ventures forth to find a cab.

Why? If Dorian is in the grip of a "mad craving"[44] and has the means of satisfying it in his hand, what would motivate him to undertake an hour's journey to a "long, low room which looked as if it had once been a third-rate dancing saloon,"[45] in order to purchase the very opium he already possessed? Wilde makes an attempt at an explanation. While in the hansom, Dorian muses that

> ugliness was the one reality. The coarse brawl, the loathsome den, the crude violence of disordered life, the very vileness of the thief and outcast, were more vivid, in their intense actuality of impression, than all the gracious shapes of Art, the dreamy shadows of Song.[46]

Dorian needs the squalor of the East End as a garish antidote to his West End habitat, the text suggests. And there is, of course, the more immediate reason of the murder—Dorian wants to get away from the house simply to put distance between himself and the memory of Basil Halliward's slashed throat. The ugliness described in the passage above is "what he needed for forgetfulness."[47]

But when the novel is considered as an urban Gothic, another reason for Dorian's cab ride suggests itself: Gothic behavior demands a Gothic environment. Opium use occurs in the East End riverside around Limehouse on the Ratcliff highway—reports by observers such as J. Ewing Ritchie and Richard Rowe say so, and Dickens's *Mystery of Edwin Drood* (1870) laid the matter to rest.[48] Wilde knows this, and so does Dorian Gray. A descent into three days of indulgence in opium (the narrator tells us that "in three days he would be free"[49]) cannot occur in Mayfair. Aside from the problem of curious acquaintances and servants, Londoners know that there is a specified locale for such vices. Dorian Gray hastens to the Chinese districts of the East End riverside to have his debauch, because, as numerous novels, newspaper articles, and social commentaries have detailed, the West End rejects it.

THE GOTHIC NEXT DOOR: CROSSING THE BOUNDARIES

But does it really? Dorian Gray's nightmare trip to Limehouse makes even less sense in light of the events of the novel up to this point. Contrary to the wisdom espoused by the texts we have considered in this chapter so far, Gothic events definitely do take place in the West End—the murder of Basil Halliward and the existence of the picture itself prove this. Dorian's stash indicates that he does not run for Limehouse every time he wants opium; it must be his usual habit to partake in Grosvenor Square. The lapis-inlaid cabinet, in fact, serves as a symbol of the vice hidden beneath Dorian's beautiful exterior, vice that is very much at home in the West End. In spite of the cross-London journey and of Lord Henry's assertion to Dorian that "crime belongs exclusively to the lower orders,"[50] Dorian Gray has spent the majority of his novel engaging in sordid activities all over London, irrespective of East, West, South, or North.

Dorian's trip to the opium den, on the surface a reinforcement of the East/West dynamic, actually highlights that dynamic as an oversimplification. Even though travel narratives and guidebooks from the Victorian era presented the dangers of the city as being narrowly defined by economic and spatial dictates, the urban Gothic doesn't allow such easy pigeonholes to sit unchallenged. If the primitive past can be locked up in self-contained districts like Limehouse or Spitalfields, then the progressive present has nothing to fear from it. The threat of the Gothic is not that these "vestigial stains" exist, but that they cannot be contained by southern Europe, or equatorial Africa, or the East End of London. The urban Gothic definitely utilizes the idea of "light" and "dark" areas defined by economy and violent crime, but it also ups the ante by acknowledging the reality of the Victorian city more fully than supposedly factual reporters like Walter Besant or Baedeker's. To a West End reader, crime and terror in Whitechapel is sensational but ultimately reassuring. The urban Gothic immerses its horrors in familiarity, and on its streets a Mayfair address is no guarantee of safety. So, as *The Picture of Dorian Gray* demonstrates, the idea of an East/West split, encompassing wealth/poverty, enlightened/primitive, and good/evil divisions, is a faulty one.

Once again we must refer to a map to explain why. In 1889, Charles Booth attached as an appendix to his *Life and Labour of the London Poor* a map of relative income levels in London. This "poverty map" is color-coded: gold areas indicate the wealthy or upper classes, red indicates middle-class, and so on. Colors become darker as they move down the scale, culminating in black, which indicates the "lowest class. Vicious, semi-criminal." Macroscopically, the map seems to reinforce the West End versus East End school of thought. There is no question that the East End and areas south of the Thames are overall much darker, all deep blue and black, than the generally lighter red and gold of the West End. However, when a particular section of Booth's map is examined in detail, something else becomes apparent—there are pockets of blue and black all over the city, not just within the established enclaves for such economic situations.

It follows that Booth's map can be read two ways. As Franco Moretti explains, "The whole is quite ordered—but its individual parts are instead largely random. It is striking how rapid the transitions are, between the urban sub-systems; how poverty replaces wealth at every unpredictable turn of the street."[51] And indeed Booth's map shows streets where houses fronting major arteries are marked in red, while the alleys directly behind those houses show dark blue ("very poor, casual; chronic want") or black. For example, the area around Lincoln's Inn shows deep red along High Holborn street, but one block north or south yields the lowest economic levels represented by the map. Likewise, Guilford Street in Bloomsbury shows a strip of black less than a block from the predominantly gold Russell Square.

How much more terrifying to middle-class readers is this London, then, a London not of two easily discernible halves, but rather a patchwork of light and dark areas existing "cheek-by-jowl in the modern metropolis"?[52] The true topography of London is complex and unknowable: the wealthier, lighter, and "safer" areas existing side by side with the poorer, darker, more "dangerous" ones in an uneasy chiaroscuro as disturbing as it is compelling. Indeed, by the time of Booth's map, "the prevailing imaginary landscape of London [shifted] from one that was geographically bounded to one whose boundaries were indiscriminately and dangerously transgressed."[53] In the urban Gothic, this proximity is a source of horror, threatening as it does the teleological superiority of the modern city. Mighall demonstrates how a wrong turn in the relatively well-to-do area of Pentonville leads Oliver Twist quickly into the range of Bill Sikes near St. Giles. We will now look at this trope of proximity in several novels, demonstrating how this Gothic next door hits closer to readers' anxieties than the relatively reassuring East/West split. All the descriptions of poverty and crime we have already seen are still in operation, but their locations are unpredictable and physically closer to us as readers than we can be comfortable with.

Perhaps the quintessential novel of the proximity trope is Stevenson's *The Strange Case of Dr. Jekyll and Mr. Hyde*. There are three sites of interaction between the savage and the enlightened in Stevenson's short novel: the houses of Dr. Lanyon, Edward Hyde, and Dr. Jekyll (see fig. 3.5). Lanyon, Henry Jekyll's estranged friend and the most overtly respectable character in the novel, lives in Cavendish Square (a neighbor, perhaps, of the unlucky Mr. Merdle from *Little Dorrit*). Cavendish Square is unequivocally prosperous and "safe"—Booth shows gold in all directions in and around the square. Cavendish is the proper place of residence for a distinguished doctor in retirement who has led an unimpeachable life, and Stevenson rightly gives Lanyon a mansion there.

Edward Hyde, on the other hand, keeps a flat in Soho, the "district of some city in a nightmare," as Utterson calls it. Soho, though in the midst of central London, carries a reputation of vice and iniquity, of prostitution and

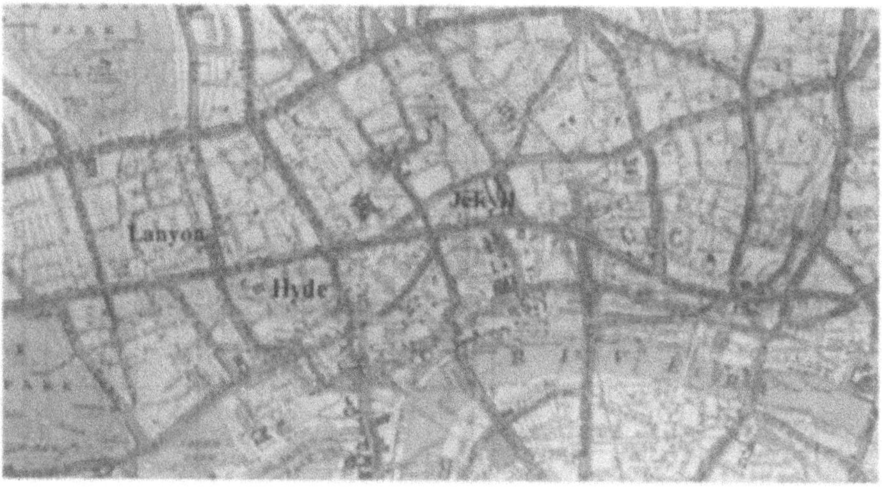

Figure 3.5. General location of the residences of Lanyon, Hyde, and Jekyll in Stevenson's novel. The relative proximity of the three houses is telling, underlining as it does the existence of wealth and poverty (and by extension virtue and crime) in relatively close quarters. Drawn from Bacon's Gem Map of London, 1910; Rare Books Room, University of South Carolina.

sexual deviance, as well as gambling and general bohemian lifestyles. "At first glance," George Augustus Sala writes of Soho in 1872, "you see nothing but dingy houses teeming with that sallow, cabbage-stalk and fried fish sort of population, indigenous to back slums."[54] No wonder then, that among the first things Henry Jekyll tells us he did as preparation to assume a life as Edward Hyde was to "take and furnish . . . that house in Soho," as if a house in Soho were the obvious place for a man like Hyde to live.[55] Like Dorian Gray, Hyde knows that Gothic behavior demands a Gothic environment. A glance at Soho on Booth's poverty map shows, if not black, in the main a field of gray (mixed) shading down to dark blues (very poor, casual). But Soho is not an East End district—it is immediately east of Mayfair and north of Leicester Square and the Strand, further from Whitechapel than St. Paul's or the Bank of England. Soho is essentially the center of London, in the West End but not of it. The fictional Edward Hyde was only one of many Victorian men who found their vices in Soho, and readers certainly knew this.

But although Soho is disturbingly close to the West End, it is actually at Henry Jekyll's house that Stevenson most fully deploys the trope of proximity. We first see the house from the rear, when Enfield tells the "story of the door" to Utterson during a Sunday afternoon walk:

> Two doors from one corner, on the left hand going east the line was broken by the entry of a court; and just at that point a certain sinister block of building thrust forward its gable on the street. It was two storeys high; showed no window, nothing but a door on the lower storey and a blind forehead of discoloured wall on the upper; and bore in every feature, the marks of prolonged and sordid negligence. The door, which was equipped with neither bell nor knocker, was blistered and distained. Tramps slouched into the recess and struck matches on the panels; children kept shop upon the steps; the schoolboy had tried his knife on the mouldings; and for close on a generation, no one had appeared to drive away these random visitors or to repair the ravages.[56]

Things look different in front, however:

> Round the corner from the by-street, there was a square of ancient, handsome houses, now for the most part decayed from their high estate and let into flats and chambers. . . . One house, however, second from the corner, was still occupied entire; and at the door of this, which wore a great air of wealth and comfort, though it was now plunged in darkness except for the fanlight, Mr. Utterson stopped and knocked.[57]

Dr. Jekyll's house, as any number of undergraduate essayists will explain, is a metaphor of Jekyll's double life. The dilapidated by-street entrance denotes Hyde's depravity, and the shabby genteel of the square is revealing of Jekyll's mixed morality, the "incongruous compound" of good and evil that is Henry Jekyll.

There has been a good deal of speculation about the exact location of Henry Jekyll's house, and in mapping the novel I have spent some time attempting to fix the good doctor's address. A strong contingent of scholars maintains that Stevenson modeled Jekyll's home on that of surgeon John Hunter, who lived in Leicester Square and had exactly the sort of living arrangements as Henry Jekyll: a large house fronting the square backed with two buildings used as dissecting rooms and an operating theater. Hunter ran a private anatomy school from this address. At the time Stevenson wrote the novel, this house had become the resting place of the Royal College of Surgeons' museum collection. It has since been demolished (a cinema is on the site).

While I admit that Stevenson may have used Hunter's house as the model for Jekyll's, it seems doubtful that he intended Leicester Square as the house's location. While standing outside Hyde's entrance, Enfield tells Utterson early in the novel that he had noticed Jekyll's address and that "he lives in some square or other."[58] It is extremely unlikely that any resident of London would forget the name of Leicester Square or that Enfield and Utterson would not know that they were standing a mere house-width away from the well-known square, no matter how squalid the alleyway.

It seems more feasible that Stevenson purposely kept Jekyll's address vague. He gives us Lanyon's location at Cavendish Square and gives a general area for Hyde's den. He even gives Portland Street as the location of the hotel Jekyll repairs to while on the run after Carew's murder. To be so exact about every other location in the novel and to obscure the most important address seems intentional. We know that it is in "some square or other" in a "busy-quarter of London"[59] and is backed by a by-street or alleyway that contains shops but is not of the highest level of Booth's hierarchy. Any number of places in the city could match this description.

In the interest of mapping the novel, I have chosen Red Lion Square between Holborn and Bloomsbury as a likely candidate. Booth's map shows the square itself as red and backed on three sides with blues and black. Red Lion Square was also the home of three Pre-Raphaelite painters: Dante Rossetti in 1851 and Edward Burne-Jones and William Morris in 1856–1859. Rossetti's landlord expressed concern over the painter's behavior toward female models, saying that "some artists sacrifice the dignity of art to the baseness of passion."[60] Whether this objection was one directed at artists generally or was perhaps due to personal knowledge of Rossetti is unclear, but the hint of sexual scandal implied by the landlord's worries and by the behavior of many of the Pre-Raphaelite Brotherhood in general lends the square additional appropriateness as Jekyll's home.

Regardless of the actual site, Jekyll's house is representative of the microscopic level of Booth's poverty map. A fairly grand house with an "air of wealth and comfort" set in a square of similar houses that have gone to seed, backing onto a by-street where tramps slouch in doorways and "no one appear[s] . . . to repair the ravages," Jekyll's house is itself fairly inclusive in its catalog of the various economics on Booth's map, functioning both as a Gothic presence within the West End, but also as a symbol of the diverse economic nature of London's geography.

The Strange Case of Dr. Jekyll and Mr. Hyde thus undermines the broad light/dark divisions of contemporary commentators. The economic confusion around Jekyll's house is an accurate reflection of the good doctor's conflicted identity, but also belies a reassuring geographic split between the classes. Even Dr. Lanyon's house becomes a Gothic site when Jekyll undergoes his transformation there before Lanyon's horrified eyes. And Jekyll's first involuntary transformation into Hyde—the point at which Hyde's location becomes completely uncontrollable and unpredictable—occurs in Regent's Park, a decidedly upper-crust site. More than being the story of the divided self of Henry Jekyll, Stevenson's novel is truly reflective of the complex play of light and shadow that is Victorian London. What better metaphor for a good man who becomes an incarnation of evil than this city of contrasts?

For a further example of the proximity trope, we turn back to Charles Dickens's most Gothic-infused novel, *Little Dorrit*. Initially, what can be

Figure 3.6. ***Little Dorrit*'s London. The Adelphi and Miss Wade's flat near Park Lane are evidence of the Gothic erupting in the city and the West End, while Bleeding Heart Yard demonstrates the non-Gothic poor. Drawn from Bacon's Gem Map of London, 1910; Rare Books Room, University of South Carolina.**

gleaned from mapping *Little Dorrit* (fig. 3.6) is a reiteration of the East/West dichotomy. The two edifices, Mrs. Clennam's house and the gray "oblong pile" of the Marshalsea, are in decidedly depressed parts of London. The Marshalsea is on the high street in the Borough, just south of London Bridge, an underprivileged area as far back as the late sixteenth century, when Shakespeare's Globe stood not too far away.[61] Little Dorrit's nighttime wanderings, partially quoted in chapter 1, occur in this area—she crosses London Bridge during the course of the evening, but quickly crosses back; the whole of that foggy night of horror takes place in the Marshalsea's immediate neighborhood. Likewise, the Clennam house, though north of the river, is given a dilapidated riverside setting only slightly less seedy than Gaffer Hexam's shack in *Our Mutual Friend*:

> [Arthur] crossed by St. Paul's and went down, at a long angle, almost to the water's edge, through some of the crooked and descending streets which lie (and lay more crookedly and closely then) between the river and Cheapside. Passing, now the mouldy hall of some obsolete Worshipful Company, now the illuminated windows of a Congregationless Church that seemed to be waiting for some adventurous Belzoni to dig it out and discover its history; . . . he came at last to the house he sought. An old brick house, so dingy as to be all but black, standing by itself within a gateway. Before it, a square courtyard where a shrub or two and a patch of grass were as rank (which is saying much) as the iron railings enclosing them were rusty; behind it, a jumble of roots.[62]

The Clennam house is unquestionably in a Gothic district, an area like that surrounding the Marshalsea which is infinitely remote from the world of Mr. Merdle, who lives in Cavendish Square in the heart of the privileged West End. These two spaces, the Clennam House's riverside and the Borough High Street of the Marshalsea, are the primary sites of the Gothic mode in *Little Dorrit*, and their locations are consistent with what we have seen of Gothicized districts in London. In many ways the novel maintains this separation—even the non-Gothic Bleeding Heart Yard is sufficiently removed from Merdle and his high society to give a spatial dimension to its class difference. Arthur Clennam's initial home in a rented flat in Covent Garden places him in the center, in Moretti's "middle space," befitting his middle-class status, and allowing him distance from but easy access to his mother and Little Dorrit in the Gothic districts.

But within this framework, Dickens completely undermines the idea of a Gothic confined by geographic area. To begin with, he makes it clear that poor doesn't necessarily mean scary; *Little Dorrit*, typically for a Dickens novel, features plenty of examples of the working poor as good-hearted and hard-working: the Plornishes and the other inhabitants of Bleeding Heart Yard, Frederick Dorrit, the Chiverys, Daniel Doyce. To underline this point, Dickens also places positive examples of impoverished living within the

Gothic confines of the Marshalsea—Amy Dorrit creates a happy domestic space in her own room and especially in her father's chambers, and the general society of debtors who live in the Marshalsea is for the most part collegial and warm.

More important to the urban Gothic mode, however, is the opposite effect, that of Gothic events and characters occurring within the confines of the wealthy or "safe" areas of London. *Little Dorrit* is full of corrupt upper-class characters who don't necessarily qualify as Gothic,[63] yet there are some genuinely sinister presences who occur in non-Gothicized spaces. One of these is the cruel Henry Gowan, who marries Pet Meagle and befriends the villain Rigaud in Italy. But the character who most violates the East/West split and thus most fully represents the urban Gothic threat is the enigmatic Miss Wade.

Miss Wade, that cold and angry seducer of Tattycoram, is a Gothic presence who doesn't seem to know her place. When Tattycoram leaves the employ of the Meagleses at Miss Wade's instigation, Arthur and Mr. Meagles visit Wade's flat, which is in "one of the dull by-streets in the Grosvenor region, near Park Lane."[64] Dull or no, the Grosvenor Square region is among the most fashionable in London, and the by-streets nearby—possibly Brook or Grosvenor Street, or even a small alley like King Street—would be less than a block from Hyde Park to the West and not more than three or four blocks from Oxford Street. Miss Wade, described early in the novel as having a face "still and scornful, set off by arched dark eyebrows," as well as "proud eyes . . . lifted nostril[s] [and a] handsome and compressed and even cruel mouth,"[65] is a vampire-like figure who plays a crucial role in the main Gothic plot. Miss Wade's characterization as a vampire has been remarked by Piya Pal Lapinski,[66] who posits Le Fanu's lesbian vampire Carmilla as a literary antecedent. Indeed, more than one critic has pointed out the latent homosexuality that seems to wait just under Miss Wade's surface—her cold manner, anti-male stance, and especially her seduction of the naïve and innocent Tattycoram all fit with contemporary stereotypes of the masculinized female. It therefore seems strange to find her with a Mayfair address: according to the East/West rule Miss Wade should be relegated to Southwark or Spitalfields, but she keeps a fashionable address and travels throughout the continent. Rigaud is properly in a Gothicized prison as the novel opens, but Miss Wade moves in the same circles and stays in the same places as the Meagleses and Arthur Clennam.

But even the mansions near Park Lane are twisted in Dickens's description. When Clennam and Meagles venture forth on foot from the "top of Oxford Street"[67] to find Miss Wade, what they find is not what readers would normally expect from the gold areas of Booth's map. The friends

> dived in among the great streets of melancholy stateliness, and the little streets that try to be stately and succeed in being more melancholy, of which there is a labyrinth near Park Lane. Wildernesses of corner-houses, with barbarous old porticoes and appurtenances; horrors that came into existence under some wrong-headed person in some wrong-headed time, still demanding the blind admiration of all the ensuing generations and determined to do so until they tumbled down; frowned upon the twilight. Parasite little tenements with the cramp in their whole frame, form the dwarf hall-door on the giant model of His Grace's in the Square, to the squeezed window of the boudoir commanding the dunghills of the Mews, made the evening doleful. Rickety dwellings of undoubted fashion, but of a capacity to hold nothing comfortably except a dismal smell, looked like the last result of the great mansions' breeding in-and-in; and, where their little supplementary bows and balconies were supported on thin iron columns, seemed to be scrofulously resting upon crutches.[68]

This is one of Dickens' most striking descriptions of London, functioning, in its effective conflation of a wealthy district with the decrepitude and decay of poorer areas, as a microcosm of the urban Gothic. Here, the conditions that characterize the Gothicized city have overtaken the mansions near Park Lane—the very buildings themselves have become diseased, rickety and scrofulous, producing the miasmic smells that infuse the darkest marks on Booth's map. And it is here that Miss Wade chooses to make her London home.

Although Miss Wade's apartment near Grosvenor Square is the most extreme example of the proximity trope in *Little Dorrit,* there are numerous other instances of Gothic locations occuring immediately adjacent to "safe" areas. For instance, in a strikingly Gothic scene that doesn't fit spatially with the conventional wisdom, Arthur follows Tattycoram and Rigaud into the Adelphi and finds them meeting with Miss Wade. The Adelphi, set on the busy and central thoroughfare of the Strand, immediately enshrouds the conspirators and their interlocutor in silence and gloom: "there is always, to this day, a sudden pause in that place to the roar of the great thoroughfare. The many sounds become so deadened that the change is like putting cotton in the ears, or having the head thickly muffled . . . the shore [was] funereal and silent after dark. . . . It was a deserted place and looked on a deserted scene."[69]

We have already seen how *Little Dorrit* presents a London marked by scenes of isolation and solitude, but these scenes take place mere steps away from the crush and light of the non-Gothic city. This is the crux of the proximity trope—that a quick turning can take one nearly instantly from a bright thoroughfare into a darkened enclave where a murderer like Rigaud can feel at home. Although the Adelphi is in the very center of progressive London, perhaps three hundred yards from Trafalgar Square, Miss Wade and Rigaud can comfortably plot their blackmail not only with impunity but in surroundings befitting the proceedings. *Little Dorrit* repeatedly reminds us that the Gothic can occur in the bright, progressive areas of the city as well, and this is its true threat.

As you may have noticed, there are actually two ways in which this proximity trope is being played out in these novels. London's social geography provides multiple opportunities to discover Gothic settings literally around the corner from wealth and safety, but at the same time we find Gothicized characters who are able to easily cross the boundaries between the light and dark areas of the city. Miss Wade makes use of the Jekyll-and-Hyde economic truths of London's topography as detailed by Booth's poverty map—she ducks into the Adelphi to meet Rigaud—but she also moves in the established progressive areas by keeping a flat near Grosvenor Square. This mobility partakes of the contamination threat we've touched on briefly already; the idea that the contagion of the East End cannot be contained by the East End's boundaries, but is able to roll across the city like a particularly insidious fog.[70]

In Richard Marsh's 1897 thriller *The Beetle*, we find a similar tendency of the Gothic monster to penetrate the "safe" areas of London. I will discuss *The Beetle* in more detail in chapters 4 and 5, but we should at least pause here to take note of the geography of the novel. Marsh's novel is concerned with a human-insect shape-shifter intent on a horrible revenge against one of the young lions of Parliament. This creature has come to London from Egypt, making it an example of the colonial anxiety that haunts much Victorian Gothic fiction (*Dracula* is another). The thing keeps a house in the suburbs near Walham Green, but it or its emissary travels quickly and repeatedly into London's West End. The Beetle itself visits Sydney Atherton's Kensington home to attempt to enlist Atherton's help (or to hypnotize him as well if he will not help). At the end of the novel, the creature travels the length and breadth of London and beyond during a protracted train chase. From the novel's very beginning, Gothic characters and events prove difficult to contain as social and geographic boundaries are crossed and erased.

Early in the narrative, the Beetle hypnotizes an out-of-work clerk named Robert Holt to use as a tool to infiltrate London, sending him to burglarize the home of Paul Lessingham, the MP targeted by the Beetle. Lessingham lives in Lowndes Square in the heart of ritzy Belgravia, and much is made of the distance Holt must walk to reach it, but the breaking and entering is accomplished with no difficulty or obstruction. It seems as if the Beetle has even sent Gothic weather to assist the proceedings: "The process of smashing a pane of glass—it was plate glass—was anything but a noiseless one. . . . [But] about that time the wind was howling wildly,—it came shrieking across the square. It is possible that the tumult which it made deadened all other sounds."[71] Holt, the possessed emissary of the Beetle, has brought a demonic force from the decrepit suburbs deep into the heart of fashionable

London, into the very home of a member of the government. The weather mirrors the events, a replication of the pathetic fallacy found in many eighteenth-century Gothic novels. Even ignoring the supernatural elements in this scene, it was a disturbing thought that burglary could penetrate Belgravia with so little resistance.

Robert Holt himself represents the permeability of London's social and geographic boundaries in a very mundane but no less terrifying way. Holt is a clerk by profession, but has lost his situation and been unable to secure another. As *The Beetle* opens, Holt has spent the day unsuccessfully searching for work and has just been denied admission to the Fulham Workhouse. That this is a new and unwelcome experience for Holt is expressed beginning in the third paragraph of the novel:

> To have tramped about all day looking for work; to have begged even for a job which would have given me money enough to buy a little food; and to have tramped and to have begged in vain,—that was bad. But sick at heart depressed in mind and in body, exhausted by hunger and fatigue, to have been compelled to pocket any little pride I might have left, and solicit, as the penniless, homeless tramp which indeed I was, a night's lodging in the casual ward,—and to solicit in vain!—that was worse. Much worse. About as bad as could be. . . .
>
> I had hardly expected to figure as a tramp; but, supposing it conceivable that I could become a tramp that I should be refused admission to that abode of all ignominy, the tramp's ward, was to have attained a depth of misery of which never even in nightmares I had dreamed.[72]

Social mobility was an established fact by the end of the nineteenth century, but here we have the reality that social mobility moves in two directions. Holt's horror is that he could have fallen so far. The social and geographic boundaries are easily transgressed, and here they are conflated—Holt's transformation into a tramp has also necessitated a move to lower-class locales; being homeless he must beg for a bed in the workhouse. This results in a mundane but very real horror that is worse than Holt's nightmares. He has become one of Jack London's "new and different race of people" and later reveals even the erosion of middle-class morals by exclaiming, "For a loaf of bread, what I wouldn't do!"[73]

This is part of the reality that the urban Gothic metaphorizes. The crossing of boundaries between the light and dark districts of London was a terrifying component of the urban Gothic, exacerbated by the unexpected placement of those boundaries. Even with a map like Charles Booth's to mark out the dangerous areas in easy-to-avoid black, there was no guarantee that the inhabitants of those black areas wouldn't simply walk around the corner to your district, your street, your house. There was little even to prevent you falling into those black areas yourself, as Robert Holt and Henry Jekyll discovered.

DRACULA

So the true power of the urban Gothic comes not from the recognition of the established ideas of where and who the criminal elements of London were, but in the knowledge that the Gothic could not be contained by geography. Bram Stoker repeatedly uses this knowledge as a pressure point in *Dracula*, perhaps the ultimate novel of the modern city being invaded by the savage past.

Like *The Picture of Dorian Gray* and *Little Dorrit*, at first glance *Dracula* utilizes the basic East/West dichotomy, and Stoker's novel goes further by combining the non-British setting of the earliest Gothics with the urban Gothic mode in vogue in the 1890s. Dracula is, after all, not a Londoner, but an eastern European immigrant. Ostensibly Romanian, the Count is described in terms of Semitic stereotypes.[74] He thus can be read as a stand-in for the waves of immigrants who flocked to London during the nineteenth century and settled in the East End, while simultaneously evoking memories of the exotic settings of many eighteenth-century Gothic novels in the imposing and isolated edifice of Castle Dracula, brooding high in the Carpathians. Indeed, the Count's journey from Transylvania to London at the beginning of the novel functions as a sort of mini-history of the Gothic novel from its crumbling, wind-swept origins to the modern metropolitan horror tale of the late nineteenth century. There is even a brief sojourn in the land of Brontëan domestic Gothic as the Count arrives in England at Whitby, a north Yorkshire port dominated by the ruins of an eleventh-century abbey and surrounded by the same moors frequented by Heathcliff and Jane Eyre.

Count Dracula does not choose the East End for his primary residence (his crumbling estate Carfax is twenty miles east of London in Purfleet), but he quickly sets up a house there. Once established at Carfax, Dracula distributes his fifty boxes of earth (necessary for his daylight beauty sleep) among three houses across London, thus allowing him to move about the city at night and always be relatively close to a sanctuary. Of these three safe houses, two are in the recognized Gothic districts of the city: one in Jamaica Lane, Bermondsey, and one in Mile End New Town at 197 Chicksand Street.

Mile End New Town, as Nina Auerbach and David Skal tell us in the footnotes to the Norton Edition of Stoker's novel, is "a continuation of London's Whitechapel district, where the Jack the Ripper murders had taken place in 1888."[75] The address at Chicksand Street is actually firmly in Whitechapel—Harker is off by a half a mile or so calling it Mile End New Town. And as if simply placing the house in Whitechapel isn't enough to conjure

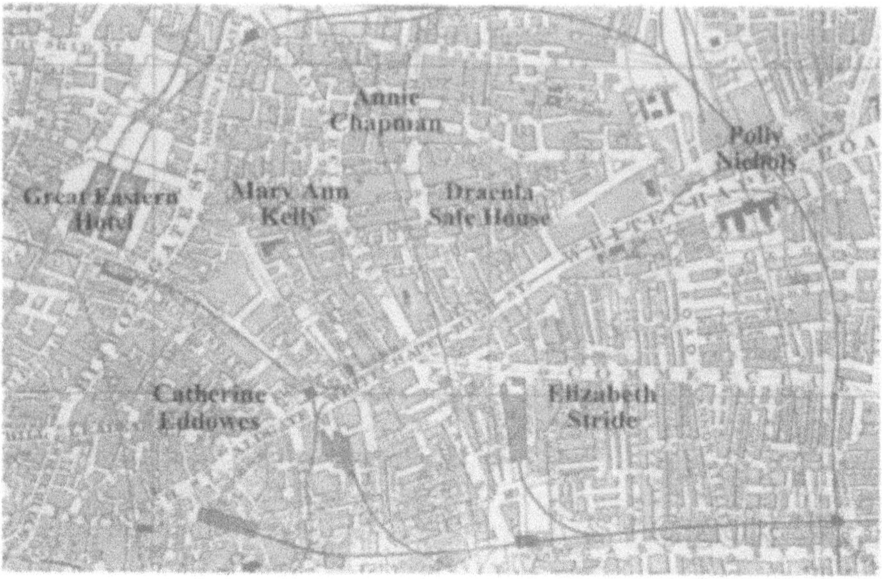

Figure 3.7. The murder sites of Jack the Ripper's victims in relation to Dracula's safe house on Chicksand Street. This map also demonstrates the proximity of these sinister loci to the Great Eastern Hotel, where Van Helsing initially stays upon his arrival in England. Drawn from Bacon's Gem Map of London, 1910; Rare Books Room, University of South Carolina.

images of the nine-year-old crimes, the Count's house at 197 Chicksand Street is roughly at the center of a circle formed by the Ripper murder sites (see fig. 3.7). This proximity may have been unintentional (Stoker may have only meant to evoke the East End generally), but it is worth noting that the house in Mile End New Town is the only one for which readers are given an actual address. Stoker is generally exact in his London locations—Jamaica Lane, Bermondsey (which is assumedly meant to be Jamaica Road); Piccadilly across from Green Park, and so on—but this is one of the only instances in the novel, excepting hotels, where he gives a street number. We may speculate about the exact location of the house on Jamaica Road, but there is only one 197 Chicksand Street. At nine years remove, the Autumn of Terror was very much within recent memory, and Stoker was, like everyone living in England and much of the rest of the Western world, aware of the details of the murders.[76] To be so specific about placing one of the Count's safe houses in the midst of the Ripper's killing ground seems hardly arbitrary. Dracula's deployment at this site allies him directly with the "vestigial stains" of the East End and deliberately evokes the horrors of the Ripper.

Both the murder sites and Dracula's Chicksand Street residence are at the very edge of the East End; in fact, the line formed by connecting Catherine Eddowes, Mary Ann Kelly, and Annie Chapman's murder sites could be used as a hypothetical border between Whitechapel and the city (although Eddowes's body was actually found a few yards inside the official bounds of the city). Stoker demonstrates the difference between the two spaces by having ur-vampire hunter Abraham Van Helsing stay at the Great Eastern Hotel the first time he comes to England in the novel. The Great Eastern is adjacent to Liverpool Street Station and is, according to the *London Encyclopaedia*, the only hotel in the city. It was and is exclusive and pricey, most definitely a high-end place to stay. The fact that the Great Eastern is a five-minute walk from Dorset Street, the "worst street in London," is irrelevant to the East/West figuration—the hotel is not in the East End and therefore is an acceptable place for Van Helsing to stay. The good doctor subsequently stays at the even ritzier Berkeley in Piccadilly, but his initial visit to the Great Eastern highlights the terror and death lurking just across Bishopsgate Street.

Stoker, then, knows and uses the dichotomy evidenced in Dorian Gray's wild cab ride. Dracula's second safe house is south of the Thames in Jamaica Road, still well within the confines of savage London on a street whose name conjures up, as Gill Davies says, "colonial links and financial importance." But what of the third house? It is in this third house that we find the Count breaking free of the class confines of the East End and threatening the teleological status quo. The third safe house is as close to the heart of the prosperous West End as can be imagined—in Piccadilly Street, across from Green Park. We are not given the exact address, but the house can be no more than a block or two from the Albemarle Hotel, where Lord Holmwood stays in London, and the Berkeley, Van Helsing's primary hotel. Dracula apparently finds this area of London agreeable, as he is earlier seen by Jonathan Harker outside Guilano's restaurant on Piccadilly, hunting a young girl.

This sighting, near Hyde Park Corner, is the first of several forays by Dracula into the heart of "enlightened" London. On September 17, the Count is sighted (again in broad daylight) looking at the wolves at the London Zoological Gardens in Regent's Park and demonstrating to the astonished keeper that he can touch and interact with the animals with impunity. Later that same evening Dracula releases the wolf Berserker, whom he uses to assist in breaking into Lucy's home at Hillingham, which is likely either in Highgate or Hampstead, both well-to-do suburbs near Hampstead Heath. When coupled with the lurking at Hyde Park Corner, Dracula's venturing into Regent's Park, and even to Hillingham in the northern suburbs, is among the most shocking aspects of the novel. Dracula's threat is not only his vampiric nature (and the cluster of readings that implies) but also that he does not know his place. Dracula's primitive savagery occurs in the very center of the modern city (see fig. 3.8).

This is the time-honored project that Dracula undertakes: the bringing of the Gothic Other, the fringe-dwelling degenerate, into the realm of the progressive Britisher. Whereas Lucy as vampire confines herself to true Gothic sites on the outlying districts of London—Hampstead Heath with its wild landscapes and history of highwaymen and crime, and Highgate Cemetery's lushly overgrown and wooded lanes[77] —Dracula seems intent on penetrating into the center of the city.

This knowledge is hardly surprising given the amount of thought the Count has given the metropolis. Dracula is fascinated by London; his desire

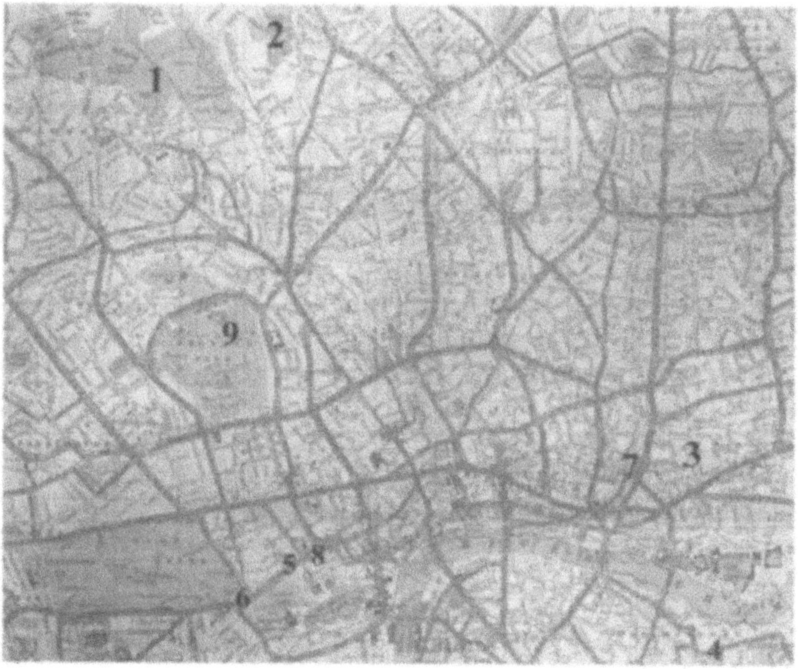

Figure 3.8. ***Dracula*'s London. This map clearly illustrates the East/West divide, demonstrating just how deeply the Count penetrates into the progressive West End. Drawn from Bacon's Gem Map of London, 1910; Rare Books Room, University of South Carolina.**

KEY: 1. Hampstead Heath, where Lucy preys on children as the "Bloofer Lady"; 2. Highgate Cemetery, the model for "Kingstead Cemetery" where Lucy is buried; 3. 197 Chicksand Street, one of Dracula's safe houses; 4. the safe house on Jamaica Road, Bermondsey; 5. the third safe house, on Piccadilly Street; 6. Hyde Park Corner, where Jonathan sights Dracula after returning from Budapest; 7. the Great Eastern Hotel, where Van Helsing first stays in London; 8. the Albemarle and the Berkeley, hotels of Arthur Holmwood and Van Helsing; 9. London Zoo, where Dracula talks with the keeper and later releases a wolf.

to be there is the precipitating factor for the entire novel. During the opening chapters dealing with Jonathan Harker's unhappy stay in Castle Dracula, we see the Count poring over maps and reference works. He asks Harker to converse with him daily so he can perfect his English. Harker even catches him "reading, of all things in the world, an English Bradshaw's Guide."[78] Dracula tells Harker that he longs "to go through the crowded streets of your mighty London, to be in the midst of the whirl and rush of humanity, to share its life, its change, its death, and all that makes it what it is."[79] The Count's real estate purchasing plan and his movements throughout the novel bear out this desire: Dracula covers the city geographically, economically, and socially, purposefully breaking down the geographic stereotypes of crime and transgression.[80]

Dracula's most obvious example of the Gothic erupting in the midst of modernity is the Count's third safe house in Piccadilly Street. The house's location is across from Green Park, putting it less than a quarter-mile from Buckingham Palace and within a few minutes' walk from Hyde Park. The fairly posh surroundings notwithstanding, when Jonathan Harker first comes upon the place,

> the house looked as though it had been long untenanted. The windows were encrusted with dirt, and the shutters were up. All the framework was black with time, and from the iron the paint had mostly scaled away. It was evident that up to lately there had been a large noticeboard in front of the balcony; it had, however, been roughly torn away, the uprights which had supported it still remaining. Behind the rails of the balcony I saw there were some loose boards, whose raw edges looked white.[81]

Later, upon gaining entrance to the house through the influence and money of Lord Godalming, the group takes note that the place smells "vilely."[82] Dracula has placed his mark here, his corrupting influence evident at the center of the city's prosperity.

Interestingly, the house on Piccadilly is also the command center for Dracula's small collection of real estate. The crew find a sheaf of documents on the dining-room table: "title-deeds of the Piccadilly house in a great bundle; deeds of the purchase of the houses at Mile End and Bermondsey; notepaper, envelopes, and pen and ink."[83] Also there was "a little heap of keys" which opened all of the houses. Though he has sanctuaries all over the city, Dracula uses his only West End home as a business office and depository for important papers and money. The West End, site of much of the wealth of the British empire and home of those who administer that wealth, serves as the vampire's economic hub as well.

Ultimately, however, Dracula's forays into the more enlightened districts of the city are doomed to failure. Though his ability to manifest outside the East/West dichotomy inherent in the Gothicized city is the most powerful and unsettling element of his sojourn in London, it is precisely the modernity of London that drives him back to Transylvania. London is, after all, the most progressive and advanced city in the world. Julian Wolfreys says that "modernity erupts through the very act of writing the city,"[84] and even though he is referring to Blake and Dickens, we can see the idea hold for Stoker. Our intrepid heroes combat Dracula through telegraph and train as much as through stake and garlic, and these things are products of the modern London. Dracula himself uses the London Directory, the Law Lists, and the Bradshaw Guide to arm himself for confronting the great city, but he cannot match the combined knowledge and skills of Van Helsing's crew—a doctor, a lawyer, a Lord, an American cowboy, and a Dutch metaphysician; the totality of the Western world seems summed up in this group that banishes the ignorant, eastern threat of the vampire. The Old World cannot compete with the "nineteenth century up-to-date with a vengeance." Nevertheless, Dracula moves further west in the city than we would expect, and pops up in several unexpected locations. Even though the modern city is ultimately able to repulse the vampire, part of the lesson of Stoker's novel seems to be that there is no place in London completely safe or enlightened.

As reassuring to nineteenth-century Londoners as the idea of a safe and happy West End set against a depressed and dangerous East End was, the reality was of course much more complex. As Booth's map demonstrates, Victorian London's economic patterns could not be summed up in a simple duality. London's patchwork of wealth, poverty, and all the gradations in between denied any easy formulation of Gothic sites, and even so the past was as apt to erupt in the heart of the West End as anywhere else, as Miss Wade, Henry Jekyll, and Count Dracula prove. The uncertainty of the Gothic's location implies an instability in the basic concept of progressive modernity. And at any rate, the experience of the urban Gothic didn't occur on maps, but in the streets those maps attempted to represent. The characters and readers who tried to negotiate through London's labyrinth had no true map to guide them, as we will soon see.

NOTES

1. Franco Moretti, *Atlas of the European Novel, 1800–1900* (London: Verso, 1998), 3.
2. Flora Tristan, *London Journal*, 1840, 631.
3. Tristan, *London Journal*, 631.
4. Tristan, *London Journal*, 631–32.
5. Moretti, *Atlas of the European Novel*, 117.
6. Moretti, *Atlas of the European Novel*, 86.
7. Asa Briggs, "The Human Aggregate," *The Victorian City: Images and Realities*, ed. H. J. Dyos and Michael Wolff, vol. 1 (London: Routledge & Kegan Paul, 1973), 83.
8. Karl Baedeker, *London and Its Environs: A Handbook for Travellers*, Facsimile Edition (1900; Moretonhampstead, Devon: Old House Books, 2002), 94.

9. Gustave Doré and Blanchard Jerrold, *London: A Pilgrimage* (1872; New York: Dover, 1970), 97.

10. Doré and Jerrold, *London*, 146.

11. Walter Besant, *All Sorts and Conditions of Men* (1882; Oxford: Oxford University Press, 1997), 323.

12. Doré and Jerrold, *London*, 124–25.

13. Judith Walkowitz, *City of Dreadful Delight: Narratives of Sexual Danger in Late-Victorian London*, Women in Culture and Society series (Chicago: University of Chicago Press, 1992), 194.

14. Walkowitz, *City of Dreadful Delight*, 195.

15. Jack London, *The People of the Abyss* (New York: Macmillan, 1903), vii.

16. Walkowitz, *City of Dreadful Delight*, 26.

17. London, *People of the Abyss*, 3.

18. London, *People of the Abyss*, 3.

19. London, *People of the Abyss*, 4.

20. "The Worst Street in London: Where Our Criminals Are Trained," *Daily Mail*, July 16, 1901.

21. The *Daily Mail* piece and McCarthy's angry response can both be read in full on the *Casebook: Jack the Ripper* website (www.casebook.org).

22. "The Worst Street in London."

23. "The Worst Street in London."

24. "The Worst Street in London."

25. Robert Mighall, *A Geography of Victorian Gothic Fiction* (Oxford: Oxford University Press, 1999), 51.

26. F. S. Schwarzbach, *Dickens and the City* (London: Athlone Press, 1979), 213.

27. For a discussion of the economic grounding of much of *Our Mutual Friend* and its Gothic language, see chapter 5.

28. Charles Dickens, *Our Mutual Friend* (1865; New York: Bantam, 1990), 30.

29. Dickens, *Our Mutual Friend*, 17.

30. Dickens, *Our Mutual Friend*, 17.

31. Dickens, *Our Mutual Friend*, 31.

32. Dickens, *Our Mutual Friend*, 166.

33. Oscar Wilde, *The Picture of Dorian Gray*, ed. Donald L. Lawler, Norton Critical Edition (1891; New York: Norton, 1988), 142.

34. London, *People of the Abyss*, 6.

35. London, *People of the Abyss*, 8.

36. Wilde, *Picture of Dorian Gray*, 142.

37. Wilde, *Picture of Dorian Gray*, 142-43.

38. See also Wilde's poem "The Harlot's House" (1885), from which much of the imagery in Dorian's cab ride is directly duplicated. Specifically, the shadows against the blinds moving like "monstrous marionettes" is repeated from the poem.

39. Wilde, *Picture of Dorian Gray*, 143.

40. London, *People of the Abyss*, 7-8.

41. Wilde, *Picture of Dorian Gray*, 141.

42. Wilde, *Picture of Dorian Gray*, 141.

43. Wilde, *Picture of Dorian Gray*, 141.

44. Wilde, *Picture of Dorian Gray*, 141.

45. Wilde, *Picture of Dorian Gray*, 144.

46. Wilde, *Picture of Dorian Gray*, 143.

47. Wilde, *Picture of Dorian Gray*, 143.

48. Ritchie describes opium dens in *Days and Nights in London* (1880), Rowe in *Life in the London Streets* (1881). Charles Dickens Jr.'s 1879 *Dictionary of London* includes this entry: "Opium Smoking Dens.— The best known of these justly-named 'dens' is that of one Johnstone, who lives in a garret off Ratcliff-highway, and for a consideration allows visitors to smoke a pipe which has been used by many crowned heads in common with poor Chinese sailors who seek their native pleasure in Johnstone's garret. This is the place referred to in the

'Mystery of Edwin Drood.' . . . A similar establishment of a slightly superior—or it might be more correct to say a shade less nauseating—class is that of Johnny Chang, at the London and St. Katharine Coffee-house, in the Highway itself."

49. Wilde, *Picture of Dorian Gray*, 143.

50. Wilde, *Picture of Dorian Gray*, 162.

51. Moretti, *Atlas of the European Novel*, 78.

52. Mighall, *Geography of Victorian Gothic Fiction*, 40.

53. Walkowitz, *City of Dreadful Delight*, 29.

54. George Augustus Sala, "Perfidious Patmos," *Gaslight and Daylight with Some London Scenes They Shine Upon,* in *The Strange Case of Dr. Jekyll and Mr. Hyde*, by Robert Louis Stevenson, ed. Martin A. Danahay (1872; Peterborough: Broadview, 1995), 174.

55. Robert Louis Stevenson, *The Strange Case of Dr. Jekyll and Mr. Hyde*, ed. Martin A. Danahay (1886; Peterborough: Broadview, 1995), 80.

56. Stevenson, *Strange Case of Dr. Jekyll and Mr. Hyde*, 32.

57. Stevenson, *Strange Case of Dr. Jekyll and Mr. Hyde*, 42.

58. Stevenson, *Strange Case of Dr. Jekyll and Mr. Hyde*, 35.

59. Stevenson, *Strange Case of Dr. Jekyll and Mr. Hyde*, 32.

60. Quoted in Ben Weinreb and Christopher Hibbert, *The London Encyclopaedia* (London: Macmillan, 1993), 658.

61. The Borough is still somewhat so today. Although much of Southwark and the Borough is undergoing a revival (the new Tate Modern and the Jubilee Riverwalk evidence this, as do the resurgence of upscale restaurants and shops), the area around St. George's Church, where the one remaining wall of the Marshalsea still stands, definitely remains somewhat derelict.

62. Charles Dickens, *Little Dorrit*, ed. John Holloway (1857; Harmondsworth, England: Penguin, 1967), 70–71.

63. This is due partially to these characters not operating out of the past/present dichotomy—the various Barnacles working in the Circumlocution Office, for example, are representatives of what is wrong with the present. The most prominent upper-class villain, Mr. Merdle, is simply not presented by Dickens as a Gothic character—the language used around Merdle is for the most part comic, and even during the chapters leading up to his suicide Merdle is represented as an object of pity more than a threatening presence. His actions may have widespread and devastating consequences, but Merdle is a very different sort of villain from *Oliver Twist*'s Monks, for example.

64. Dickens, *Little Dorrit*, 373.

65. Dickens, *Little Dorrit*, 62.

66. In "Dickens's Miss Wade and J. S. Le Fanu's Carmilla: The Female Vampire in *Little Dorrit*," *Dickens Quarterly* 11, no. 2 (August 1994): 81–87.

67. Dickens, *Little Dorrit*, 344.

68. Dickens, *Little Dorrit*, 344–45.

69. Dickens, *Little Dorrit*, 555–56.

70. Several literary and social historians have written compellingly about Victorian fear of contamination and miasma theory, among them Tina Young Choi in "Writing the Victorian City: Discourses of Risk, Contamination, and Inevitability," *Victorian Studies* 43, no. 4 (Summer 2001): 561–89, and Pamela Gilbert's excellent *Mapping the Victorian Social Body* (Albany: SUNY Press, 2004).

71. Richard Marsh, *The Beetle*, ed. Julian Wolfreys (1897; Peterborough: Broadview, 2004), 71–72.

72. Marsh, *The Beetle*, 41.

73. Marsh, *The Beetle*, 46.

74. From chapter 2: "His face was a strong—a very strong—aquiline, with high bridge of the thin nose and peculiarly arched nostrils; with lofty domed forehead, and hair growing scantily around the temples, but profusely elsewhere. His eyebrows were very massive, almost meeting over the nose" (23). Later, a zookeeper at the London Zoo describes Dracula as "a tall, thin chap, with a 'ook nose and a pointed beard" (126). Bram Stoker, *Dracula,* ed. Nina Auerbach and David J. Skal, Norton Critical Edition (1897; New York: Norton, 1997).

75. Stoker, *Dracula*, 229n2.

76. Stoker also drew direct connections between his novel and Jack the Ripper. In an introduction to the Icelandic translation of *Dracula* in 1901, Stoker inexplicably attributed vampiric origins to the Whitechapel murders. Attempting apparently to give additional believability to his novel, Stoker describes the narrative as if it actually happened, writing that "this series of crimes has not yet passed from the memory—a series of crimes which appear to have originated from the same source and which at the time created the same repugnance in people everywhere as the notorious murders of Jack the Ripper." Quoted in Barbara Belford, *Bram Stoker and the Man Who Was Dracula* (Cambridge, MA: De Capo Press, 2002), 272.

77. In the novel, Lucy is buried in "Kingstead Cemetery," a fictional location. I believe Stoker modeled Kingstead on Highgate Cemetery, despite Auerbach and Skal's suggestion of Hampstead Cemetery in the Norton *Dracula*. The novel's clues to the cemetery's location are that it is adjacent to Hampstead Heath, and that after rescuing a child from Lucy in the graveyard, Seward and Van Helsing "got a cab near the Spaniard's" (178), the old inn and restaurant on the north-eastern side of the Heath. It would make little sense for the doctors to travel so far north from Hampstead Cemetery to catch a cab at the Spaniard's when cabs and train stations are abundant nearby. Jumping the wall to the west of Highgate, however, would require a trip across the Heath, and the Spaniard's would indeed be the first place where finding a cab would be feasible. It is also unlikely that the vampire Lucy could have abducted children from the Heath and moved through the inhabited streets necessary for her to reach Hampstead Cemetery. Coupled with the creepy and tree-lined description of the cemetery, these clues seem to me to suggest Highgate as a model much more than Hampstead.

78. Stoker, *Dracula*, 28.

79. Stoker, *Dracula*, 26.

80. Gill Davies does a fine job of diagramming the way Dracula surrounds London's perimeter before penetrating into the center of the city. Davies also spends time considering the economic implications of Dracula's locations within London. Gill Davies, "London in *Dracula*; Dracula in London," *Literary London: Interdisciplinary Studies in the Representation of London* 1, no. 3 (March 2004), http://homepages.gold.ac.uk/london-journal/davies.html.

81. Stoker, *Dracula*, 232.

82. Stoker, *Dracula*, 262.

83. Stoker, *Dracula*, 262.

84. Julian Wolfreys, introduction to *The Beetle,* by Richard Marsh (1897; Peterborough: Broadview, 2004), 13.

Chapter Four

Walking in the City of Dreadful Night

The Gothic Flâneur

Look at the construction of the place. The Gordian knot was all very well in its way: so was the maze of Hampton Court. . . . But what involutions can compare with those of Seven Dials? Where is there such another maze of streets, courts, lanes, and alleys . . . as in this complicated part of London?—Charles Dickens, *Sketches by Boz*, 1839

After a hundred steps I became aware / Of something crawling in the lane below.—James Thomson, *The City of Dreadful Night*, 1874

In May 2007, I led a group of students on a ten-day trip to London and its environs. During a day trip into Kent, four or five students and I found ourselves in the hedge maze in the gardens at Leeds Castle. The purpose of this maze, as with most, is to reach the center, where a series of steps lead up to a sort of tower that allows the intrepid traveler to look back down from a height at the maze he has successfully conquered. The maze isn't large, and we confidently strode into it expecting to quickly make it to the tower. Fifteen minutes later we were hopelessly lost, a situation made more frustrating by the proximity of the tower, looming close at hand but very much out of reach. No matter how we attempted to map out the maze in our heads as we moved through it—systematically moving in a single direction, taking alternative turnings when we came to the same intersection a second time, and so forth—we got no closer to the center. We might have been there still, but a couple of visitors who had made it to the top took pity on us and began to shout down directions: "Turn right!" "Take the middle path!" With their help, we made it to the tower in less than five minutes. The people on the tower could see the whole of the maze, and therefore understood its construction in ways that we, walking below, could never hope to.

The difference in these two perspectives forms the crux of this chapter. Until now, we have been looking at London from above, as it were. The mapping of Gothic London is a useful way to see at a glance the broad sweep of contemporary attitudes toward the city, to see which are the sites of anxiety and which of security. But this sort of overarching view of the city is a luxury of the author, who lays London out before him like a text. For the text's inhabitants, the characters of the urban Gothic, there is a more difficult path to navigate. To walk in Gothic London is to give up any idea of map or guide; it is to duck the head and enter a labyrinth which is, as Dickens says of Seven Dials, more treacherous than any Gordian knot or Thebian trial. In London, Baudelaire's *flâneur* becomes an anxious wanderer, lost and terrified, at constant risk of encountering the grotesque and Gothic dwellers at the heart of the maze. To some degree, the reader experiences this Gothic *flânerie* along with the characters, but she partakes of the disorientation of the London walker only as far as the author forces her to. With the author as a guide, the reader can ultimately be led out of the maze.

In this chapter I look at two types of walkers on Gothic London's streets. First, I will consider the characters who walk the streets of the Gothic city, showing how their experience differs from the standard Baudelairean *flâneur* and demonstrating how the Gothic's sense of anxiety is multiplied when set in the labyrinth of London's streets and alleys. But I will also expose the minotaurs at the heart of London's labyrinth, the atavistic lurkers who threaten and transform the unwary walker. These monsters may be the truest *flâneurs* on the streets of London—creatures completely at home in the twisted alleys and back streets of the city. But before we meet these haunted walkers, we should first take a look at the sort of labyrinth we are dealing with. Let us begin with a look at why London was (and is) especially suited to the maze metaphor.

LONDON AS LABYRINTH

The source of what the 1900 Baedeker's guide calls London's "labyrinthine topography" was the city's rapid and unplanned growth. The speed of London's expansion during the nineteenth century, coupled with its lack of a municipal governing body prior to the formation of the London County Council in 1888, resulted in an unstructured urban evolution sprawling in all directions, unlike the more organized growth of New York or Paris, cities that were largely mapped out as grids. "London," Roy Porter offers, "was not a coherent development, dictated by government, given form by a rational road grid. In the century of Darwin—himself living beyond Bromley on

London's outskirts—it was likened to some natural phenomenon, evolving spontaneously."[1] The city's continual and seemingly organic increase spawned a rabbit's warren of streets and alleys repeatedly described as labyrinthine by those who experienced it. "To one already impressed by the immensity of London," writes Mary Krout in her 1899 travel book *A Looker-On in London*, "the first sight of its tangled streets is like surveying an interminable labyrinth, which is without beginning and without end."[2]

Krout's description of a labyrinth that is "without beginning and without end" is evocative of what Umberto Eco, drawing on the theories of Deleuze and Guattari, calls the "rhizome" labyrinth. In the explanatory notes to his novel *The Name of the Rose* (1983), Eco delineates three types of labyrinth: the Greek labyrinth, which "does not allow anyone to get lost" because of its predictable structure; the mannerist maze, which is like a tree with roots—there are "many blind alleys" but the whole is ultimately structured hierarchically and thus understandable; and the rhizome: "The rhizome is so constructed that every path can be connected to every other one. It has no center, no periphery, no exit, because it is potentially infinite."[3]

London is not a rhizome, of course. The city has a beginning and an end. It is possible, though difficult, to step outside London and contemplate the whole. The traveler who moves in a single direction long enough will leave the city, and even in the Victorian era the popular balloon ascents were able to provide something like an omniscient overview, as did views from high vantage points such as the top of St. Paul's or the Monument. Indeed, the desire to step outside the whole is in large part the reason behind the Victorian passion for panopticons, panoramas, and dioramas. Daguerre's diorama, opened in 1829, featured a 126-foot open dome into which visitors were lifted by steam powered lifts, revealing a realistic circular painting of the whole of London as seen from the top of St. Paul's. By the time of the Great Exhibition of 1851, these panoramas "had become a mania of the London public."[4] These map-like representations of the city were reassuring proof that London had limits, if only you could get far enough removed to see them.

Twentieth-century cultural theorist Michel de Certeau makes explicit the difference between those who have maps and those who do not. In his essay "Walking in the City," de Certeau contemplates New York City while on the 103rd floor of the World Trade Center, from which vantage he can see most of the city at once. Ascending to this height, says de Certeau, is "to be lifted out of the city's grasp."[5] The totality of vision allowed by this all-encompassing view is like that of the mapmaker or city planner—it enables an understanding of the city's entire topography impossible from the street, but also divorced from any sort of real urban experience. As de Certeau explains:

> When one goes up there, he leaves behind the mass that carries off and mixes up in itself any identities of authors or spectators. An Icarus flying above these waters, he can ignore the devices of Daedalus in mobile and endless labyrinths far below. His elevation transfigures him into a voyeur. It puts him at a distance. It transforms the bewitching world by which one was "possessed" into a text that lies before one's eyes. It allows one to read it, to be a solar eye, looking down like a god. . . . Must one finally fall back into the dark space where the crowds move back and forth, crowds that, though visible from on high, are themselves unable to see down below?[6]

The answer, of course, is yes. To see the city in its entirety is to be god-like, omniscient as an author. De Certeau's reference to the original Greek myth of the labyrinth at Knossus reminds us that even in its earliest forms the need to look down was inherent in the conception of the labyrinth—Icarus's solution to the maze is not to find his way through but to fly up and out. But this experience is not one shared by the majority of those who come into contact with the city. Most of us cannot fly Icarus-like above the streets (and perhaps this isn't a bad thing, given the ultimate fate of that too-ambitious aviator). To de Certeau, the opposite of "voyeur"—his word for the omniscient overseer on high—is "walker," one of the crowd who "though visible from on high" is "unable to see down below." These walkers are effectively blind, threading their way through the maze of streets with no knowledge of the larger pattern. Again, de Certeau:

> The ordinary practitioners of the city live "down below," below the thresholds at which visibility begins. They walk—an elementary form of this experience of the city; they are walkers, *Wandersmänner*, whose bodies follow the thicks and thins of an urban "text" they write without being able to read it. . . . The networks of these moving, intersecting writings compose a manifold story that has neither author nor spectator, shaped out of fragments of trajectories and alterations of spaces: in relation to representations, it remains daily and indefinitely other.[7]

It is not my purpose to completely explore de Certeau's theories of spatial narrative, but his ideas here are especially apt for Victorian London, a city composed of no regular pattern of streets, no recognizable design for logical movement. Thomas Rice tells us that

> complex systems exhibit design, orders more akin to the rhizome forest than the hierarchical trees. Individuals are unable to perceive those orders, however, because they can never achieve a panoptic position in a system that contains them, where there is no up (or down), no place from which to map the system, no external point of reference.[8]

Rice and Eco use mapping as a metaphor for complex systems in general, for what Eco calls "the space of conjecture,"[9] but the metaphor holds truth for the actual topography of Victorian London. The whole can be mapped, of course, but to those within the object itself, "who can never achieve a panoptic vision," London is unending and unknowable. To those walking the streets of the city, London might as well be infinite.

Joseph Conrad makes humorous use of the confusion of London's streets, especially the incongruity of house numbers, in his 1907 novel *The Secret Agent*:

> With a turn to the left Mr. Verloc pursued his way along a narrow street by the side of a yellow wall which, for some inscrutable reason, had No. 1 Chesham Square written on it in black letters. Chesham Square was at least sixty yards away, and Mr Verloc, cosmopolitan enough not to be deceived by London's topographical mysteries, held on steadily, without a sign of surprise or indignation. At last, with business-like persistency, he reached the Square, and made diagonally for number 10. This belonged to an imposing carriage gate in a high, clean wall between two houses, of which one rationally bore the number 9 and the other was numbered 37; but the fact that this last belonged to Porthill Street, a street well-known in the neighborhood, was proclaimed by an inscription placed above the ground-floor windows by whatever highly efficient authority is charged with the duty of keeping track of London's strayed houses. Why powers are not asked of Parliament (a short Act would do) for compelling those edifices to return where they belong is one of the mysteries of municipal administration.[10]

Conrad is having fun here, indulging in a Dickensian satire on municipal government and on the bewilderment of those who walk in London. But below the surface of Conrad's humor is a marked uneasiness. The idea of houses that move around and refuse to stay where they belong is unsettling; as an explanation for the labyrinthine nature of London's topography it borders on the outright scary.[11] What Conrad does illustrate in this passage is Londoners' resignation to the incongruities and confusion of the city's layout. Difficulty in understanding the London map at street level seems here to be an accepted fact. Mr Verloc may be cosmopolitan enough not to be disturbed by such geographic anomalies, but the mention of his unperturbedness implies that not everyone has such sophistication. For most walkers in London, the city seems designed to confound.

In his *London: A Biography*, Peter Ackroyd invokes the labyrinth tag, adding that the city "cannot be conceived of in its entirety but can only be experienced as a wilderness of alleys and passages, courts and thoroughfares, in which even the most experienced citizen may lose the way."[12] Travelers in New York or Paris who missed a turning could take the next cross-street and double back to right themselves; in London this could result in becoming irretrievably lost.[13] Any sort of confident movement through the city required the omniscience of de Certeau's mapmaker. In 1844, *Mogg's New Picture of London and Visitor's Guide to Its Sights* pressed upon its readers the necessity of carrying a detailed map of the city while sightseeing: "like the clue of Ariadne [a good map], will conduct [the traveler] through the labyrinth, and, occasionally consulted, will enable him, unattended, to thread with ease the mazes of this vast metropolis."[14] Mapless, the wanderer runs the risk of joining "that floating population of foreigners and provincials who are continually in a chronic condition of being 'lost in London.'"[15]

But even with a map, some areas of London are ultimately unknowable. The areas which the middle and upper classes insisted on seeing as Other, the large Gothicized areas considered in chapter 3, are not navigable even with a map. As Franco Moretti reports:

> In early-nineteenth-century maps, detail is rapidly lost as the map moves away from the West End; the London maps published by Bowles (1823), Wyld (1825), and Fraser (1830), for instance, all agree on the number of streets that intersect Bond Street, or lead into Grosvenor Square—but they are in total disagreement on those that lead into Smithfield (13, 9, 10), or on the alleys around Saffron Hill (in Bowles, one third fewer than in the others), or on the number of lanes that run into the river between Blackfriars and Southwark Bridge (9, 12, 16).[16]

Thus the areas understood by West Enders to be savage and vague are rendered as such in the reality of the map. There is no text that can accurately guide the traveler through those labyrinths.

But some texts do at least attempt to guide the reader. The Gothic's frequent reliance on first-person narration, either directly or through documentary narratives couched within the novel proper, results at times in the reporting of routes and landmarks—a sort of travel guide to Gothic London. Thus, in *Dracula*, when Mina and Jonathan encounter Dracula near Hyde Park, the reader is told (by Mina through her journal) the path the couple have taken: omnibus to Hyde Park Corner, a walk up Rotten Row, then up Piccadilly, seeing the Count outside Guiliano's, and finally a calming turn in Green Park.[17] Likewise the two journeys described in chapter 3 (those of Wrayburn and Lightwood in *Our Mutual Friend* and of Dorian Gray in his novel) give signposts and routes fairly explicitly, as do other novels we will discuss later. Many authors provide specificity of location in their descriptions of London. But the main idea of de Certeau's theory—that the walker is a blind wanderer with no clear knowledge of his environment—is reinforced repeatedly in Gothic narratives in which the reporting of routes or landmarks does nothing to alleviate the sense of being lost and threatened. And more often than not, the sense of being threatened is justified.

In the opening chapter of Richard Marsh's *The Beetle*, Robert Holt tells the story of how he comes to find the house with the open window, which will become the locus of evil for the events to come. An out-of-work clerk, Holt has spent the day vainly looking for a position. Having failed that, he finally resorts to the humiliation of attempting to gain admission to the Hammersmith workhouse, only to be told that there are no beds available. He is thus obliged to continue walking through the London suburbs:

> Retreating from the inhospitable portal of the casual ward, I had taken the first turning to the left,—and, at the moment, had been glad to take it. In the darkness and the rain, the locality which I was entering appeared unfinished. I seemed to be leaving civilisation behind me. . . . Exactly where I was I could not tell. I had a faint notion that, if I only kept on long enough, I should strike some part of Walham Green. How long I should have to keep on I could only guess. Not a creature seemed to be about of whom I could make inquiries. It was as if I was in a land of desolation.[18]

Holt is hopelessly lost in the labyrinth, unaware of all but a vague sense of the spatial relationship of his location with his destination. His unsettling impression is that he is "leaving civilisation behind," entering the realm of the savage, the primeval past. The seemingly abandoned house he finally discovers, "one of those so-called villas which are springing up in multitudes all around London,"[19] is the home of the eponymous Beetle. The villain's placement is in an appropriately non–West End area of the city, one which would have been inadequately represented on the early-nineteenth-century maps Moretti examines. The emphasis in these opening passages, however, is on the disquiet of the traveler in this area. We are given descriptions of Walham Green that characterize it as ugly and unfinished, adjectives that are suggestive also of the misshapen and mutable body of the Beetle. Holt is uneasy not because of the dweller in the house but because he is disoriented and unable to find his way. It is only later that his knowledge of the house alters his unease into outright fear.

LOST IN LONDON: THE *FLÂNEUR* IN THE DARK

In this way, Holt differs from the most often discussed walker in the nineteenth-century city: the *flâneur*, who is eminently at home in the streets. First fully conceived and described by the French poet Charles Baudelaire and then adopted by Walter Benjamin as the hero-figure of his *Arcades* project, the figure of the *flâneur* was originally strongly associated with nineteenth-century Paris. As conceptualized by Baudelaire, the *flâneur* is a stroller, a poet who idly walks the streets of the city. The *flâneur*'s ambition is to observe those around him,[20] to watch the individuals that compose the crowd. According to Benjamin:

> The street becomes a dwelling for the *flâneur*; he is as much at home among the façades of houses as a citizen is in his four walls. To him the shiny, enamelled signs of businesses are at least as good a wall ornament as an oil

> painting is to a bourgeois in his salon. The walls are the desk against which he presses his notebooks; news-stands are his libraries and the terraces of cafés are the balconies from which he looks down on his household after his work is done.[21]

Baudelaire, writing in his 1863 essay "The Painter of Modern Life," is even more explicit. The poet tells us that

> the crowd is [the *flâneur*'s] domain, just as the air is the bird's, and water that of the fish. His passion and his profession is to merge with the crowd. For the perfect idler, for the passionate observer it becomes an immense source of enjoyment to establish his dwelling in the throng, in the ebb and flow, the bustle, the fleeting and the infinite. To be away from home and yet to feel at home anywhere; to see the world, to be at the very centre of the world, and yet to be unseen of the world, such are some of the minor pleasures of those independent, intense and impartial spirits.[22]

An important component of Baudelaire's definition is the *flâneur*'s separateness from those he observes. Though the *flâneur* is at home in the crowd, he is not of it. "The literature of rambling," writes Deborah Nord, "fed on the exhilaration of disconnection and anonymity."[23] This quality of being sundered from those he observes allows the *flâneur* to maintain a critical distance, to become a "connoisseur of human nature."[24] Marc Eli Blanchard tells us that "at the beginning of every *flâneur*'s experience, there is the perception of his own lack of identification with anything or anyone in particular."[25] In order to negotiate the waters of the metropolitan cityscape, it is necessary to have an outsider's understanding of those who dwell within it. "The more uncanny a big city becomes," writes Benjamin, "the more knowledge of human nature—so it was thought—it takes to operate in it."[26]

The *flâneur*'s idleness and languor make him a fitting character to be appropriated by fin de siècle writers such as Oscar Wilde (who implicates Baudelaire's *Les Fleurs du mal* as one of the wicked influences on Dorian Gray), and his role as detached observer allows him to be cast perfectly as the poet-hero of modernity. The *flâneur*'s urban encounters also contain more sinister overtones, however. "The interplay between the city as bestial and the city as beautiful," writes Graeme Gilloch, "was both the essential theme of, and the very source of inspiration for, Baudelaire's poetry."[27] Thus the *flâneur* existed from the beginning in the Gothic city. But the walkers in the urban Gothic are different from Baudelaire's original, at home as he was in the streets. The Gothic *flâneur* is in a state of nearly constant anxiety; the disorientation of London's streets and the threat of the minotaur unsettle and frighten the traveler, transforming Baudelaire's sense of aloof detachment into a terrifying isolation that leaves the walker alone and at the mercy of the city and its denizens.

The possibility of the Gothic *flâneur* was also inherent in the construction from the very beginning. Baudelaire cites American Gothic writer Edgar Allan Poe's London-set story "The Man of the Crowd" (1840) as formative for the character of the poet-observer. Poe was not often an urban author. Discounting the August Dupin mysteries, which despite some similarities to the form are more detective stories than Gothics, most of Poe's horror tales have more traditional Gothic settings; the House of Usher's wild and desolate landscapes have more in common with the writings of Ann Radcliffe than with those of Charles Dickens. "The Man of the Crowd" is a rare detour for Poe into the area of the urban Gothic. Poe's story features an old man who constantly moves through the crowded streets, adjusting his wanderings to keep him in the most populated areas as the day progresses. The narrator attempts to follow the old man, but gives up after twenty-four hours of unceasing motion. The wanderer's travels take him on a circuitous and unending route first through the "great thoroughfares"[28] and then, as the night wears on, into "noisome" districts "where everything wore the impress of the most deplorable poverty, and of the most desperate crime."[29] This is *flânerie* of an anxious sort, not Baudelaire's walker "at home in the crowd." For although the old man is himself very much of the multitude, the speaker-observer is made apprehensive by the man he follows. Baudelaire sees the old man as the *flâneur*, always moving with the crowd, "at home in the streets." Benjamin agrees, although he feels that Poe's old man is motivated less by a desire to be among others as by being "someone who does not feel comfortable in his own company."[30] But in terms of the urban Gothic, Poe's narrator fills the *flâneur*'s role much more fully. Beginning explicitly as an observer of those around him (one of the primary elements of Baudelaire's hero-poet), and continuing on to walk the streets expressly to observe the old man, the narrator of "The Man of the Crowd" is a true Gothic *flâneur*, made more and more anxious by his wanderings. Poe's story also differs from Baudelaire's poetry in its setting: "The Man of the Crowd" takes place in London.

The narrator of "The Man of the Crowd" begins his tale in a coffeehouse on one of London's "principal thoroughfares."[31] He is looking at the crowd passing by outside the bow-window in which he sits and describing each type of person he sees to the reader. Among them are "noblemen, merchants, attorneys, tradesmen, stock-jobbers,"[32] as well as clerks of various standing. The narrator is more interested, however, in the "swell pick-pockets," "gamblers," "Jew pedlars,"[33] and others whom he considers at the low end of the "scale of gentility."[34] He spends a fair amount of time describing the different character-types of the prostitutes loitering nearby:

> women of the town of all kinds and ages—the unequivocal beauty in the prime of her womanhood, putting one in mind of the statue in Lucian, with the

> surface of Parisian marble, and the interior filled with filth—the loathsome and utterly lost leper in rags—the wrinkled, bejewelled and paint-begrimed beldame, making a last effort at youth—the mere child of immature form, yet, from long association, an adept in the dreadful coquetries of her trade, and burning with a rabid ambition to be ranked the equal of her elders in vice.[35]

Combined with the people observed before and after ("professional street beggars," "drunkards innumerable"), this catalog of street-walkers helps create a vision of the elements of the city most threatening to the middle-class observer. After depicting the milling Londoners at length (two-and-half pages of a five-page story), the narrator spies the old man of the title and is compelled to rush out of the coffeehouse to follow the strange wanderer. The lingering sketches of the criminals and more threatening denizens of the streets have prepared the reader for the old man, who is a sort of embodiment of all that is terrifying about the crowds in London:

> He was short in stature, very thin, and apparently very feeble. His clothes, generally, were filthy and ragged; but as he came, now and then, within the strong glare of a lamp, I perceived that his linen, although dirty, was of a beautiful texture; and my vision deceived me, or, through a rent in a closely-buttoned and evidently second-hand *roquelaire* which enveloped him, I caught a glimpse both of a diamond and a dagger.[36]

The Man of the Crowd is old, even decrepit, and exhibits the clothing and hygiene of the worst of London's slum dwellers. At the same time, however, there is a hint of wealth and of threat about him in the diamond and the dagger. In some ways this man embodies not only the crowds of the city, but the city itself—old and dirty, but possessed of affluence and of danger. "The man of the crowd *is* the crowd," writes Richard Lehan, "and, metonymically, the city as well."[37]

The subsequent chase through London's streets results in a pursuit cum walking tour, from the "street of the D— Hotel" (an opulent boulevard in the West End, possibly the Strand) to the "noisome quarter" mentioned above. The chase is marked by anxiety and a growing horror. Interestingly, the affluent areas of the city are mentioned in passing, but when the narrator pursues the old man into the poorer districts, the narrative lingers over descriptions:

> By the dim light of an accidental lamp, tall, antique, worm-eaten, wooden tenements were seen tottering to their fall, in directions so many and capricious that scarce the semblance of a passage was discernible between them. The paving stones lay at random, displaced from their beds by the rankly growing grass. Horrible filth festered in the dammed-up gutters. The whole atmosphere teemed with desolation.[38]

This "noisome quarter" is the lengthiest portrayal Poe gives of London itself. The West End is described in a few sentences as "brilliantly lighted, and overflowing with life."[39] It is the dark and dirty regions that draw the narrator's attention, just as the old man's most obvious qualities are age and decay.

If we can accept the Man of the Crowd not just as a *flâneur* prototype but a personification of London, then two other observations are worth noting here. One is that the speaker explicitly identifies the old man with crime: "'This old man,' I said at length, 'is the type and genius of deep crime.'"[40] If the man is read as an incarnation of London, then this statement is a telling commentary on Poe's perception of the British capital, recalling the lengthy descriptions of criminal types the narrator observed earlier in the story. It is also significant that this "genius of crime" walks through the whole of London, not just the more deprived areas. This specter of the criminal exists wherever there are masses of people, thus tingeing the entirety of the metropolis with a Gothic taint.

More correlative to our consideration of London as an unmappable and unknowable labyrinth, however, is the sentence with which Poe chooses to end his story. The heart of this man, the heart of London, says the narrator, is "a grosser book than the 'Hortulus Animæ,' and perhaps it is but one of the great mercies of God that *es lässt sich nicht lesen.*"[41] As de Certeau will do over a hundred and twenty years later, Poe compares the cityscape to a text. The *Hortulus Animæ*, a popular prayer book from the sixteenth century, obviously does not encompass all that exists in London, if only because it does not expose the ugliness of crime and desolation that lurks there. More importantly, the city is a text that "*lässt sich nicht lesen*" (won't let itself be read). Richard Leman, in *The City in Literature*, interprets this sentence as proof of the city's impenetrability:

> While the narrator's sense of acute impression leaves him with an indelible picture of the man of the crowd, the circular journey which encompasses—that is, encloses—the city finally breaks down short of meaning, and we are left with a sense of the mysterious and uncanny. . . . The narrator is thus left with intense impressions of the man of the crowd (that is, impressions of the city), but what such sensory data may mean beyond the realm of impression—what they tell him about the meaning of the city itself—he cannot say.[42]

Leman has identified an important element of Poe's story: the obscurity of London as an understandable object. But Leman's translation of the final German phrase of the story has itself hidden a further point. The reflexive "*sich*" is crucial here. Leman's translation, "it can't be read," is more accurately rendered as: "it will not allow itself to be read." London, Poe suggests, is not unreadable simply by virtue of its complex layout or its size. At some level, it *chooses* to remain obscure, purposefully concealing its true nature.

The great city is consciously Gothic, then, willfully dark and purposively threatening. London intentionally obscures itself from the *flâneur*'s comprehension.[43]

MINOTAURS

Labyrinths are the home of monsters. This has always been so, beginning with the minotaur at Knossus, or perhaps with the spiders at the center of webs throughout history. A maze the size of London has too many minotaurs to count, and walkers lost on its streets must eventually encounter one or more. In the urban Gothic, these monsters range from the ordinary—pickpockets, murderers, rapists, even prostitutes—to infernal and supernatural creatures such as Dracula, Hyde, or the strange Egyptian insect that haunts Richard Marsh's *The Beetle*. What Poe describes in "The Man of the Crowd" is the experience of following one of these monsters through the labyrinth.

This is often the apex of the experience of walking in the urban Gothic novel—the sense of anxiety mounts until the walker comes upon a monstrous person or thing who is much more at home in the streets than the walker. These encounters, these meetings with the minotaur at the heart of London's Knossus, occur precisely because the walker has no true knowledge of his surroundings. As Blanchard says in *In Search of the City*: "The question, then, is one of approach, of denying one's knowledge and sense of context in order to make possible, in this very absence of one's self, the appearance of something other and strange, yet close enough to be felt as a part of one's own being."[44] The monsters lurking in the twisted streets of London are the "vestigial stains," predators from the savage past, hunting for walkers grounded in the present. Those who encounter the minotaur find themselves altered in some way, often for the worse. As an example, consider the experience of Florence Dombey.

Florence Dombey, the daughter of business magnate Paul Dombey in Charles Dickens's *Dombey and Son* (1848), takes to the streets of London alone on two occasions during the course of her novel: once as a child when she becomes separated from her party, and once later in her life when she leaves home to live at Sol Gill's shop. The first of these is the most terrifying, the most Gothic. In chapter 7 of *Dombey and Son*, eight-year-old Florence is taken on an excursion to the home of Polly Toodle, young Paul Dombey's wet nurse, in an economically depressed part of Camden-town.[45] On the way back, Florence is separated from her party when the Stagg's Garden marketplace is thrown into confusion by "a thundering alarm of 'Mad Bull.'"[46] Florence does not realize she has been cut off from her friends until it is too late:

> Florence screamed and ran. She ran till she was exhausted, urging Susan to do the same; and then, stopping and wringing her hands as she remembered that they had left the other nurse behind, found, with a sensation of terror not to be described, that she was quite alone.[47]

Florence now attempts to negotiate the labyrinth. Scared and wandering through the unfamiliar streets, she soon encounters a minotaur in the form of Good Mrs. Brown, an opportunistic old woman who preys on children. Brown is a grotesque apparition, identified as a savage throwback by her ugliness and dirt and by the skins she carries over her arm like some primitive Neanderthal:

> She was a very old woman, with red rims around her eyes, and a mouth that mumbled and chattered of itself when she was not speaking. She was miserably dressed, and carried some skins over her arm. She seemed to have followed Florence some little way at all events, for she had lost her breath; and this made her even uglier still, as she stood trying to regain it: working her shrivelled yellow face and throat into all sorts of contortions.[48]

Good Mrs. Brown quickly takes charge of Florence. Promising the girl a reunion with her companions, the old woman leads her "down a dirty lane, where the mud lay in deep black ruts down the middle of the road," stopping at a "shabby little house, as closely shut up as a house that was full of cracks and crevices could be."[49] The interior of this abode contains "a great heap of rags of different colors lying on the floor; a heap of bones, and a heap of sifted dust or cinders; but there was no furniture at all, and the walls and ceiling were quite black."[50] Age and dilapidation are the hallmarks of Mrs. Brown's abode; Florence has been brought to the underside of London, into the depths of a black mark on Booth's poverty map.

Once inside, Mrs. Brown forces Florence to hand over her frock, bonnet, petticoats, and shoes. After overcoming her desire to cut off Florence's hair as well, the old woman dresses Florence in rags and leads her "through a labyrinth of narrow streets and lanes and alleys" to the edge of the progressive city (where "the roar of the great thoroughfare made itself audible"[51]), and releases her. Pertinent to our consideration of the monster as *flâneur* is the fact of Mrs. Brown's knowledge of the streets, especially the dark and confusing side streets she guides Florence through at the end of this episode. Florence is merely a visitor to the streets of London; Good Mrs. Brown is completely at home there.

In the space of an hour, Florence is taken by the monster in the labyrinth and transformed. Her flight and subsequent accosting by Mrs. Brown have been described by Erik Bond as "a terrifying maturation mapped onto Camden's streets."[52] Bond sees the experience, rightly, as a trauma for the young girl, saying that "Brown forces Florence to physically alter herself and mirror the mental changes this abduction is producing in her,"[53] causing her psychological damage and moral staining (her loss of innocence) to be reflected in her outward appearance. Florence is dragged abusively out of childhood by the street-hag; a difficult psychological journey is mapped out through a dangerous physical one.

At the same time, Good Mrs. Brown has remade Florence in her own image. The innocent middle-class girl who gets lost in the market quickly becomes a rag-clad street urchin stranded on the edge of progressive London. As a representative of London's hidden primitivism, Mrs. Brown's function in the narrative is to drag others down into her dirty past, staining them with her history. As an example of middle-class Londoners' fears of being somehow contaminated by the lower classes, the episode is nearly primal in its metaphoric force.

Even after her escape from Good Mrs. Brown, however, Florence still has to deal with the confusion of peripatetic London. Her newfound knowledge and hard-won experience haven't made her at home as a walker in the metropolis. She tries to reach her father's offices in the city, but is hampered by her lack of knowledge of the streets:

> All she knew of her father's offices was that they belonged to Dombey and Son, and that that was a great power belonging to the City. So she could only ask the way to Dombey and Son's in the City; and as she generally made the inquiry of children—being afraid to ask grown people—she got very little satisfaction indeed. But by dint of asking her way to the City after a while, and dropping the rest of her inquiry for the present, she really did advance, by slow degrees, toward the heart of that great region which is governed by the terrible Lord Mayor.[54]

Here we have a glimpse of the knowledge that Florence has gained. People on the streets of London are to be feared, and it is difficult to find anyone who can give accurate guidance through the city. Even the slow advancement towards her goal only brings Florence in range of a region "governed by the terrible Lord Mayor," who is made by Dickens to sound like some ogre from a dark fairy tale—as if the head of London's government is himself a minotaur waiting to catch all the population in his net.

Florence Dombey's trip through the labyrinth is terrifying, and her encounter with Good Mrs. Brown evidence of the savagery lurking in London's Gothic districts. According to this account, the risks of wandering the city's streets are manifold—not only can the traveler lose her way irrevocably, but London's minotaurs are waiting to catch her when she does.

Enfield is describing the experience of the Gothic *flâneur* in the first chapter of *The Strange Case of Dr. Jekyll and Mr. Hyde*, when he tells Utterson of his first encounter with Hyde. Coming home "from some place at the end of the world," Enfield describes the anxiety of walking the night streets of London, streets that are "lighted up as if for a procession and all as empty as a church," by saying that he wishes for the sight of a patrolling bobby.[55] It is at that point that Enfield meets the minotaur in the form of Edward Hyde:

> All at once, I saw two figures: one a little man who was stumping along eastward at a good walk, and the other a girl of maybe eight or ten who was running as hard as she was able down a cross street. Well, sir, the two ran into one another naturally enough at the corner; and then came the horrible part of the thing; for the man trampled calmly over the child's body and left her screaming on the ground. It sounds like nothing to hear, but it was hellish to see. It wasn't like a man; it was like some damned Juggernaut.[56]

Hyde is truly a monstrous dweller in the city, and this encounter leaves a sinister impression upon Enfield. But there are in fact two wanderers in the nocturnal city in Enfield's story—the other walker here, the little girl, fares even worse. Though she is not killed (she was "not much the worse, more frightened"[57]), it is likely that her run-in with Edward Hyde will haunt her the rest of her life, just as Hyde's atavism haunts the narrative.

Edward Hyde is as comfortable walking in the city as those who meet him are uneasy. He is a minotaur, and as such the labyrinth of London is his home. Hyde operates through much of his novel as a random violent element loose in the streets of London, and anyone unfortunate enough to have a chance encounter with him is likely to suffer for it.

When Sir Danvers Carew meets Hyde in the street and asks directions of him, the consequences are even more dire than those that met the little girl of Enfield's story. A maid who is watching from a second-story window describes this random meeting, telling at first how Sir Danvers asks information of Hyde "with a very pretty manner of politeness." Hyde's response is anything but polite:

> He had in his hand a heavy cane, with which he was trifling; but he never answered a word, and seemed to listen with an ill-contained impatience. And then all of a sudden he broke out in a great flame of anger, stamping with his foot, brandishing the cane, and carrying on (as the maid described it) like a madman. The old gentleman took a step back, with the air of one very much surprised and a trifle hurt; and at that Mr. Hyde broke out of all bounds and clubbed him to the earth. And next moment, with ape-like fury, he was trampling his victim under foot and hailing down a storm of blows, under which the bones were audibly shattered and the body jumped upon the roadway.[58]

Hyde displays himself here in full atavistic ferocity, a thinly veiled Darwinian throwback who is unable to keep a civilized hold on his "ape-like fury." This scene is the quintessential encounter between the lost and anxious Gothic *flâneur* and his counterpart, the minotaur who is both more knowledgeable and more dangerous. Sir Danvers's only mistake is in losing his way—something all too easy on these streets. Stopping to ask for directions is the last attempt to make sense of his surroundings he will ever make.

The various depictions of Edward Hyde meeting with walkers who are scarred or killed serve almost as cautionary tales for the foot traveler. Stevenson's focus is less on the *flâneur* than on the violence of the encounter as understood by an observer—Enfield sees the little girl get trampled, the maid watches the murder of Sir Danvers. By placing the reader's perceptions as analogous to those watching the results of the *flâneur*'s Gothic meetings, Stevenson reinforces the danger of the streets through example. It would be best, he seems to suggest, to avoid wandering the streets of London, especially during the fog-bound gaslit nights such as those that perpetually occur in his novel.

The urban Gothic's characters, along with the reader, are essentially strangers on the streets on London. Even the native Londoner (Enfield, Sir Danvers, etc.) who finds himself in these unsettling situations becomes as unfamiliar with his hometown topography as any rustic on a day trip. This is especially dangerous because, as Edward Hyde demonstrates, the monsters that roam the labyrinth are completely at home there. This fact becomes startlingly clear to Gabriel Syme, the protagonist of G. K. Chesterton's *The Man Who Was Thursday* (1908). Chesterton's novel, one of several about secret anarchist societies written during the early twentieth century that frequently lapse into the urban Gothic mode,[59] tells the story of Syme, a police detective who infiltrates a high-level council of anarchists (taking the code name "Thursday"). Syme's confidence is shaken when the president of the council ("Sunday") announces that there is a traitor among them. Fearing exposure, Syme walks through London as a snowstorm begins. It is then that Syme encounters a familiar minotaur, a member of the anarchist council called Professor de Worms:

> He was considerably astonished to see, standing quite still outside the shop and staring into the window, a man. His top hat was loaded with snow like the hat of Father Christmas, the white drift was rising round his boots and ankles. . . . That any human being should stand in such weather looking into a shop was a matter of sufficient wonder to Syme; but his idle wonder turned suddenly into a personal shock; for he realised that the man standing there was the paralytic old Professor de Worms.[60]

Professor de Worms has earlier been described as ancient and decrepit, a dying old man who somehow personifies for Syme the inherent immorality of the anarchists:

> The red flower in his buttonhole showed up against a face that was literally discoloured like lead; the whole hideous effect was as if some drunken dandies

> had put their clothes upon a corpse. When he rose or sat down, which was with long labour and peril, something worse was expressed than mere weakness, something indefinably connected with the horror of the whole scene. It did not express decrepitude merely, but corruption. Another hateful fancy crossed Syme's quivering mind. He could not help thinking that whenever the man moved a leg or arm might fall off.[61]

The Professor is described here in terms of a zombie, a walking corpse rotten to the point of dissolution. Syme is therefore rightfully disturbed to discover that Professor de Worms is pursuing him through London with a speed and agility that seems to violate the laws of physics. Syme enters a restaurant in Soho for lunch, only to find the Professor there before him. Likewise in a coffeehouse, Syme finds the Professor entering moments after him. "Can that old corpse be following me?" he wonders,[62] before running a hundred yards to catch a moving omnibus. When the Professor soon struggles lamely up the steps to sit near Syme, the detective loses his composure and leaps from the bus "with the vague idea, if this incomprehensible jack-in-the-box was really pursuing him, that in the labyrinth of little streets he could soon throw him off the scent."[63] The Professor is much more a creature of this maze of side streets than Syme, however, and it is soon evident that he cannot be shaken off so easily. The chase is eerily silent because of the snow on the ground, until at one point Syme crosses a cobblestone square that has been cleared of snow:

> He thought little of this as he passed it, only plunging into yet another arm of the maze. But when a few hundred yards farther on he stood still again to listen, his heart stood still also, for he heard from that space of rugged stones the clinking crutch and labouring feet of the infernal cripple.[64]

The relentless and inexplicable pursuit causes Syme to mistrust his surroundings and eventually to become claustrophobic within the knot of streets he thought would hide him. The "impulse to break out of this hive of houses, and to get once more into the open and lamp-lit street"[65] sends Syme rushing through the maze, becoming disoriented. Even though he finds the large open street he's looking for, "he struck it much father up than he fancied,"[66] breaking into the open in front of St. Paul's, quite a way from the Soho of his flight's beginning. The Professor soon catches up, and the ensuing chase sends Syme into familiar Gothic territory, down by the river into a "foul tavern, sprinkled with foreign sailors, a place where opium might be smoked or knives drawn."[67]

Syme's experience is terrifying and, to him, without natural explanation. He is lost in a labyrinth of alleyways, pursued by a walking corpse. The streets are strangely empty, and the alleys through which Syme scrambles are "blind and featureless; there was no little window or any kind of eye."[68] The "sealed and sullen" sunlight itself is described as "sickly, green, dead red, or decaying bronze."[69] Even the subsequent revelation that the Professor is a police detective as well,[70] a much younger man disguised as a dying senior citizen, does not alleviate the terror of the chase itself or Syme's unnerving impression that he had been somehow dropped into a city of nightmare—indeed during the chase we are told that Syme remembers every nightmare he ever had. Syme's experience is the frightening sense of being irretrievably off course, of encountering a sinister and powerful creature and being unable to withstand or escape it in a confusing cityscape with no logical pattern.

This sort of experience occurs repeatedly in urban Gothic novels during the fin de siècle. We turn now to a novel that multiplies the effect of the Gothic *flâneur* by replicating it on two narrative levels. The interwoven tales of Arthur Machen's *The Three Impostors* (1895) carry the reader throughout the south of England and Wales, from the city to the desolate countryside, even to the Rocky Mountains of North America. It is a distinctly urban book, however, and the frame story as well as the most compelling of the interpolated tales take place in London. Lin Carter, in her introduction to the 1972 Ballantine paperback of *The Three Impostors*, says the novel "reads rather as if Machen were trying to look at London as Scheherazade looked at Baghdad—through eyes that saw everyday life as a tangle of incredible coincidences, chance meetings, overheard anecdotes, and marvelous encounters. . . . Through the eyes of Arthur Machen, London becomes a fantastic metropolis, filled with intrigue and mystery and marvels."[71] Carter is correct—Machen repeatedly uses the Gothic *flâneur* as a device to begin the urban portions of *The Three Impostors*, though it is not always immediately obvious who is the wanderer and who the minotaur. And even though several of the interpolated tales take place in non-urban and even non-British settings, it is difficult to forget that the telling of each of these stories takes place on the streets of London at or near the places where the tellers are first encountered.

Machen's episodic novel concerns the experiences of Dyson and Phillips, two friends intrigued by intellectual pursuits, science, and literature. Avid walkers, the pair also act as interlocutors for various individuals they meet in the city. The stories told by these individuals make up the bulk of the narrative in *The Three Impostors*, and the tellers' appeals to Dyson and Phillips for assistance drive the frame narrative.

Dyson in particular has two encounters that initiate the novel. The first incident establishes Dyson as a Gothic *flâneur* and simultaneously an observer of a Gothic encounter. Going out in the early evening, Dyson wanders through the Oxford Street area of "stucco and prosperity"[72] but then moves eastward: "It was quite dark when I passed along a sombre little by-street, ill-lighted and empty. I did not know at the time in the least where I was, but I found out afterwards that it was not very far from Tottenham Court Road."[73]

He is in a deserted warehouse district when he sees two people in rapid succession. The first is a man fleeing for his life, who rushes by "flinging something from him as he ran."[74] Dyson picks up the gold coin the man has thrown away and then ducks into a darkened mews as he hears another person approaching quickly:

> A man went by with a rush a few paces from where I was standing, and I felt uncommonly pleased that I was hiding. I couldn't make out much feature, but I saw his eyes gleaming and his teeth showing, and he had an ugly-looking knife in one hand, and I thought things would be very unpleasant for gentleman number one if the second robber, or robbed, or what you like, caught him up.[75]

Dyson consults Phillips, who identifies the gold piece as a unique and very valuable Roman coin. During this conversation Dyson refers again to his witnessing of the murderous chase near Tottenham Court Road:

> It is queer enough what I saw; a man is sauntering along a quiet, sober, everyday London street, a street of grey houses and blank walls, and there, for a moment, a veil seems drawn aside, and the very fume of the pit steams up through the flagstones, the ground glows, red-hot, beneath his feet, and he seems to hear the hiss of the infernal cauldron. A man flying in mad terror for his life, and furious hate pressing hot on his steps with knife drawn ready; here, indeed, is horror.[76]

An accurate description of the Gothic experience on the streets, this passage also neatly sums up the sense, repeatedly invoked in *The Three Impostors*, that the world we see hides a much more disturbing reality just below its surface.

Additionally, the impetus for this action—a Roman coin—is an explicit reference to London's earliest past. The Romans, in taking the southern regions of Britain from the pagan Celts under Queen Boudicca, were the original forces of historical telos in the Thames valley, and the founding of Londinium by the Roman empire initiated the city as a site of cultural progress. The Romans were in their time the most advanced culture in the world—Roman innovations in architecture, government, and engineering were the outward signs of modernity two thousand years ago. That they themselves have become the antiquated past is indicative of the forward march of progress. Dyson's Roman coin evokes both London's history of growth and modernity, while itself becoming a physical expression of that history's inability to stay buried.

Dyson's second foray into *flânerie* occurs at the beginning of the section entitled "The Encounter of the Pavement." The opening of this section deliberately casts Dyson in the role of Baudelaire's poet-walker, emphasizing the air of idle detachment Baudelaire felt so important to the *flâneur*:

> Mr. Dyson, walking leisurely along Oxford Street, and staring with bland inquiry at whatever caught his attention, enjoyed in all its rare flavours the sensation that he was really very hard at work. His observation of mankind, the traffic, and the shop windows tickled his faculties with an exquisite bouquet; he looked serious, as one looks on whom charges of weight and moment are laid; and he was attentive in his glances to right and left, for fear lest he should miss some circumstance of more acute significance.[77]

In Baudelairean terms, Dyson is ripe for an encounter, and indeed the title of this section of Machen's novel should have prepared us for this. It is no surprise then, when Dyson meets a highly emotional man pursuing a "young man in spectacles" who has just gotten into a cab in front of Dyson. The pursuer, accosting Dyson and asking if he had seen the other man, is singular in appearance and action:

> The words bubbled and boiled out of the man's mouth in the fury of his emotion, his face went from red to white, and the beads of sweat stood out on his forehead; he stamped his feet as he spoke, and tore with his hand at his coat, as if something swelled and choked him, stopping the passage of his breath.[78]

Neither is the man physically reassuring. Like Edward Hyde and Professor de Worms, the man, who gives his name as Mr. Wilkins, is dressed well, but the clothes seem somehow incongruous on him:

> His silk hat, Dyson thought, should have been a high bowler of odious pattern, worn with a baggy morning-coat, and an instinct told him that the fellow did not commonly carry a clean pocket-handkerchief. The face was not of the most agreeable pattern, and was in no way improved by a pair of bulbous chin-whiskers of a ginger hue, into which moustaches of like colour merged imperceptibly.[79]

Dyson's inherent aversion to Mr. Wilkins, reminiscent of Enfield's dislike of Edward Hyde, stems from the sense that Wilkins's outward appearance hides some baser nature within, a nature that Dyson perceives in terms of class.

Overcoming his distaste, Dyson goes with Mr. Wilkins "down a sober street" and "into what seemed a narrow passage past an iron-barred gate thrown back."[80] Here Mr. Wilkins tells "The Novel of the Dark Valley," the first long interpolated tale of the novel. Wilkins is the victimized protagonist of his tale, but the manner in which Dyson meets him betrays his true nature. Because we know that someone with Mr. Wilkins's strange appearance and manner met on the streets of London can only be a minotaur, it is difficult not to be suspicious of him. Consequently, Mr. Wilkins is ultimately revealed as one of the three impostors of the title, and his story a fabrication intended to ensnare Dyson.

More interesting than Dyson's meeting of Mr. Wilkins, however, is the parallel experience of Mr. Phillips, who meets someone able to describe what happens to the *flâneur* permanently taken by the monster in the maze. Mr. Phillips, the more scientifically minded of the two protagonists, meets a young woman, Miss Lally, in Leicester Square who seems to want to speak with him. The story she tells him becomes "The Novel of the Black Seal," one of the centerpieces of Machen's episodic narrative. Before she tells her tale, however, Miss Lally relates that she is looking for her brother, who is missing somewhere in the city, taken by a supernatural entity.

Miss Lally tells Phillips that her brother, who turns out to be the young man with spectacles earlier referenced in Wilkins's tale, has been employed as a classical master at a private school in Highgate. The siblings have always been close and met each Saturday in Leicester Square to spend the day together, the sister coming up from her position as a governess in Tooting to the south. This Saturday, however, a strange event happens. She sees her brother approaching from the south (instead of the north as usual), accompanied by another man. She is immediately seized by a "bristling fear, the fear of a child in the dark, unreasonable and unreasoning, but terrible, clutching at my heart with the cold grip of a dead man's hands."[81] Miss Lally then looks closely at the man with her brother:

> I noticed that this man was leading my brother rather than walking arm-in-arm with him; he was a tall man, dressed in quite ordinary fashion. He wore a high bowler hat, and, in spite of the warmth of the day, a plain black overcoat, tightly buttoned, and I noticed his trousers, of a quiet black and grey stripe. The face was commonplace too, and indeed I cannot recall any special features, or any trick of expression; for though I looked at him as he came near, curiously enough his face made no impression on me—it was as though I had seen a well-made mask.[82]

As the two figures pass her, Miss Lally hears her brother's voice speaking to her, though his lips do not move. The voice "came to my ears as if mingled with splashing water and the sound of a shallow brook flowing amidst stones,"[83] telling her that he cannot stay. It is then that the strange encounter turns unequivocally nightmarish:

> As my brother passed me, I saw the hand that held him by the arm, and seemed to guide him, and in one moment of horror I realized that it was a formless thing that has mouldered many years in the grave. The flesh was peeled in strips from the bones, and hung apart dry and granulated, and the fingers that encircled my brother's arm were all unshapen, claw-like things, and one was but a stump from which the end had rotted off.[84]

Recovering herself enough to follow the pair, Miss Lally runs from the square and sees "the two figures walking amidst the crowd"[85] and follows them into a side street, but then loses them completely in the crowd. She returns to Leicester Square, and it is there that Phillips meets her.

Miss Lally's experience is horrific and understandably unsettling. She appeals to Phillips to confirm that she isn't losing her mind. What she has seen is the aftermath of her brother meeting the minotaur. He is being taken away (northward from Leicester Square into Soho, haunt of Edward Hyde and Conrad's Mr. Verloc), transformed into the same sort of zombie as the man that guides him, unable to speak or turn his head to look at his sister. Perhaps more disturbing than what lies in store for Miss Lally's brother, though, is the physical appearance of the thing which is spiriting him away. He is dressed "in quite ordinary fashion," and his face makes no impression whatsoever on the closely observant Miss Lally. As she says, it is as if the man's face were a "well-made mask." Except for the bizarre rotting appendage with which he grasps the brother's arm, this creature is virtually indistinguishable from any other middle-class worker in the city. Miss Lally's description (perhaps even down to the mask-like face) would fit any of the thousands of clerks who make their way to work in the city every day. The zombie-clerk could be a comment on the stultifying effects of the repetitiveness of modern life, in which case every city dweller becomes simultaneously both minotaur and *flâneur*, both monster and human. Moreover, the walking dead is a clear metaphor for the recurring past, for history that will not stay dead. The truth behind the façade of the corpse-clerk is that which is always imparted by the urban Gothic—the "normal" and modern exterior is only the crust over a festering core of primitive savagery.

We never discover anything else about the sinister figure who carries off Miss Lally's brother, however, because the whole story has been invented. The real minotaur here is Miss Lally herself, the second of the eponymous impostors, who has invented her story to trap Phillips. It is necessary, then, to retrace our steps somewhat and examine how Mr. Phillips first meets Miss Lally.

Phillips has gone out on this Saturday to escape from his home for a while, recalling Baudelaire's requirement that the *flâneur* be uncomfortable in his own dwelling and thus prefer the streets. In this case, Phillips's landlady has thrown some important artifacts he had been studying into the rubbish bin, and Phillips takes a walk to cool off:

> Unlike Dyson he walked fast, with his eyes on the pavement, absorbed in his thoughts, and oblivious of the life around him; and he could not have told by what streets he had passed, when he suddenly lifted up his eyes and found himself in Leicester Square.[86]

Phillips is not being a typical *flâneur*, as he is not observing the streets around him, but he does lose track of where he is walking and seems surprised to find himself in Leicester Square. Likewise, the woman he meets on the park bench in the square doesn't seem at first to have any of the characteristics of the Gothic monster—she is "neatly dressed"[87] and appears to be "a young girl with a quaint and piquant rather than a beautiful face" with "charming eyes of a shining hazel."[88] It is actually her understated attractiveness and "all-beseeching"[89] attitude that causes Phillips to hear her out.

But this is the same woman, whose real name is Helen (her surname is not given), who colludes with Richmond and Davies to kill the young man with the spectacles because of his theft of the golden Tiberius. The spectacled man, Joseph Walters, is tortured before being burned alive, and Helen keeps a severed finger as a souvenir. The three impostors, members of a sinister secret organization modeled loosely on the Order of the Golden Dawn,[90] are among the most dangerous characters to be encountered on the streets of Victorian Gothic fiction. Like the zombie-clerk in Helen's story, it is perhaps the very fact of their innocuous first impression that makes them so frightening.

Helen's choice to build her story around an undead creature who looks like any other man in the street is indicative of her own duplicitous nature, but also of the uncertainty of the Gothic *flâneur*. The characters who walk in the Gothicized city are in unfamiliar territory; no map is available to guide them to safety. The minotaur, the only creature truly comfortable on the streets of darkest London, lurks in wait for the unwary; encounters with the inhabitants of labyrinthine London realize the fears inherent in the Gothic *flâneur*, making concrete the uncertainty and dread in the heart of the modern cityscape.

THE CITY OF DREADFUL NIGHT

Perhaps the ultimate evocation of walking in Gothic London occurred twenty-one years earlier than Machen's novel of urban paranoia. In 1874, James Thomson published his long paean to the Gothic cityscape, *The City of Dreadful Night*, a poem which repeats over and over again the experience of meeting the minotaur. Thomson's work is not, of course, a novel, but *The City of Dreadful Night* is, nonetheless, a primary text in the urban Gothic tradition.

The City of Dreadful Night is a recounting of the narrator's *flânerie* in the city of the title, a nightmare city never actually named as London but which carries the stamp of the capital in its urban Gothic mode. Among the clues to Thomson's city being London are the presence of an Embankment by the river where the narrator wanders (the Victoria, Albert, and Chelsea Embankments, begun in 1868, were completed in 1874, the year *The City of Dreadful Night* was completed), the river itself, which "girds the city west and south,"[91] and of course Thomson's own residence in London for much of his life. London is further implicated by the firm establishment by the 1870s of the urban Gothic mode—by the time Thomson wrote his epic, nearly all Gothicized cityscapes that appeared in the work of British writers were set in London.

Thomson evokes a deserted metropolis through which the narrator walks endlessly, a city "of Night, but not of sleep"[92] through which a dark river flows, haunted by suicides. As the speaker traverses the alleys and thoroughfares of this City of Night, he repeatedly relies on the language and imagery of the Gothic to depict his surroundings. These lines are from the beginning of section III:

> Although Lamps burn along the silent streets,
> Even when the moonlight silvers empty squares
> The dark holds countless lanes and close retreats;
> But when the night its sphereless mantle wears
> The open spaces yawn with gloom abysmal,
> The sombre mansions loom immense and dismal
> The lanes are black as subterranean lairs.[93]

These lines would not seem out of place in a verse retelling of *The Strange Case of Dr. Jekyll and Mr. Hyde*. Moonlit and gaslit, Thomson's city is labyrinthine and huge, a London trapped in perpetual midnight from which the speaker has no escape. And, as with all walkers of London's Gothic streets, the narrator of Thomson's poem frequently meets the minotaur.

The sad and frightening denizens of Thomson's stylized London are remarkable first for their scarcity. His city is one of spatial isolation, lonely and nearly empty. The wanderers in the city are few, and they don't seem to interact with one another. Each person encountered by the narrator is involved in a private ritual or drama; the only gathering of people is in the cathedral, where the speaker muses that "perchance they were not a great multitude / Save in that city of so lonely streets / Where one may count up every face he meets."[94] And even there the members of the congregation do not speak to each other, sitting silently and separately while listening to the existential message of the dark figure William Thesing calls the "anti-preacher."[95]

If the emptiness of the city seems to highlight the people Thomson's narrator does meet, it also creates an atmosphere conducive to the marked peculiarities of those people. The residents of the City of Dreadful Night are of a kind with their metropolis: they are dark and ruined, damaged by the city in which they wander and transformed into figures both pitiable and horrifying—evolutionary throwbacks that belie their modern surroundings. In many ways, these Gothic dwellers reflect the poorer classes of the actual city, unfortunates modified by urban conditions into distorted reflections:

What men are they who haunt these fatal glooms,
And fill their living mouths with dust of death,
And make their habitations in the tombs,
And breathe eternal sighs with mortal breath,
And pierce life's pleasant veil of various error
To reach that void of darkness and old terror
Wherein expire the lamp of hope and faith?

They have much wisdom yet they are not wise,
They have much goodness yet they do not well,
(The fools we know have their own Paradise,
The wicked also have their proper Hell);
They have much strength but still their doom is stronger,
Much patience but their time endureth longer,
Much valor but life mocks it with some spell.[96]

In spite of, or perhaps because of, this humanized core at the heart of Thomson's minotaurs, they are extremely disquieting to both narrator and reader. The man in section IV who declaims endlessly in the "spacious square,"[97] the couple talking by the river who denounce "He / Who formed such creatures to His own disgrace,"[98] these are all once-normal citizens corrupted by the poisonous influence of the city. The threat here is not of physical harm or death, but that the unwary traveler will become trapped, that the fate of these broken and insane men "who haunt these fatal glooms" may await the unfortunate *flâneur* who stumbles too long down the dark lanes. There is a danger that, like Florence Dombey in her own meeting with the minotaur, the monster may take the unlucky walker in and remake her in its own image.

The extremity of this fear is reached in section XVIII, when the narrator wanders "in a suburb of the north"[99] and chances on "something crawling in the lane below."[100] Upon closer inspection, the wounded thing that drags itself along the lane is seen to be a grotesquely altered fellow traveler: "But coming level with it I discerned / that it had been a man."[101] The thing looks at the narrator, showing a "haggard filthy face with bloodshot eyes,"[102] and begins to spit vituperatives, claiming that the speaker has come to take the thing's prize away. It becomes evident that this quasi-human beast lives in greedy, paranoid pursuit of some goal or treasure it has forgotten, looking for the "sacred secret of the clue"[103] that it cannot recall. The narrator rightly concludes that the only solace such a creature could find would be to have been spared the pain of life by not being born: "What weary way were planned / To seek oblivion through the far-off gate / Of birth, when that of death is close at hand!"[104]

The City of Dreadful Night is a dark and ominous painting of a city and its inhabitants without light or hope: Thomson's poetic vision constitutes a "complete negation of Blake's optimistic hope of building a New Jerusalem"[105] and relies instead on a repeated invocation of Dante's hell.[106] Lack of hope for the future is a direct refutation of the teleological worldview, in which the present must be understood to be superior to the past. Thomson not only drags the past into the light in the form of his atavistic inhabitants, but he also deliberately defies the idea of London as a progressive city moving toward higher and more advanced levels. The Gothic mode has here made good on its threat—the past has won. Indeed, what seems to set *The City of Dreadful Night* apart, even from other urban Gothic works, is its overwhelming atmosphere of despair. Amy Levy, in her elegiac essay "James Thomson: A Minor Poet" (1883), calls Thomson "essentially the poet of mood" and classifies *The City of Dreadful Night* as

> the very sign and symbol of that attitude of mind which we call Weltschmerz, Pessimism, what you will; i.e., the almost perfect expression of a form of mental suffering which I can convey by no other means than by the use of a very awkward figure—by calling it "grey pain," "the insufferable inane" which makes a man long for the "positive pain."[107]

She goes on to say that the poem's view of life is one which "does not exist for the perfectly healthy human being" but that such an attitude "is one of the phenomena of our world."[108]

Levy's assessment is accurate: *The City of Dreadful Night* is particularly concerned with mood—in this way Thomson is closely allied aesthetically with Poe. Indeed, "The Man of the Crowd" complements Thomson's *City* in several ways, not least in anticipating a similar narrative situation in section II of Thomson's poem. The eight stanzas of section II find the narrator following an old man on a repetitive and unending circuit of various sites in the city. Like the narrator of Poe's tale, Thomson's speaker follows the old man "because he seemed to walk with an intent,"[109] and he describes the pursued as "shadowlike and frail,"[110] compared with Poe's old man, who was called "very thin, and apparently very feeble."[111] Likewise, the speaker in *The City of Dreadful Night* is led on an interminable journey: "We travelled many a long dim silent street,"[112] "we travelled weary roads without suspense,"[113] and "we travelled streets and lanes with wondrous strength."[114] Three times the man stops, each time at the site of a death—the metaphorical deaths of Faith, Love, and Hope. Also like Poe's narrator, the speaker here quits following the old man when he realizes the repetition of the circuit, realizing that "he circled thus for ever tracing out / The series of the fraction left of Life."[115] Additionally there is the sleeplessness of Poe's tale—the narrator follows the Man of the Crowd all night and into the next day, through a city which is, as Thomson tells us, "of Night, but not of Sleep."[116] The atmosphere of the two works is also similar; although Poe's story is one less of despair than of a sort of increasing horror and paranoia, it nevertheless concerns itself, as does Thomson's poem, with chiaroscuro, urban wandering, and districts of the city where the air seems to "teem with desolation."[117] And both works tell of the dangers inherent in walking the labyrinth of London.

Thomson's poem, as well as Poe's "The Man of the Crowd," contains within it the shadow of the Gothic *flâneur* as he appears in the fin de siècle urban Gothic. De Certeau's unknowable city, here a labyrinth filled with grotesques and monsters, is the medium through which the Gothic *flâneur* wanders, and his observations and encounters make him not at home in the city and its crowds but rather disoriented, uneasy, and ultimately terrified. The minotaurs within the labyrinth, the true *flâneurs* of these evocations of the dark city, are brought to the fore in Dickens, Stevenson, Machen, Conrad, Chesterton, and many others as the most dangerous aspect of London's impenetrable construction.

The construction of these Gothic Londons, however, must be ultimately acknowledged to be accomplished by the architectural expedients of pen and ink. For these are *representations* of London, and as such are merely words on a page. We have moved from a bird's-eye view of the city to the concrete experience of walking its streets. In the next chapter, I'd like to descend even further, through the streets and onto the page itself.

NOTES

1. Roy Porter, *London: A Social History* (Cambridge, MA: Harvard University Press, 1994), 209.
2. Mary H. Krout, *A Looker-On in London*, 1899, *The Victorian Dictionary*, http://www.victorianlondon.org/publications2/ lookeron-1.htm.
3. Umberto Eco, "Postscript," in *The Name of the Rose*, trans. William Weaver (San Diego: Harcourt, 1994), 525–26.
4. Ben Weinreb and Christopher Hibbert, *The London Encyclopaedia* (London: Macmillan, 1993), 597.
5. Michel de Certeau, "Walking in the City," *The Practice of Everyday Life* (Berkeley: University of California Press, 1984), 92.
6. de Certeau, "Walking in the City," 92.
7. de Certeau, "Walking in the City," 93.
8. Thomas J. Rice, "Mapping Complexity in the Fiction of Umberto Eco," *Critique* 44 no. 4 (Summer 2003): 365n5.
9. Eco, "Postscript," 526.
10. Joseph Conrad, *The Secret Agent: A Simple Tale* (1907; New York: Penguin, 1990), 53.
11. If not actually scary, this passage takes on darker implications as the novel progresses. Conrad's complex interweaving of mistaken and alternative identities lends a metaphoric force to the idea of houses being in the wrong place, or being somehow mislabeled.
12. Peter Ackroyd, *London: The Biography* (New York: Nan A. Talese, 2001).
13. I discovered the truth of this firsthand while doing research for this book. I missed a turning while walking on Oxford Street in central London and attempted to "cut the block" by taking the next side street and doubling back. Even though I consider myself familiar with that part of London, it was nearly forty-five minutes before I found my way back to Oxford Street.
14. *Mogg's New Picture of London and Visitor's Guide to Its Sights*, 1844, *The Victorian Dictionary*, http://www.victorianlondon.org/entertainment/sightseeing.htm.
15. George Augustus Sala, *London.*

16. Franco Moretti, *Atlas of the European Novel, 1800–1900* (London: Verso, 1998), 83.
17. *Dracula* frequently takes on the tone of a travel narrative, most explicitly during the opening chapters where Jonathan Harker relates his trip through eastern Europe to Transylvania. His reporting of hotels, native dress, and local cuisine seems a homely beginning to a horror novel.
18. Richard Marsh, *The Beetle*, ed. Julian Wolfreys (1897; Peterborough: Broadview, 2004), 5.
19. Marsh, *The Beetle*, 6.
20. The Baudelairean *flâneur* is always a male figure. Deborah Nord, in the introduction to her 1995 study *Walking the Victorian Streets: Women, Representation, and the City* (Ithaca, NY: Cornell University Press), discusses the gender of walkers in nineteenth-century fiction, concluding that the female counterpart to the male *flâneur* is a different kind of streetwalker altogether: the prostitute. She does acknowledge Dickens's Florence Dombey and writers such as Elizabeth Gaskell as women who attempt to "escape the status of spectacle and become a spectator" (12), but ultimately admits the "virtual impossibility of the *flâneuse*" (11). Having said that, the Gothic *flâneur* does occasionally cross gender lines, as seen in the discussion of Machen's *The Three Impostors* in this chapter.
21. Walter Benjamin, *Charles Baudelaire: A Lyric Poet in the Era of High Capitalism* (London: NLB, 1973), 37.
22. Charles Baudelaire, "The Painter of Modern Life," 1863, *JahSonic: Sharing Tastes*, http://www.jahsonic.com/PoML.html.
23. Nord, *Walking the Victorian Streets*, 2.
24. Benjamin, *Charles Baudelaire*, 40.
25. Marc Eli Blanchard, *In Search of the City: Engels, Baudelaire, Rimbaud* (Saratoga, CA: Anma Libri, 1985), 91.
26. Benjamin, *Charles Baudelaire*, 40.
27. Graeme Gilloch, *Myth and Metropolis: Walter Benjamin and the City* (Cambridge: Polity, 1996), 139.
28. Edgar Allan Poe, "The Man of the Crowd," in *Great Works of Edgar Allan Poe* (New York: Chatham River Press, 1987), 244.
29. Poe, "A Man of the Crowd," 245.
30. Benjamin, *Charles Baudelaire*, 48.
31. Poe, "Man of the Crowd," 240.
32. Poe, "Man of the Crowd," 241.
33. Poe, "Man of the Crowd," 241–42.
34. Poe, "Man of the Crowd," 242.
35. Poe, "Man of the Crowd," 242.
36. Poe, "Man of the Crowd," 243.
37. Richard Lehan, *The City in Literature: An Intellectual and Cultural History* (Berkeley: University of California Press, 1998), 81.
38. Poe, "Man of the Crowd," 245.
39. Poe, "Man of the Crowd," 244.
40. Poe, "Man of the Crowd," 245.
41. Poe, "Man of the Crowd," 245.
42. Lehan, *The City in Literature*, 81–82.
43. Implying as he does a sentience at play in the great city, Poe here anticipates an important theme of twentieth-century urban Gothic literature—that of the city itself as a living, malevolent organism. This theme would reach a sort of apex in Fritz Leiber's urban ghost stories including "Smoke Ghost" (1941) and the novel *Our Lady of Darkness* (1977), which situates the urban Gothic in San Francisco.
44. Blanchard, *In Search of the City*, 91.
45. It is in this section that Dickens gives his famous description of the coming of the railroad, quoted in chapter 2.
46. Charles Dickens, *Dombey and Son*, ed. Alan Horsman, Oxford World's Classics (1848; Oxford: Oxford University Press, 2001), 74.
47. Dickens, *Dombey and Son*, 71.

48. Dickens, *Dombey and Son*, 74.
49. Dickens, *Dombey and Son*, 77.
50. Dickens, *Dombey and Son*, 77.
51. Dickens, *Dombey and Son*, 79.
52. Erik Bond, "Flights of Madness: Self-Knowledge and Topography in the Cities of Burney and Dickens," *Literary London: Interdisciplinary Studies in the Representation of London* 1 no. 1 (2003), http://homepages.gold.ac.uk/london-journal/bond.html, 4.
53. Bond, "Flights of Madness," 4.
54. Dickens, *Dombey and Son*, 80.
55. Robert Louis Stevenson, *The Strange Case of Dr. Jekyll and Mr. Hyde*, ed. Martin A. Danahay (1872; Peterborough: Broadview, 1995), 33.
56. Stevenson, *Strange Case of Dr. Jekyll and Mr. Hyde*, 33.
57. Stevenson, *Strange Case of Dr. Jekyll and Mr. Hyde*, 33.
58. Stevenson, *Strange Case of Dr. Jekyll and Mr. Hyde*, 46.
59. Another is Conrad's *The Secret Agent*, discussed earlier.
60. G. K. Chesterton, *The Man Who Was Thursday* (New York: Boni and Liveright, 1908), 102.
61. Chesterton, *The Man Who Was Thursday*, 81
62. Chesterton, *The Man Who Was Thursday*, 104.
63. Chesterton, *The Man Who Was Thursday*, 107.
64. Chesterton, *The Man Who Was Thursday*, 107–8.
65. Chesterton, *The Man Who Was Thursday*, 108.
66. Chesterton, *The Man Who Was Thursday*, 108.
67. Chesterton, *The Man Who Was Thursday*, 111.
68. Chesterton, *The Man Who Was Thursday*, 108.
69. Chesterton, *The Man Who Was Thursday*, 109.
70. It is the great in-joke of Chesterton's novel that every member of the anarchist council turns out to be a police detective in disguise and that Sunday is the detective chief who hired them all, a shadowy figure who may or may not be God. No anarchist council exists, merely a group of earnest men attempting to expose a nonentity.
71. Lin Carter, "Baghdad-on-the-Thames: Introduction to Arthur Machen's *The Three Impostors*," November 20, 1999, *The Order of the Twilight Star*, http://www.cafes.net/ditch/carter.htm.
72. Arthur Machen, *Three Impostors* (1895; New York: Knopf, 1923), 13.
73. Machen, *Three Impostors*, 13–14.
74. Machen, *Three Impostors*, 14.
75. Machen, *Three Impostors*, 15.
76. Machen, *Three Impostors*, 19.
77. Machen, *Three Impostors*, 21.
78. Machen, *Three Impostors*, 22–23.
79. Machen, *Three Impostors*, 24.
80. Machen, *Three Impostors*, 25.
81. Machen, *Three Impostors*, 64.
82. Machen, *Three Impostors*, 64.
83. Machen, *Three Impostors*, 65.
84. Machen, *Three Impostors*, 65.
85. Machen, *Three Impostors*, 65.
86. Machen, *Three Impostors*, 59.
87. Machen, *Three Impostors*, 59.
88. Machen, *Three Impostors*, 60.
89. Machen, *Three Impostors*, 60.
90. Machen himself belonged to this mystical organization and modeled the impostors on specific high-ranking members. Other members of the Golden Dawn were Aleister Crowley (the self-styled "wickedest man in Britain") and W. B. Yeats, the model for the young man in spectacles.

91. James Thomson, *The City of Dreadful Night,* in *Broadview Anthology of Victorian Poetry and Poetic Theory*, ed. Thomas J. Collins and Vivienne J. Rundle (Peterborough: Broadview, 1999), I l.22.
92. Thomson, *City of Dreadful Night*, I l.71.
93. Thomson, *City of Dreadful Night*, III l.1–3.
94. Thomson, *City of Dreadful Night*, XIV l.10–12.
95. William Thesing, *The London Muse: Victorian Poetic Responses to the City* (Athens: University of Georgia Press, 1982), 144.
96. Thomson, *City of Dreadful Night*, XI ll.1–14.
97. Thomson, *City of Dreadful Night*, IV l.1.
98. Thomson, *City of Dreadful Night*, IV l.2–4.
99. Thomson, *City of Dreadful Night*, XVIII l.1.
100. Thomson, *City of Dreadful Night*, XVIII l.14.
101. Thomson, *City of Dreadful Night*, XVIII l.19–20.
102. Thomson, *City of Dreadful Night*, XVIII l.25.
103. Thomson, *City of Dreadful Night*, XVIII l.30.
104. Thomson, *City of Dreadful Night*, XVIII l.73–75.
105. Thesing, *London Muse*, 135.
106. This happens most overtly in the poem's initial epigram, "Through me is the way to the city of pain" (from the *Inferno* 3.1), and in section I, line 78: "They leave all hope behind who enter there," mirroring the *Inferno* 3.9. Throughout the poem, however, Thomson's insistence on the city as a sort of Hell and the Dantesque encounters with other damned wanderers touts the poet's debt to *The Divine Comedy*.
107. Amy Levy, "James Thomson: A Minor Poet," in *The Broadview Anthology of Victorian Poetry and Poetic Theory*, ed. Thomas J. Collins and Vivienne J. Rundle (Petersborough, ON: Broadview, 1999), 1358–59.
108. Levy, "James Thomson," 1359.
109. Thomson, *City of Dreadful Night*, III l.1.
110. Thomson, *City of Dreadful Night*, III l.2.
111. Poe, "Man of the Crowd," 243.
112. Thomson, *City of Dreadful Night*, III l.6.
113. Thomson, *City of Dreadful Night*, III l.14.
114. Thomson, *City of Dreadful Night*, III l.20.
115. Thomson, *City of Dreadful Night*, III l.45–46.
116. Thomson, *City of Dreadful Night*, I l.71.
117. Poe, "Man of the Crowd," 245.

Chapter Five

Dialogues in the Dark

Bakhtin in London

> *There was a quality in that voice which I cannot describe. Not only an accent of command, but a something malicious, a something saturnine. It was a little guttural, though whether it was a man speaking I could not positively have said; but I had no doubt it was a foreigner. It was the most disagreeable voice I had ever heard.*—Richard Marsh, *The Beetle*, 1897

In chapter 4 we looked at the urban Gothic walker, juxtaposing his experience with that of the mapmaker or author, who can see the totality of the city at once. As we found, and as Dickens confirmed in his own perambulations, London walked is not as easily quantifiable as London mapped. Michel de Certeau felt that walkers in a city create a text with their routes, writing a narrative in which they participate as author and character. In this way, according to de Certeau, a walker creates the city as he negotiates passage through its streets. The urban Gothic novel provides its readers with multiple examples of this process.

In reality, however, the opposite is happening in an urban Gothic novel. The author controls the routes of his walkers and like a mapmaker sees the totality of the city and the narrative. The city is not actually created by Florence Dombey, Edward Hyde, or the various walkers in *The Three Impostors*, but by the author's descriptions of these characters' journeys. It is, in fact, the text that builds these Londons: these Gothic cities are composed not of stones and wood but of words. Thus, after hovering above London and mapping the urban Gothic, followed by moving down onto the streets of the literary city, we now descend even further, into the text itself. There we will consider the language of the urban Gothic, using as examples Dickens's *Our Mutual Friend* and Richard Marsh's *The Beetle*. And just as de Certeau provided a framework from within which to understand the Gothic walker, we will be guided in our exploration of language by Russian theorist Mikhail Bakhtin.

BAKHTIN AND THE GOTHIC

Robert Mighall claims that the Gothic "adopts a number of rhetorical and textual strategies to locate the past and represent its perceived iniquities, terrors, and survivals."[1] In *Reading Gothic Fiction: A Bakhtinian Approach*, Jacqueline Howard finds these "rhetorical and textual strategies" to involve Mikhail Bakhtin's heteroglossia, that shifting patchwork of voices in dialogue that the Russian theorist held to be the primary constituent of language systems and therefore the fundamental component of every novel.

Bakhtin writes that, at any specific moment in history, language "represents the co-existence of socio-ideological contradictions between the present and the past, between differing epochs of the past, between different socio-ideological groups in the present, between tendencies, schools, circles and so forth, all given in bodily form."[2] In the Gothic mode, the first of these contradictions is of primary importance. The past is always threatening to rise up from the dead, and what Mighall calls "vestigial stains" are recognizable even in the modern cityscape. Heteroglossia in the Gothic mode foregrounds questions of "pastness." Whether these questions concern themselves with the historical past or with the past of the novel and its characters, that past's possible resurgence into the present (and the implied threat of the present socio-ideological structure being thereby subverted) is the major anxiety of a Gothic text, and it is expressed through the novel's heteroglossia. In the urban Gothic, this knot of discourses is concerned with the spaces, architecture, conditions, and inhabitants of the city.

Howard finds fault with earlier (mainly psychological) readings of the Gothic that are "based on the belief that the novel, at its best, is a unified, seamless whole."[3] She turns instead to Bakhtin to understand the ways in which the mode functions, saying that the Gothic

> can most satisfactorily be viewed in a Bakhtinian way as a *plural* form, that is, as a novelistic genre which draws on and recontextualizes or transforms prior discursive structures, fragments of "the already said," both literary and non-literary. As such, it is constituted by numerous speech genres which have arisen from historically concrete situations of social interaction. These ways of speaking can include professional jargons (medical, legal, pedagogical, aesthetic, theological discourses, for example) and more everyday communicative practices such as lists, letters, diaries, anecdotes, travel accounts, folk-tales, songs, and superstitions.[4]

Heteroglossia, then, occurs in a number of ways in the Gothic mode. It is most easily recognized in epistolary elements, what Bakhtin refers to as a "special group of genres"[5] that includes diaries and letters, of many of the better-known Gothic works. Indeed, the narrative use of documents and "outside" voices is a staple of the Gothic traceable back to the earliest examples of the form; interpolated stories are found in many of Ann Radcliffe's novels (e.g., *The Italian*), and Charles Maturin's *Melmoth the Wanderer* is a veritable set of narrative nesting dolls, each story hidden within the next until it seems likely Melmoth's true tale will never be told. In the Victorian era, *Dracula* develops the epistolary Gothic to its furthest extent, telling the entire story in a series of diaries, journals, newspaper clippings, and recorded memoranda that function within the narrative as characters read each other's writing to keep themselves up to date with the story they are enacting. Stoker's method of narration makes *Dracula* an excellent case study for this sort of surface heteroglossia; the use of found documents to tell the story seems to effectively erase any easily recognizable authorial voice, leaving a babble of disparate but equal discourses.

Gothic heteroglossia occurs in more subtle ways as well. In examining the ways in which eighteenth-century Gothic writers appropriated a variety of discourses, Howard finds contemporary discourses of taste and sensibility informing much of Matthew Lewis's *The Monk*, for example, and also points out the contradictory nature of the dialogue between these discourses. When considering the alleged anti-Catholicism of Lewis's novel (exemplified through the character of Lorenzo), Howard tells us that "diverse and contradictory patterns of tone and meaning problematize any attempt to read Lorenzo's combination of 'Protestant' rationalism and sensibility as morally normative or ideal."[6] She thereby highlights the inherent open-endedness and unresolvedness which the Bakhtinian lens exposes in these novels. Howard would argue, through Bakhtin, that this very unresolved complexity elevates the Gothic from the status of forgettable pop phenomenon to which it was relegated during the hundred and fifty years prior to Robert Hume's 1969 reassessment.

But although Howard does aptly demonstrate how the various discourses of the Gothic situate each novel in its own unique historical context, her ideas can be taken even further. The Bakhtinian dialogism of any given Gothic work is also complementary to and in many cases constitutive of its modality. To see how a novel's discourse actually produces the Gothic mode, let us turn back to Dickens.

GOTHIC LANGUAGE IN *OUR MUTUAL FRIEND*

"Dickensian" is not a synonym for "Gothic"; it is a larger term that encompasses a vaster expanse of style, as can be seen in the discussion of the previous chapter. But many of the elements we think of as Dickensian are Gothic—the complex narratives, the grotesque characters, the huge and labyrinthine city. And some of the ways in which Dickens thinks about the world can be called Gothic as well—the past and our relationship to it is one of Dickens's major preoccupations. Whether Dickens can be said to share the Gothic's teleological view of history is open to debate; his attitude toward progress and industrialization is too complicated for an easy answer. But the ways in which Dickens returned to his childhood traumas in narrative after narrative shows that he certainly believed history could trouble the here-and-now.

Our Mutual Friend, like most of Dickens's later works, makes a conscious effort to encompass the entire multiverse of mid-Victorian society. The result is a sprawling novel that offers a cacophony of discourses to the reader armed with a Bakhtinian lens. The novel's cohesiveness lies in its multifacetedness, a concept at the very heart of Bahktinian prosaics, and the disparate voices within the text create a tension based on a perceived rift between the modern, enlightened present and the savage, primitive past, thus using what Bakhtin calls "heterogeneous stylistic unities" to create a Gothic text.

Midway through chapter 16 of the first book of *Our Mutual Friend*, washerwoman Betty Higden tells John Rokesmith and the Boffins that her seemingly idiotic mangle-turner Sloppy is more talented than he appears. "You mightn't think it," she says, "but Sloppy is a beautiful reader of a newspaper. He do the Police in different voices."[7] Thanks to T. S. Eliot's use of the final sentence of that quotation as the original title of the poem that became *The Waste Land*, this off-handed comment by a fairly minor character has gained a sort of mythical half-life in literary critical circles; the MLAIB indexes no less than six articles of that title in the last ten years or so, most of them Eliot-related.[8]

But aside from its status as clever modernist anecdote, Mrs. Higden's description of Sloppy's reading prowess is a pithy summation of Bakhtin's dialogic theory of the novel; the primary marker of the novel as a genre, according to Bakhtin, is the presence of overlapping, contradictory but mutually informing discourses. Novelists like Dickens offer excellent proving grounds for Bakhtin's theories, of course. The sheer size and complexity of a novel like *Our Mutual Friend* provides dozens of discernible discourses merely among the book's characters, to say nothing of the heterogeneity of the authorial voice. But Bakhtin argues that dialogism is the major characteristic of *any* novel; as long as there is an author and a character, says Bakhtin, there are enough voices to ensure the emergence of a dialogue. The tensions and exchanges in this dialogue, often conflicting and seldom resolved, are for Bakhtin the marks of a successful novel. As David Lodge says in his *Art of Fiction*, "novelists do the Police in different voices."[9]

Our Mutual Friend paradigmatically illustrates the Gothic mode as a consequence of dialogism. Charles Dickens's last completed novel, published in installments between May 1864 and November 1865, *Our Mutual Friend* is dark and expansive; like many of Dickens's later works, it paints on a huge canvas that attempts to encompass all of London, and by extension all of Victorian society. Paul Schlicke calls *Our Mutual Friend* "the most complexly plotted of all Dickens's novels,"[10] a true statement that is remarkable when considered alongside *Bleak House* or *Little Dorrit*. It is a novel of hyperbole, concerned almost compulsively with waste and excess, with greed and obsession.[11] The vast array of voices Dickens utilizes to tell his tale(s) is one of the hallmarks of the grand and hyperbolic narrative of *Our Mutual Friend*, as in most of his larger works.

Bakhtin himself carefully explored Dickens's use of a wide range of discourses. "Discourse in the Novel" specifically looks at heteroglossia in *Little Dorrit*, focusing on the ways in which "the speech of another is introduced into the author's discourse (the story) in *concealed form*."[12] By "concealed form" Bakhtin means that Dickens appropriates these discourses with none of the formal markers that usually designate another's speech; rather he presents them as authorial utterances. Bakhtin uses several specific examples from Dickens's narration of events around the Merdles in *Little Dorrit* to demonstrate dialogism and to define various terms (hybrid construction, pseudo-objective motivation, etc.). As he freely admits, Bakhtin focuses exclusively on passages that are satirical or parodic in nature, because he believes that it is in comic writing that Dickens's heteroglossia is most evident. "Comic style," Bakhtin writes, "(of the English sort) is based . . . on the stratification of common language."[13] Bakhtin does not at all imply, however, that dialogic discourse only occurs in comic writing. He focuses on this sort of writing in his analysis of Dickens (with references to earlier British comic writers like Smollett and Fielding) because it is in Dickens's satiric mode that such stratification of language can be best seen in conscious use. Dickens's commandeering of high epic syntax, for example, is something of which Dickens himself was very aware, having chosen that sort of language for a specific effect.

The same is as true of *Our Mutual Friend* as of *Little Dorrit*, but in neither novel is comic style the only sort of writing in which Dickens engages. Both are dark, ominous works that filter character, setting, and plot through uneasy relationships with various unsavory occurrences from the novelistic and historical past. Both are, in short, novels in the Gothic mode.

The surface trappings of traditional Gothics are much in evidence in *Our Mutual Friend.* The opening sequence sets the tone: it is the darkest opening of any novel by Dickens, and even detractors of the novel frequently remark on it for its powerfully sinister atmosphere. Lizzie Hexam and her father fishing for corpses in the filthy Thames provides a setting of horror, but the scene also introduces the book's primary themes. As F. S. Schwarzbach explains:

> The text is extremely reticent about the river itself, withholding all the details of physical description. What we do see is the man lean into the river, and emerge with his arms "wet and dirty" and with money in his hand. From this brief incident three associations are born: the river and death, the river and dirt, and the river and money. [14]

Schwarzbach identifies the three major themes of *Our Mutual Friend.* Death, dirt, and money are in many ways the only subjects of *Our Mutual Friend*'s 800-plus pages. And importantly, the languages of death, dirt, and money are repeatedly called upon to evoke imagery in the novel.

The reader searching for evidence of the Gothic mode in *Our Mutual Friend* finds her attention drawn most immediately to the discourse of death and decay in the novel. The opening chapter, in addition to using the father and daughter corpse-fishers to metaphorize the Thames, repeatedly refers to death, most notably when Gaffer Hexam waxes philosophic in his opinions that a dead man can't be robbed. Later Jenny Wren exhorts Riah to "come back and be dead," an entreaty to leave the toils and worries of life behind: And still as they went down they heard the sweet little voice, more and more faintly, half calling and half singing, "Come back and be dead, Come back and be dead!"[15] And of course the novel's protagonist, John Harmon, is presumed dead, creates another life to be able to remain dead, and continually refers to himself *as* dead:

> "It is a sensation not experienced by many mortals," he says, "to be looking into a churchyard on a wild windy night, and to feel that I no more hold a place among the living than these dead do, and even to know that I lie buried somewhere else, as they lie buried here."[16]

In addition to these references to death in the language of the novel, the plot itself features multiple corpses, at least two attempted murders, and one murder/suicide, as well as Riderhood's false drowning.

Likewise, language about dirt is evident throughout, beginning with the elder John Harmon making his fortune as a dust collector and filtering through the text until Bradley Headstone and Rogue Riderhood are "found, lying under the ooze and scum" of Plashwater Weir Mill Lock[17] and Silas Wegg is hurled headlong into a scavenger's cart (most likely full of solid waste of animal or human origin). Boffin's Bower, surrounded by towering mounds of "dust," a catch-all term encompassing dead cats, broken pottery, coal dust, and human and animal waste, is a memorable image that is emblematic of the novel as a whole. We are given repeated instances of the grit of the city getting in our eyes and hair. In fact, London in *Our Mutual Friend* is grimier than usual for a Dickens novel, even dirtier than *Little Dorrit*'s prison-haunted ruin. In the opening passage of book III, we find fog and dirt oppressively combined: "It was a foggy day in London, and the fog was heavy and dark. Animate London, with smarting eyes and irritated lungs, was blinking, wheezing, and choking; inanimate London was a sooty spectre, divided in purpose between being visible and invisible, and so being wholly neither."[18]

Dickens's repeated invocation of filth and pollution becomes Gothic rhetoric by playing on middle-class readers' perceptions equating dirt with disease and degeneration. He utilizes not only the language of the eighteenth-century Gothics but contemporary discourse concerning the poor or the criminal. Consider this description of the Six Jolly Fellowship Porters, a riverside pub frequented by the Hexams and Rogue Riderhood:

> The Six Jolly Fellowship Porters, already mentioned as a tavern of a dropsical appearance, had long settled down into a state of hale infirmity. In its whole constitution it had not a straight floor, and hardly a straight line; but it had outlasted, and clearly would yet outlast, many a better-trimmed building, many a sprucer public-house. Externally, it was a narrow lopsided wooden jumble of corpulent windows heaped one upon another as you might heap as many toppling oranges, with a crazy wooden verandah impending over the water; indeed the whole house, inclusive of the complaining flag-staff on the roof, impended over the water, but seemed to have got into the condition of a faint-hearted diver who has paused so long on the brink that he will never go in at all.[19]

Dickens here makes use of urban discourse to highlight Mighall's "vestigial stains." The decaying Six Jolly Fellowship Porters is markedly different from other, safer areas of London (such as the Veneerings'), and Dickens Gothicizes the pub through recourse to the language of dirt.

The most striking strains of discourse in *Our Mutual Friend*, however, concern money. Thematically, the novel dwells on speculation—actual speculation as evinced by Fascination Fledgby, the Veneerings, and others; criminal speculation in the form of the "friendly move" of Wegg and Venus, the Lammles, and Bradley Headstone; and emotional speculation in the romantic plots of Lizzie Hexam and Bella Wilfer. Dickens's project of denigrating selfishness and greed in favor of selflessness and generosity is reinforced in economic terms throughout the novel. Thus Mr. Boffin wants to prove that Bella is "true golden gold at heart,"[20] and we see that Fledgby is "sensible of the value of appearances as an investment."[21] Dickens even refers to the trash in the streets as "that mysterious paper currency that circulates in London when the wind blows."[22]

In his "A Speculative Resurrection: Death, Money, and the Vampiric Economy of *Our Mutual Friend*," Daniel Scoggin connects Dickens's economic concerns in the novel with the figure of the vampire, itself a symbol of a past that will not stay dead. Scoggin notes that "the image of the vampire could be used to portray the person who engages in the direst of Victorian economic sins: market speculation";[23] he also references other vampire-like figures in Victorian fiction, such as Eliot's Bulstrode in *Middlemarch* and *Bleak House's* Vholes. The economic vampires in *Our Mutual Friend*, among them the Lammles, the Veneerings, Silas Wegg, and Rogue Riderhood, attempt to suck the money from other characters and the culture in general. Dickens purposefully uses Gothic language to taint our perceptions of economic villains like Mr. Lammle:

> And thus the Lammles got home at last, and the lady sat down moody and weary, looking at her dark lord engaged in a deed of violence with a bottle of soda water as though he were wringing the neck of some unlucky creature and pouring its blood down his throat.[24]

Just as important as this vampiric language to the Gothic mode in *Our Mutual Friend* is the economic force of dust, trash, and waste. The past cannot be avoided in the London of *Our Mutual Friend,* because it is always strewn in the streets or, more strikingly, piled in great heaps in the outer yard of Boffin's Bower, an abode described as "an enclosed space where certain tall dark mounds rose high against the sky, and where the pathway to the Bower was indicated, as the moonlight showed, between two lines of broken crockery set in ashes."[25] Dickens spends much of the novel showing the reader how waste and refuse are transformed into money. Jenny Wren buys scraps of rag from Riah and Fledgeby to make dolls' dresses; Riah tells his employer that "our waste goes into the best of company, sir, on her rosy-cheeked little customers. They wear it in their hair, and on their ball-dresses, and even . . . are presented at court with it."[26] Mr. Venus makes his living by articulating bones and recycling the dead. And the huge fortune that catches nearly every character up in its influence, precipitating most of the plot(s), is that of the Golden Dustman—wealth accrued from the cast-off remains of the past.

The three major themes of death, dirt, and money weave themselves in Bakhtinian fashion into the very language of *Our Mutual Friend.* The pervasiveness of these discourses is complete, and each theme makes the suggestion of the past somehow encroaching on the present. To see this process illustrated, consider this passage from book II, chapter 15:

> A grey dusty withered evening in London city has not a hopeful aspect. The closed warehouses and offices have an air of death about them, and the national dread of colour has an air of mourning. The towers and steeples of the many house-encompassed churches, dark and dingy as the sky that seems descending on them, are no relief to the general gloom; a sun-dial on a church-wall has the look, in its useless black shade, of having failed in its business enterprise and stopped payment for ever; melancholy waifs and strays of housekeepers and porters sweep melancholy waifs and strays of papers and pins into the kennels, and other more melancholy waifs and strays explore them, searching and stooping and poking for anything to sell. The set of humanity outward from the City is as a set of prisoners departing from gaol, and dismal Newgate seems quite as fit a stronghold for the mighty Lord Mayor as his own state-dwelling.[27]

In this passage we find all three discourses painting a dark and dreary portrait of the city. The "air of death" and the "air of mourning" denote decay and lifelessness, as does the "withered evening." Dirt is particularly in evidence—the sky itself is "dark and dingy" and the night is "grey" and "dusty." The destitute search through the day's sweepings. The churches offer no solace from the murk. The city is characterized as a prison and the city's most notorious prison as a statehouse for the mayor. Most interestingly, Dickens has incorporated here the economic discourse pertinent to so much of *Our Mutual Friend.* The useless sun-dial seems to be a failed businessman who has "stopped payment." The scavenging waifs are digging through the trash hoping to find some piece of detritus to convert into money. The effect of the heteroglossia of these three discourses is typical of the way in which the narrative dialogues in *Our Mutual Friend* operate.

But what of conventional dialogue? Up to this point we have examined various strains of discourse as they appear in the authorial narrative voice. What of the myriad of characters that move and think and act and talk in *Our Mutual Friend*? Bakhtin writes that heteroglossia in the novel is perceived as "another's speech in another's language,"[28] and this is most evident when an actual person steps on stage and speaks:

> the human being in the novel is first, foremost, and always a speaking human being; the novel requires speaking persons bringing with them their own unique ideological discourse, their own language. The fundamental condition, that which makes a novel a novel, that which is responsible for its stylistic uniqueness, is the *speaking person and his discourse.*[29]

During the course of his career, Charles Dickens created 989 characters, each with his or her own distinctive speech patterns.[30] It is interesting to note that an author known on the one hand for the distinctiveness of his narrative voice (albeit a voice that is a composite of the many discourses we've alluded to) is also so adept at creating so many distinct voices among his characters. Critics have continuously discussed, reviled, and defended Dickens's characterization since the first installments of *The Pickwick Papers*, with much emphasis on his use of grotesques. Bakhtin would point out, as I do now, that the primary way in which Dickens grants autonomy to individual characters is through speech. Robert Newsom reminds us that Dickens often defined characters through the "use of tags—frequently repeated expressions (sometimes mere noises) tied to an individual."[31] Thus Mr. Snagsby's expressive coughing in *Bleak House*, Flora Finching's stream-of-consciousness rambling and William Dorrit's "hum" and "ha" in *Little Dorrit*, and Captain Cuttle's numerous misquotations in *Dombey and Son*. Such a tag in *Our Mutual Friend* is Jenny Wren's repeated references to her bad back and queer legs and her frequent assurance that she knows everyone's tricks and manners. Likewise, Rouge Riderhood's repeated references to living by the sweat of his brow constitutes an identifying verbal tag. Beyond this sort of superficial identifier, though, discourses of death, dirt, and money weave their way into the language of Dickens's characters in *Our Mutual Friend*, making the Gothic mode inextricable from the voices that create the novel.

A case in point is Mr. Venus, the taxidermist and junior partner in Wegg's "friendly move." Mr. Venus's tag is his recurring referral to the letter from Pleasant Riderhood rejecting him because she cannot bear "to be regarded, in that boney light."[32] Venus is disconsolate at this sentiment from the noble Pleasant, but it appears to be a valid complaint; judging by his speech, Mr. Venus regards everything in a "boney light." As an articulator of human bones, Mr. Venus (whose given name is never revealed) tells Silas Wegg early in the novel that "if you was brought here loose in a bag to be articulated, I'd name your smallest bones blindfold equally with your largest, as fast as I could pick 'em out, and I'd sort 'em all, and sort your wertebræ, in a manner that would equally surprise and charm you."[33] So proud is Mr. Venus of this ability that he uses it as a gauge of his own emotional state, as seen in this statement of his pain at being rejected by Pleasant: "My very bones is rendered flabby with brooding over it. If they could be brought to me loose, to sort, I should hardly have the face to claim 'em as mine."[34] Or later in the same passage, referring to the parrot he had bought from Pleasant: "Yes, there it lies on its side, dried up; except for its plumage, very like myself."[35] Even later, he reveals that his involvement in the "friendly move" has "told upon my heart, and almost equally upon my skeleton."[36] Mr. Venus's reliance on and constant referral to his profession serve to disconcert Wegg, who is never comfortable in Mr. Venus's "dark and greasy" shop and who would rather not be reminded of his partner-in-crime's abilities and employment.

But it is Mr. Venus's role to remind. His use of boney metaphors is indicative of more than his being "an enthusiast of his art."[37] Because Mr. Venus cannot speak without referencing taxidermy or the sorting of bones, he continually reinforces the novel's preoccupation with death and its return.

After finally succumbing to his conscience and deciding to reveal Wegg's plot, he tells Noddy Boffin that "having prepared your mind in the rough, I will articulate the details."[38] In case this allusion should be missed, Dickens immediately calls it a "professional exordium." The word is an important one. Mr. Venus is an articulator, after all, and performs that service both for the bones of "humans warious" and for the deathly subtext of the novel. Although chiefly a comic character, Mr. Venus's contribution to *Our Mutual Friend* is of the gloomy, Gothic sort.

Bradley Headstone, conversely, cannot be described as a chiefly comic character. Peter Schlicke refers to Headstone as "the most terrifying psychological portrait Dickens ever drew,"[39] and indeed the reader's anxiety mounts as the narrative progresses and Headstone becomes more and more unhinged. He does not have a verbal tagline or specific professional jargon to draw on. Headstone is a teacher, but the discourse of teaching doesn't inform his speech in any demonstrable way. His speech, in fact, is remarkable less for the information it provides than for the manner in which it provides its information. Headstone's discourse is that of barely repressed violence—the strangled utterances of a man attempting to stave off a murderous impulse, a man who will ultimately fail. Bradley Headstone, perhaps, is the character in *Our Mutual Friend* who most profoundly realizes the Gothic struggle between the savagery of the past and the refinement of civilization.

Eugene Wrayburn at one point calls Bradley Headstone a "curious monomaniac,"[40] and though Wrayburn is in full arrogant idle mode, he is quite correct. Headstone's fixation on Lizzie Hexam and his hatred of Wrayburn as a successful rival push him further and further down the road toward murder. John Kucich has noted the systems of repression and indulgence in passionate emotion in *Our Mutual Friend*, concluding that what separates Wrayburn and Harmon from Headstone is their ability to repress their violent impulses. This is true in due course, and Kucich's argument is convincing. But through much of the novel Headstone *is* able to control himself, albeit barely, and his restraint seeps through his speech in terrible ways. The following exchange occurs during Lizzie Hexam's final rejection of Headstone:

> "Mr. Eugene Wrayburn," he repeated.
>
> "Why do you mention that name again and again, Mr. Headstone?"
>
> "Because it is the text of the little I have left to say. Observe! There are no threats in it. If I utter a threat, stop me, and fasten it upon me. Mr. Eugene Wrayburn."
>
> A worse threat than was conveyed in his manner of uttering the name, could hardly have escaped him.[41]

Later in the same scene, Headstone's increasing fixation (monomania) emerges fully into his discourse:

> "I knew all this about Mr. Eugene Wrayburn, all the while you were drawing me to you. I strove against the knowledge, but quite in vain. It made no difference in me. With Mr. Eugene Wrayburn in my mind, I went on. With Mr. Eugene Wrayburn in my mind, I spoke to you just now. With Mr. Eugene Wrayburn in my mind, I have been set aside and I have been cast out." . . .
>
> "O, Mr. Headstone, you talk quite wildly."
>
> "Quite collectedly. I know what I say too well. Now I have said all."[42]

Headstone speaks simultaneously wildly and collectedly. His speech, forcibly restrained and "half-choked,"[43] demonstrates the immense struggle within him. "I don't show what I feel," he tells Lizzie at one point; "some of us are obliged habitually to keep it down."[44] Even as he topples into the weir with Riderhood at the end of the novel, Headstone speaks in a "desperate, clenched voice."[45] A civilized, modern man would have been able to resist the compulsion to lash violently out at Wrayburn. Headstone, not quite civilized, is unable to do so. His struggle represents savagery set against modernity; it is the most overt element of the Gothic in *Our Mutual Friend*, and it is conveyed, until the attack on Wrayburn, almost entirely through language. Savagery's victory with Headstone sharply undermines the neat wrapping up Dickens effects in the other plot lines.

Mr. Venus and Bradley Headstone are but two examples of the way Dickens's characters participate in the heteroglossia of *Our Mutual Friend.* Jenny Wren's dreams of a future suitor are likewise frequently complicated by her familial past intruding into her romantic vision, a sort of Gothic-to-come that implies the inescapability of her abusive upbringing. Such constructions are common in the novel. The speech of Dickens's characters, always distinctive, serves as a series of threads woven throughout *Our Mutual Friend* to highlight crucial thematic ideas.

VOICES IN *THE BEETLE*

Dickens's London is a dirty, decaying locus of economic muscle; it is a Gothic site for murder, swindling, hidden identities, and violent passion. The city for the characters in *Our Mutual Friend* is thus a repressive obstacle to be overcome—a repository for all the crime and primitive impulses of its meanest inhabitants. Contrastingly, in Richard Marsh's *The Beetle*, London makes a valiant effort to put forth its most modern face, a progressive façade proud of its civilized and civilizing role on the world stage. But the Darwinian nightmare of Britain's colonial Others, erupting in the heart of London to strike at the voice of governmental reason in the form of Paul Lessingham, combines with the language of racial prejudice and superiority to belie the idea of a city sitting easily at the forefront of modernity.

The actual language of the city's inhabitants in *The Beetle* encapsulates the powers of modernity being used to combat the ancient pagan threat of the Beetle. Marsh chooses to utilize multiple narrators in his novel, an approach similar to that of Wilkie Collins in *The Woman in White* (1860). As previously mentioned, the use of multiple narrators is a staple of Gothic novels going back through *Melmoth* to Matthew Lewis. Usually, however, the various voices in a Gothic novel are explained by the use of found documents—the long letter at the end of *Jekyll and Hyde* and especially the aforementioned journals and diaries of *Dracula* are prime examples of this. Marsh, like Collins, differs in that he simply shifts between narrators in order to elucidate different parts of the narrative.

Each of *The Beetle*'s four narrators—Richard Holt, Sydney Atherton, Marjorie Lindon, and Augustus Champnell—has distinctive verbal mannerisms that reflect the jargons of the day. The narrators' manners of speech identify them as agents of modernity, much as the repeated references to and uses of cutting-edge technology do in *Dracula*, published in the same year.

As in Stoker's book, the characters who work together against the Beetle use "the modern technologies of telegraph and public transport,"[46] especially during the final chapters where Atherton, Lessingham, and Champnell are pursuing the Beetle and the kidnapped Marjorie through train stations across southern England.[47] London in *The Beetle* is as much an ally as a site of horror although, as discussed in chapter 4, the suburbs where the Beetle lives are presented in decidedly desolate and derelict terms. Ultimately, the superior forces of modernity defeat the Egyptian threat in Marsh's novel, and three of the four narrators are unequivocally drawn as up-to-date and progressive. Sydney Atherton is an inventor, a creator of what have now come to be called "weapons of mass destruction." (Atherton calls it "legalised murder—on the biggest scale it ever has been planned."[48]) Augustus Champnell is a confidential agent/consulting detective; as Julian Wolfreys points out in his introduction to the Broadview edition of the novel, Champnell owes a great debt to previous literary consulting detectives, including Arthur Conan Doyle's famous specimen. Marjorie Lindon, perhaps the most interesting character in the novel, is a representative of the New Woman—her independence, opinions on politics, and defiance of her father (a powerful conservative MP) all mark her as a member of that group of women who elicited such disparate responses from Victorian society.[49] All three of these characters—along with the non-narrating major character Paul Lessingham, fast-rising liberal lion of the House of Commons and Marjorie's fiancé—are members of modernity's vanguard. They represent scientific innovation, political progressiveness, cutting-edge criminal investigation, and the changing climate of gender roles at the end of the century. As Jonathan Harker would have said, they are "the nineteenth century up-to-date with a vengeance." London as bright progressive beacon, as the essence of historical telos, is embodied in the city-dwellers who engage battle with the shape-shifting Egyptian menace, and their status as modern is reinforced repeatedly through their language.

Sydney Atherton's speech is the most obvious example of this phenomenon. Atherton's use of slang at times nearly dominates his speech, making the inventor occasionally seem to be trying too hard. His quips and clever retorts put the reader in mind of the Oscar Wilde of four or five years previous. Atherton suffers from a crisis of self-assurance where Marjorie is concerned, but otherwise he is replete with poise and confidence about his role (and that of his country and city) as one at the forefront of progress. Responding to the Beetle's profession "I am of the children of Isis!" Atherton coolly asserts, "Is that so?—it occurs to me that you have made a slight mistake—this is London, not a dog-hole in the desert."[50]

Even when using his smooth exterior as a façade to mask his jealousy and fear, Sydney Atherton's language is consummately that of the self-confident Englishman. Much of *The Beetle*'s subtext is concerned with the desire to maintain the imperial social order in the face of invasion by the colonial Other, represented in the novel by the Beetle-woman and her "oriental" magic. As Wolfreys acknowledges, Atherton frequently (and apparently subconsciously) maintains the civilizing mission of the British empire, and the concept of British teleological superiority, in his references to other cultures. When the Beetle first enters Atherton's laboratory unannounced, Sydney describes the Egyptian in terms of overt racial stereotypes:

> His costume was reminiscent of the "Algerians" whom one finds all over France, and who are the most persistent, insolent, and amusing of pedlars. . . . This individual was like one of the originals, yet unlike,—he was less gaudy, and a good deal dingier, than his Gallic prototypes are apt to be. Then he wore a burnoose,—the yellow, grimy-looking article of the Arab of the Soudan, not the spick and span Arab of the boulevard. Chief difference of all, his face was clean-shaven,—and whoever saw an Algerian of Paris whose chiefest glory was not his well-trimmed moustache and beard?
>
> I expected that he would address me in the lingo which these gentlemen call French,—but he didn't.[51]

The use of quotation marks around the word "Algerian" is telling, implying as it does not actual Algerians, although not necessarily *not* actual Algerians, but Arabs in general. The differences Atherton notices between "this individual" and the street Arabs of France appear to be that the person in his lab is more Arabian than the "pedlars" Atherton is comparing him with. This person, Atherton implies, is so offendingly Arab that he can't even clean himself up to the level of a French street peddler.

Atherton's condescension toward racial and cultural Others is repeated throughout the novel so many times that it is impossible to ignore. In particular, he uses the word "Oriental" as a catch-all to mean any sort of eastern culture. Julian Wolfreys notes that Atherton "uses [the word Oriental] in a general sense to mean Eastern, non-European cultures or, more specifically, discourses constructing representations of those cultures from a Western perspective."[52] And Atherton is only the most vocal of the proponents of the imperial view in the novel. Threats to Lessingham and Marjorie Lindon aside, a basic motivation of the little group of protagonists in Marsh's novel is the excisement from London of an oriental scourge—a scourge repeatedly characterized not just by its harmful magic or weird appearance but by its ethnic and cultural origins of which the supernatural trappings are merely symptoms. Atherton's language reinforces this motivation by its clever self-assurance and by its easy, almost unconscious racism.

The most powerful voice in Marsh's novel, in a very real sense, is that of the object of Atherton's prejudice, the Beetle itself. Possibly the most self-consciously Other of any Gothic villain in fin de siècle literature, the sexually ambiguous insect-human who comes to London to punish Paul Lessingham is first encountered by out-of-work clerk Robert Holt. As discussed in the previous chapter, Holt climbs through the open window of the house where the Beetle has established its lair in the city because the place appears abandoned and because he fears a permanent collapse if he continues walking through the night. He has barely gotten through the window when he is approached and possibly attacked (at the very least probed) by a large creature that seems to be an insect. Holt runs screaming back toward the window and trips, falling at full length on the floor. Then a match is struck behind him and he meets the person/creature who lives in the house.

Holt's first sensory impression in this encounter is of the Beetle's voice. The creature strikes a light behind Holt and immediately tells him to keep still:

> There was a quality in the voice which I cannot describe. Not only an accent of command, but a something malicious, a something saturnine. It was a little guttural, though whether it was a man speaking I could not positively have said; but I had no doubt it was a foreigner. It was the most disagreeable voice I had ever heard, and it had on me the most disagreeable effect; for when it said, "Keep still!" I kept still. It was as though there was nothing else for me to do.[53]

Several things are remarkable about this piece of Gothic heteroglossia. The Beetle's voice is commanding and "malicious"; there is something about it that is inherently bad. On one level, the "something malicious" in the voice is a form of instant mesmerism—Holt spends a great deal of time describing the humiliating aspect of losing control of his body during most of his narrative.[54] The Beetle is able, then, to strip independence from this representative of the British working class simply by speaking, a form of deadly heteroglossia beyond Bakhtin's darkest imaginings. Germane to considerations of the other forms of discourse in *The Beetle*, however, is Holt's strong sense that the speaker was a foreigner. Although he is unable to even give a confident opinion concerning the speaker's gender, Holt knows for a certainty that this creature is no Englishman. The Beetle's powerful and sinister voice marks it, before Holt has even glimpsed its appearance, as something not of England. It is allied not only with the supernatural, but with the hordes of immigrants swelling the population of London and with a primitive past of multitheistic savages.

The threat to complacent empire represented by the Beetle achieves a sort of summation in the character of Paul Lessingham. *The Beetle*'s most accomplished speaker in the formal sense, Lessingham is Marjorie Lindon's fiancé and Sydney Atherton's rival and unlikely partner. His prominence in London society is due to his very public role—that of the young up-and-comer in the House of Commons. As a representative of England's civilized superiority, the reader can do no better than Paul Lessingham, who so embodies the God-given rights of Britain that he is known as St. Paul, or the Apostle. The power of the Apostle's voice is vividly displayed during an important parliamentary speech given in the first third of the novel. Atherton is in attendance and describes the effect:

> It was very far from an "oration" in the American sense; it had little or nothing of the fire and fury of the French Tribune; it was marked neither by the pomposity nor the sentiment of the eloquent German; yet it was as satisfying as are the efforts of either of the three, producing, without doubt, precisely the effect which the speaker intended. His voice was clear and calm, not exactly musical, yet distinctly pleasant, and it was so managed that each word he uttered was as audible to every person present as if it had been addressed particularly to him. His sentences were short and crisp; the words which he used were not big ones, but they came from him with an agreeable ease; and he spoke just fast enough to keep one's interest alert without involving a strain on the attention.[55]

Atherton's remarkable description of Lessingham's "parliamentary triumph of almost the highest order"[56] has several points of interest. To begin with, Atherton takes pains to separate Lessingham's style from that of other nationalities of powerful speech-makers (all of the other forms and styles of national speech mentioned are, interestingly, Western). The Apostle's speech is perceived by Atherton as quintessentially British. Lessingham is devoid of pretension but smart and convincing. He is inclusive, intelligent, forward-thinking, and beneficent—in short he is the British empire's own image of itself, and as such he is the face of progressive London. In fact, by nicknaming Lessingham after one of the most recognizable buildings in London's skyline, Marsh unequivocally links the character with the city. Paul Lessingham then, can be profitably read as the voice of London. It is not surprising, then, that Paul Lessingham is the most haunted character in the novel.

Twenty years earlier, Lessingham was held captive in Egypt by a cult (the "children of Isis") and forced to be a sort of sexual slave to an Egyptian priestess for "two unspeakable months,"[57] as well as being forced to watch multiple human sacrifices of women (women who were "as white as you or I"[58]). His escape from that confinement and his defiling of the subterranean temple where he had been held are what has brought the Beetle, possibly the same priestess who held Lessingham captive, to London seeking revenge. Lessingham continues to be haunted by this episode.

But the Lessingham who tells this story to Champnell is a very different man than the shining symbol of empire who so impresses Atherton in the House of Commons. Though it is necessary to tell the tale in order to enlist Champnell's assistance, the Apostle has lost the powerful discourse that characterized him earlier in the narrative. Indeed, he cannot even give specific details about what happened to him in the Temple of Isis:

> To dwell in detail on what occurred during my involuntary sojourn in that fearful place is beyond my power. I cannot even venture to attempt it. The attempt, were it made, would be futile, and, to me, painful beyond measure. I seem to have seen all that happened as in a glass, darkly,—with about it all an element of unreality. As I have already remarked, the things which revealed themselves, dimly, to my perception, seemed too bizarre, too hideous, to be true.[59]

Lessingham's discourse betrays other examples of his inability to tell this tale. The period of time he spent there was unable to be expressed. "How I reached the open air," Lessingham says of his final escape, "I cannot tell you."[60] The Apostle's experience robs him of the ability to articulate. "Unspeakable" becomes the most fitting word for Lessingham's tale.

When he is actually confronted with evidence of the creature that pursues him, the results are even more remarkable. Atherton at one point asks Lessingham outright about his involvement in the strange happenings of the book's opening. The Apostle loses speech altogether as Atherton asks:

> "What is the nature of the delusion? Does it take the shape of a—beetle?" . . .
>
> Without the slightest warning, he collapsed,—was transformed; I can describe the change which took place in him in no other way. He sank in a heap on the floor; he held up his hands above his head; and he *gibbered,*—like some frenzied animal. A more uncomfortable spectacle than he presented it would be difficult to find. I have seen it matched in the padded rooms of lunatic asylums, but nowhere else.[61]

This is a far cry from the triumphant speechmaker taking his seat in Parliament amid thunderous applause. The man cowering on the floor in Sydney

Atherton's laboratory has undergone some sort of reverse Darwinian regression to become an animal. He is quite literally at a loss for words. The man who had been described earlier as having "all his faculties under complete command"[62] has now been reduced to a "heap on the floor." The transformation has been effected verbally, as well—the word "beetle" is sufficient to cause the complete undoing of the young MP, another example of the Beetle's powerful Gothic heteroglossia.

Paul Lessingham can be read as a microcosm of Gothic dialogism. His discourse and occasional lack thereof reflect the central conflict that instigates the novel's Gothic mode. If Lessingham in some way is London—if his powerful articulation of liberal politics represents London's progressive telos—then it is fitting in the urban Gothic mode that he be haunted by his past, that his past be culturally and ethnically Other, and that it be characterized by images of animality and savagery. More importantly to a Bakhtinian reading of Lessingham's character, in the face of the recurring past, the voice of telos becomes hysterically mute; haunted London cannot speak its own modernity, it can only gibber like a "frenzied animal." In this way, Lessingham embodies the dialogue between the two basic Gothic heteroglossia: he speaks the modern while barely repressing a savage and literally unspeakable history.

As Bakhtin points out, it is in the nature of novels to be dialogic, and the scope of *Our Mutual Friend* and *The Beetle* provides ample opportunity to explore the form's inherent dialogism. In *Our Mutual Friend*, Dickens's own authorial voice is mitigated by various forms of discourse, chiefly those of death, dirt, and money. This heteroglossia is scattered so thoroughly throughout the text that it becomes difficult to find a passage in the novel that doesn't utilize one of these discourses as metaphor or descriptor. Furthermore, the characters themselves contribute to the Gothic mode by their own recourse to language that highlights Gothic concerns. In *The Beetle*, an assortment of characters' discourses highlights the anxieties attendant on the British imperial identity, showing the ways in which telos is adulterated by the returning repressed. The Gothic, in the form of the oriental beetle-priestess, rises out of the past to plague Paul Lessingham's progressive city, a haunting expressed through the speech of Atherton, Lessingham, and the Beetle itself.

These overlapping voices, author and character, participate in the Gothicization of the plot, the city, and the novel itself. The voices in both novels serve to unsettle the status quo, to engage in what Bakhtin called "social commentary" by showing us a clear picture of London as a haunted city. The discourses interlaced throughout *Our Mutual Friend* and *The Beetle* represent the past's dialogue with the present, an ongoing conversation that troubles and defines the narrative moment in the urban Gothic mode. The very language of these works, used by the authors to describe the city and by the city's inhabitants to express beliefs and faiths, drift uneasily through the fog of Victorian London and ultimately become the foundations of the Gothic city, a city created by the language of the Gothic narratives it haunts.

NOTES

1. Robert Mighall, *A Geography of Victorian Gothic Fiction* (Oxford: Oxford University Press, 1999), xiv.

2. Mikhail Bakhtin, "Discourse in the Novel," in *The Dialogic Imagination*, ed. Michael Holquist (Austin: University of Texas Press, 1981), 291.

3. Jacqueline Howard, *Reading Gothic Fiction: A Bakhtinian Approach* (Oxford: Clarendon Press, 1994), 14. As Howard rightfully points out, this unified view of the novel led to constructions of the Gothic as a monomyth or archetype, a sort of ahistorical generalizing (with an attendant discounting of heteroglossia) that results in a misunderstanding of the main thrust of Gothic fiction, and thereby an underappreciation of the form in general. Indeed, most declaimers of the Gothic as "subliterary" point to its failure in moral and/or aesthetic terms. See, for example, Elizabeth Napier's *The Failure of the Gothic: Problems of Disjunction in an Eighteenth-Century Literary Form* (Oxford: Clarendon Press, 1987). Napier in particular comes under fire from Howard for her failure to consider the intentionality of the Gothic's dialogism.

4. Howard, *Reading Gothic Fiction*, 16.

5. Bakhtin, "Discourse in the Novel," 321.

6. Howard, *Reading Gothic Fiction*, 197.

7. Charles Dickens, *Our Mutual Friend* (1865; New York: Bantam, 1990), 198.

8. Some do concern Dickens, such as D. A. Miller's well-known "Discipline in Different Voices: Bureaucracy, Police, and *Bleak House*" (in Steven Connor, ed., *Charles Dickens* [London: Longman, 1996]), which examines neither language nor *Our Mutual Friend*, but the role of the police in *Bleak House*.

9. David Lodge, *The Art of Fiction* (New York: Viking, 1992), 128.

10. Paul Schlicke, "*Our Mutual Friend*," in *The Oxford Reader's Companion to Dickens* (Oxford: Oxford University Press, 2000), 437.

11. It was also one of the most hotly contested of Dickens's novels from a critical standpoint. Henry James famously called *Our Mutual Friend* "the poorest of Mr. Dickens's works," while Italo Calvino calls the novel "an unqualified success, both in its plot and in the way it is written." The truth is most likely in between: as F. S. Schwarzbach writes, "The book certainly does have creative power [but that power] was used to structure a novel whose overall plan was given preeminence over detail" (F. S. Schwarzbach, *Dickens and the City* [London: Athlone Press, 1979], 213).

12. Bakhtin, "Discourse in the Novel," 303.

13. Bakhtin, "Discourse in the Novel," 308.

14. Schwarzbach, *Dickens and the City*, 198.

15. Dickens, *Our Mutual Friend*, 279.

16. Dickens, *Our Mutual Friend*, 360.

17. Dickens, *Our Mutual Friend*, 781.

18. Dickens, *Our Mutual Friend*, 417.

19. Dickens, *Our Mutual Friend*, 67.

20. Dickens, *Our Mutual Friend*, 752.

21. Dickens, *Our Mutual Friend*, 269.

22. Dickens, *Our Mutual Friend*, 147.

23. Daniel Scoggin, "A Speculative Resurrection: Death, Money, and the Vampiric Economy of *Our Mutual Friend*," *Victorian Literature and Culture* (2002): 102.

24. Dickens, *Our Mutual Friend*, 265.

25. Dickens, *Our Mutual Friend*, 62.

26. Dickens, *Our Mutual Friend*, 278.

27. Dickens, *Our Mutual Friend*, 386.

28. Bakhtin, "Discourse in the Novel," 324.
29. Bakhtin, "Discourse in the Novel," 332.
30. David Pariossien, "Characterization," in *The Oxford Reader's Companion to Dickens*, ed. Paul Schlicke (Oxford: Oxford University Press, 1994), 74.
31. Robert Newsome, "Style of Dickens," in *The Oxford Reader's Companion to Dickens*, ed. Paul Schlicke (Oxford: Oxford University Press, 1994), 543.
32. Dickens, *Our Mutual Friend*, 90.
33. Dickens, *Our Mutual Friend*, 89.
34. Dickens, *Our Mutual Friend*, 492.
35. Dickens, *Our Mutual Friend*, 483.
36. Dickens, *Our Mutual Friend*, 565.
37. Michael Cotsell, "Mr Venus Rises from the Counter: Dickens's Taxidermist and his Contribution to *Our Mutual Friend*," *The Dickensian* 80, no. 2 (Summer 1984): 109.
38. Dickens, *Our Mutual Friend*, 565.
39. Schlicke, "*Our Mutual Friend*," 438.
40. Dickens, *Our Mutual Friend*, 291.
41. Dickens, *Our Mutual Friend*, 391.
42. Dickens, *Our Mutual Friend*, 392.
43. Dickens, *Our Mutual Friend*, 391.
44. Dickens, *Our Mutual Friend*, 339.
45. Dickens, *Our Mutual Friend*, 781.
46. Julian Wolfreys, introduction to *The Beetle,* by Richard Marsh (1897; Peterborough: Broadview, 2004), 25.
47. Julian Wolfreys (introduction to *The Beetle*) points out that, also similar to *Dracula*, this group of protagonists, while using modern technology, operate out of the "irrational desire for violent retribution and destruction" (25), thus complicating their roles within a Gothic milieu.
48. Richard Marsh, *The Beetle*, ed. Julian Wolfreys (1897; Peterborough: Broadview, 2004), 102.
49. Marjorie Lindon's role as the New Woman is given a much more positive spin in *The Beetle* than in other fin de siècle Gothics such as *Dracula*. However, the threat of the New Woman is shown, and Marjorie's agency mitigated, by the closing chapters during which the Beetle kidnaps Marjorie, cuts her hair, and dresses her as a man. While perfectly dovetailing with the novel's overall unsettling ambiguity toward gender, this transformation of Marjorie undermines much of the tolerance Marsh shows for the New Woman throughout the rest of the narrative.
50. Marsh, *The Beetle*, 106.
51. Marsh, *The Beetle*, 103.
52. Wolfreys, introduction to *The Beetle*, 104n1.
53. Marsh, *The Beetle*, 52.
54. Both Holt and Paul Lessingham describe the experience of being held in thrall to the Beetle's mesmerism as an emasculating one. Lessingham later says, while describing an attempt by the Beetle to mesmerize him, that "she was putting out her utmost force to trick me of my manhood" (245). In Marsh's novel, agency is a specifically masculine province. The Beetle's gender is part of her/its monstrosity.
55. Marsh, *The Beetle*, 126.
56. Marsh, *The Beetle*, 127.
57. Marsh, *The Beetle*, 243.
58. Marsh, *The Beetle*, 244.
59. Marsh, *The Beetle*, 243.
60. Marsh, *The Beetle*, 245.
61. Marsh, *The Beetle*, 180, emphasis mine.
62. Marsh, *The Beetle*, 126.

Chapter Six

In Which Our Teleological Superiority Is Eroded

> *Watch your step. Keep your wits about you; you will need them. This city I am bringing you to is vast and intricate, and you have not been here before. You may imagine, from other stories you've read, that you know it well, but those stories flattered you, welcoming you as a friend, treating you as if you belonged. The truth is that you are an alien from another time and place altogether.*—Michel Faber, *The Crimson Petal and the White*, 2002

It is no wonder that London became a primary site for Gothic fiction from the late 1830s onward—the tensions and dichotomies expressed through the Gothic mode found a perfect topographical representation in the empire's first city. Late Victorian London was in many ways a summation of its era, embodying all the innovations and advances of the Queen's long reign while simultaneously displaying the darkest parts of its underside.

Even as the Victorian era began to fade, London remained the world's premier city, and writers still utilized the capital's potential for anxious terror. We have already looked briefly at Conrad's *The Secret Agent* and Chesterton's *The Man Who Was Thursday*, both urban Gothics written during the final gloaming of the Victorian era.

During the mid- to late twentieth century, after the British empire's fall from supremacy, London was still a haunted city, and writers continued to have recourse to the Gothic as a mode of urban representation. Many of the specters haunting London in the twentieth and twenty-first centuries would be familiar to Victorian authors: poverty, crime, the wide disparity between classes and genders. Contemporary urban Gothic fiction is still concerned with the past returning, whether the actual past or a metaphorical one in the form of Mighall's "vestigial stains." And so a new ghost impresses itself more and more insistently in contemporary Gothic fiction—the ghost of Victorian London itself.

VICTORIAN LONDON AS "ELSEWHERE"

I first went to London in 2002, to participate in a conference on "Literary London" and to begin preliminary research for this project. At that early stage, I wanted to find some of the actual locations in the novels I was working with. My plan was to find the sites of Dracula's safe houses, the locations of the Marshalsea and the Clennam house, the possible addresses of Henry Jekyll and Edward Hyde. In short, I wanted to see the Victorian remnants in the modern city. While I was planning my trip, a professor friend warned me that I might be disappointed. "Victorian London isn't there anymore," he told me. "I went one time looking for the London I had read about in Dickens, and try as I might I couldn't find it." I went in spite of his advice. And I found he was wrong.

Okay, maybe not completely wrong. London has definitely changed in the past 150 years. The modern glass and steel skyscrapers of the city's financial centers certainly bear little resemblance to the city of Dickens and Thackeray. An ultra-modern makeover has changed the face of the once-derelict Isle of Dogs considerably since the days when Dorian Gray visited opium dens nearby in Oscar Wilde's novel. As a testament to London's continuing forward impetus, some of the city's most iconic sites—the London Eye, the Millennium Bridge—are little more than a decade old. The soaring bulk of council tower blocks is the dominant image of the first ring of suburbs around the city to the south and west. The twentieth century, aided immeasurably by the German Blitz of World War II, seems at times to have wiped London clean of any historical taint.

But that does not mean that you can't find the Victorian city hidden beneath the millennial glitter. There are cobbled streets in Southwark; dark, narrow alleys in Whitechapel. A wall of the Marshalsea still stands, and Highgate Cemetery retains a moss-draped ambience that leaves no doubt why Bram Stoker buried Lucy there. Victorian neo-Gothic architecture still reaches up from between more modern structures (most spectacularly in the spires of St. Pancras station). You can even attend a play at the Lyceum Theatre, though instead of Mansfield's *Jekyll and Hyde* it will most likely be the long-running musical version of Disney's *The Lion King*. It is possible to walk in the footsteps of Stoker's Van Helsing and Conrad's Monsieur Verloc. Traces of Gothic London are scattered throughout the modern metropolis—if you know where to look.

And there are quite a few people more than willing to show you where to look. History is a booming cottage industry in modern London; the majority of the London tourist trade, a huge business by any standards, operates through the remembrance of historical fact or anecdote. The famous blue plaques commemorate this or that famous author or bygone politician's former residence, and pubs painstakingly attempt to recreate an "olde world" feel, even though this and other heritage industry ploys are often less recreations than reinventions. London's past is constantly being paraded for public consumption, and it is often the darker portions of that past that draw the most attention. The London Dungeon, the Clink Prison Museum, the Old Operating Theatre Museum—tourism in London often leans toward historical violence, and the Victorian era's presence is strongly felt in these teleological tourist traps.

As an example, the London Walks company, which gives historically themed guided walking tours of the city, ran six walks dedicated to various aspects of Victorian London during the summer of 2004, a remarkable number considering the two thousand plus years of history the company attempts to represent. And despite the rich cultural, scientific, political, and military history of Victoria's reign, four of the six walks were based on Gothic or quasi-Gothic literature or authors: Dickens's London, the London of Oscar Wilde, and two based on the London of Sherlock Holmes. The remaining two Victorian walks were titled "Haunts of Jack the Ripper" and "Darkest Victorian London." The blurb for this last walk on London Walks's website sums up the appeal:

> Elsewhere is always surprising. Especially when elsewhere is the dark side of the moon: the Victorian underside of 21st century London. And this is how we get there. We poke around in forgotten corners of "the real London" just over the river. We make some thrilling—and chilling—"finds." Everything from trace evidence—archaeological fragments—to the whole kit and caboodle. Stuff from the old, furtive, toil-worn, hard-scrabble, soon-to-be-passing, villainous past: a paupers' burying ground, a ragged school, "model dwellings," a prison, Octavia Hill's cottages, etc. We see the stones. And hear the people. Really hear them. Because they speak through Jean. And she does them in character: chimney sweeps, prostitutes, the soon-to-be-executed "Black Maria," pickpockets, street sellers, the Body Snatching Borough Gang, etc. This is history as a séance. And for added value . . . at the end of the walk you'll be able to get into the Old Operating Theatre at half price!

This advertisement neatly demonstrates Victorian London's role as the haunting past. The text begins by making very clear that the London featured in the walk is "elsewhere," so elsewhere that it is "the dark side of the moon." The past itself is given a long list of adjectives emphasizing the difficulty of life in the Victorian era, but also including the odd descriptors "furtive" and "villainous," implying both sentience and evil intent. Guide Jean performs a list of characters (she does the past in different voices!) that reads like a catalog of the poor classes of the nineteenth-century city, evoking those middle-class fears that helped create the urban Gothic a hundred and fifty years ago. Victorian London has become a ghost, capable of being conjured through historical séance, but divorced from the modern city, a savage, haunting "elsewhere."

Only once does the London Walks staff writer break the wall he has built between the breathless public and the "villainous" past, but that stumbling results in what may be the most telling phrase in the blurb. The writer tells us that the walk will take place in "the real London." He is referring to the Southwark/Borough district immediately south of London Bridge, an area rife with associations to the Victorian urban Gothic—the steps below the bridge where Nancy meets Brownlow and Rose Maylie in *Oliver Twist*, the site of the Marshalsea Prison and Dracula's Bermondsey safe house, as well as the London Dungeon wax museum, The Clink Prison wax museum, and other artificial repositories of violent history. To call this London "real" (as opposed to the modern glass and steel city evident north of the river) is to speak directly to the heart of the urban Gothic: the fear that the progressive metropolis is actually just a shell over a corrupt and threatening past that could savagely erupt at any time. It is obviously fascinating stuff—London Walks are among the most popular and successful city walking-tour companies in the world—but it's also unsettling. As the blurb says, the urban Gothic is "thrilling—and chilling."

As we have repeatedly seen, Victorian London was itself haunted by the ghosts of primitivisms past, be they historical, familial, Darwinian, or sociological. But the Victorian era, haunted by its own past, functions particularly well as a haunting presence itself. Why does the Victorian era become the most often recurring past in contemporary urban Gothics? What makes the mid- to late nineteenth century hold sway over the Gothic imagination more than, say, the seventeenth century or the medieval era, both of which are decidedly more primitive than the years when Victoria held the throne?

Roger Luckhurst posits that "London has encouraged these tropes [only] since the huge expansion of the metropolis in the nineteenth century. As the first megalopolis of the modern era, London becomes a sublime object that evokes awe and evades rational capture."[1] Thus Victorian London created the urban Gothic, and so it continues to revisit the mode from beyond the temporal grave.

In addition to London's particular suitability as a Gothic locus, the Victorian era itself has become a measuring tool for our era's own progressivity. The twentieth century (and the twenty-first) most often characterizes the Victorian age (a relatively recent past) as stuffy, rule-bound, and sexually repressed. Clichés based on such ideas, such as Victorian matrons covering piano legs to prevent the inspiration of prurient thoughts, have served to reinforce the image of the 1800s as socially and culturally inferior to the present day. The similarities of the Victorians to our own society only serve to highlight the perceived differences. Thus the twentieth century, and now the twenty-first, uses the mid- to late nineteenth century as reassurance of historical telos; the Victorians seem to represent everything we have overcome in ourselves. Though the Victorians were responsible for important advances in industry, medicine, and various sciences, contemporary commentators regularly focus on Victorian pseudosciences such as phrenology, spiritualism, or the now-disproved criminal theories of Cesaré Lombroso and Max Nordau. Even more mainstream Victorian science is often implicitly denigrated for being hopelessly outdated.

By way of example, consider the Old Operating Theatre Museum, located in an attic space above St. Thomas's church in Southwark. Originally part of St. Thomas's Hospital (famous partially for being the site of Florence Nightingale's nursing school during the nineteenth century), the theatre was abandoned and walled off when the hospital relocated to Lambeth in 1862. Almost a century later, the room was rediscovered during renovations to the church and was itself renovated into a museum. The theater now features exhibits on the history of medicine as it relates to the theatre itself and to St. Thomas Hospital. As a specimen of the early nineteenth-century operating theater, the room is remarkable; complete with tiered seats and a low-hanging gaslight, the theater is as authentic a historical interior as can be found in London.

Much of the exhibit's focus however, seems to be on the theater use during the pre-anesthetic (and pre-antiseptic) era. Visitors are told that nineteenth-century surgeons' skills were gauged primarily by how fast an amputation could be performed (important to the anaesthetized patient), and attention is drawn to the box of sawdust under the wooden operating table, strategically placed to absorb the large quantities of blood produced by the surgeon's ministrations. Coupled with the narrow spiral staircase entrance and the claustrophobic garret that houses the theater, visitors come away with an overall impression largely of relief that we have advanced beyond such barbarism. Museums are thus able to preserve little bubbles of the Victorian era for education but also, and perhaps more importantly, for reassurance. Surgical savagery can be safely gawked at in the Old Operating Theatre, but twenty-first-century Londoners have no need to worry about ninety-second amputations or unsterilized bone-saws.

TIME-HAUNTED LONDON

In the contemporary urban Gothic, this telos manifests itself in a predictable way: modern London is invaded by the Victorian city. The modern city is represented as being plagued by a past that won't go away or stay neatly tucked behind glass in a museum. The same tropes that became standard in nineteenth-century urban Gothic novels are still operative. Stephen King's short story "Crouch End" (1993), set in a north London suburb, is a striking modern evocation of Gothic *flânerie* that serves as an interesting companion piece to Poe's "The Man of the Crowd." King's story, a pastiche of H. P. Lovecraft's Cthulhu Mythos stories, hinges on the confusing topography of London's streets and on the lurking things that roam within them. In China Miéville's 2007 young adult novel *Un Lun Dun*, everything old, used-up, or obsolete in modern London seeps into an alternative city made up of the cast-off and unwanted. UnLondon is itself threatened by the Smog, an intelligent manifestation of a nineteenth-century London particular. Both King and Miéville conjure up the idea that London's past does not fade away with time, but remains somehow woven into the fabric of the modern city.

Even nonfiction writers maintain the impression that London's two-thousand-year history is in some way still in evidence. Describing the nonchronological arrangement of his *London: A Biography*, Peter Ackroyd writes:

> Contemporary theorists have suggested that linear time is itself a figment of the human imagination, but London has already anticipated their conclusions. There are many different forms of time in the city, and it would be foolish of me to change its character for the sake of creating a conventional narrative. That is why this book moves quixotically through time, itself forming a labyrinth.[2]

London, suggests Ackroyd and the numerous authors of the new London Gothics, is as labyrinthine temporally as it is physically. The Guildhall Library and Art Gallery, perhaps unknowingly, evoked this very idea in the "local history fair" it presented in London on October 11, 2003. Featuring guided walking tours, booths manned by historical societies, "expert talks," and "demonstrations of 19th century surgery techniques" (!), the event attempted to encompass the entirety of London's two-thousand-year history. It was called "The London Maze." Among the many novels that explicitly explore Ackroyd's idea of the time labyrinth is Neil Gaiman's *Neverwhere* (1996).

Neverwhere reads London as a historical palimpsest in a very concrete manner. Specifically, the novel's narrative is built around the idea of a second, more primitive London that exists below the established city in the extensive network of sewer, electrical, and transportation tunnels that honeycomb London's substrata. In London Below, the history of the city is a fully realized force that operates on a tangible level.

The protagonist of Gaiman's novel, Richard Mayhew, moves to London from Scotland three years before the beginning of the narrative. Early on he describes the city as he has experienced it during his time there:

> It was a city in which the very old and the awkwardly new jostled each other, not uncomfortably, but without respect; a city of shops and offices and churches, of ignored monuments and remarkably unpalatial palaces; a city of hundreds of districts with strange names—Crouch End, Chalk Farm, Earl's Court, Marble Arch—and oddly distinct identities; a noisy, dirty, cheerful, troubled city, which fed on tourists, needed them as it despised them, in which the average speed of transportation through the city had not increased in three hundred years, following five hundred years of fitful road-widening and unskilful compromises between the needs of traffic, whether horse-drawn, or, more recently, motorised, and the needs of pedestrians; a city inhabited by and teeming with people of every colour and manner and kind.[3]

What Mayhew senses about London is the imprint of the past on the present day. The "very old and the awkwardly new" are the faces of the teleological tension that permeates the urban Gothic. In fact, everything about Mayhew's view of London is a conflict, between traffic and pedestrians, between purpose and practice ("ignored monuments"), between the past and the present—a city where the average rate of travel hasn't increased in three hundred years has to question its definition of "progress."

This dichotomous worldview makes Richard Mayhew well suited for the events to come. After helping an apparently homeless girl found bleeding on the sidewalk, Richard awakes the next morning to find his life erased; friends don't recognize him, his job is gone, his ATM card no longer works. He is then swept quickly into the world of London Below. The girl he has helped is Door, a princess of the underworld who is fleeing a pair of killers who have butchered her family and are now after her. Richard accompanies Door on her quest through London Below to discover the secret her parents died for and incidentally to restore Richard's life in London Above.

London Below is a twisted reflection of the surface world, a funhouse mirror that refracts what Richard knows of London into strange but oddly apt distortions. His first taste of the breadth of London Below is at the Floating Market, a monthly marketplace that moves to different locations every thirty days. The Market Richard attends is held in Harrod's department store, and the spectacle he finds there is reminiscent of both bustling Victorian markets such as Covent Garden or Smithfield's and of some medieval festival day:

> Stalls had been set up all through the shop, next to, or even on, counters that, during the day, had sold perfume, or watches, or amber, or silk scarves. Everybody was buying. Everybody was selling. Richard listened to the market cries as he began to wander through the crowds. . . .
>
> "Rubbish!" screamed a fat, elderly woman, in Richard's ear as he passed her malodorous stall. "Junk!" she continued. "Garbage! Trash! Offal! Debris! Come and get it! Nothing whole or undamaged! Crap, tripe, and useless piles of shit. You know you want it."[4]

Gaiman has neatly summarized his opinions on contemporary materialism, and the metaphor is underlined by holding the market in Harrod's. It is more than metaphor, actually—Gaiman takes figures of speech, street names, and folktales and reifies them. Richard at one point observes that "he had gone beyond the world of metaphor and simile, into the place of things that *are*."[5] Thus we discover that there is a monastery of dark-skinned monks underneath Blackfriars, that the Earl's Court is held in a ghostly Underground train, and that the stories of herds of wild pigs living in the sewers have been personified in the terrifying Beast of London. Important people in London Below society are also named after specific places: Hammersmith the blacksmith, Old Bailey the bird-keeper, the Angel Islington. The repeated warning to "Mind the Gap," heard by millions of passengers on Tube platforms across London, is given sinister new meaning when Richard sees the ancient tentacled thing that lives in the space between platform and train.

London Below does not eschew the labyrinth trope of earlier urban Gothics. Richard requires guides throughout his time in the underworld, and there are even indications that routes create reality, an idea reminiscent of de Certeau's assertion that walkers write texts as they negotiate the streets. While being led to the Floating Market by an underworlder called Anaesthesia, Richard asks if the dangerous bridge they are approaching can be circumvented: "'Do we have to go across it?' he asked. 'Can't we get to the market some other way?' Anaesthesia shook her head. 'We can get to the place it's in,' she said. 'But the market wouldn't be there.'"[6] And the final obstacle to Richard and his companions reaching the stronghold of the Angel Islington (the ultimate goal of the quest) is an actual labyrinth, with an actual monster at its heart. The Great Beast of London lives in this maze, which Richard is told is among the oldest places in London, Above or Below: "'Before King Lud founded the village on the Thames marshes, there was a labyrinth here.'"[7] In Gaiman's novel, London is founded on a labyrinth, preordaining its twisted and unknowable topography. The subterranean maze, lying at the deepest level of London below and housing the fearsome Beast, is the physical expression of the Gothic *flânerie* of so many earlier novels.

But most crucial to *Neverwhere*'s Gothic mode is the way history recurs in London Below. While walking beside a subterranean river, Richard and Door encounter a London particular. The fog makes Richard choke, and he asks:

> "Why do you have fogs down here, when we don't have them up there anymore?"
>
> Door scratched her nose. "There are bubbles of old time in London, where things and places stay the same, like bubbles in amber," she explained. "There's a lot of time in London, and it has to go somewhere—it doesn't all get used up at once."[8]

More explicitly, as Door is later being led by her captors Mr. Croup and Mr. Vandemar through the labyrinth at the bottom of London Below, the reader is given this commentary:

> The labyrinth itself was a place of madness. It was built of lost fragments of London Above: alleys and roads and corridors and sewers that had fallen through the cracks over the millennia, and entered the world of the lost and the forgotten. The two men and the girl walked over cobbles, and through mud, and through dung of various kinds, and over rotting wooden boards. They walked through daylight and night, through gaslit streets, and sodium-lit streets, and streets lit with burning rushes and links. It was an ever-changing place: and each path divided and circled and doubled back on itself. . . .
>
> They walked down a tiny alleyway, which had once been part of a Victorian "rookery" (a slum comprised in equal parts of theft and penny gin, of twopenny-halfpenny squalor and threepenny sex), and they heard it, snuffling and snorting somewhere nearby.[9]

The labyrinth of London is not temporally stable. Instead, there are numerous pockets of "old time" lying in wait, erupting into the present when someone stumbles through the maze into them. It is one of the clearest representations of the recurring past in the contemporary urban Gothic, and the image of an unmappable city composed of scraps of its past is perhaps a fitting encapsulation of the modern-day Gothic city.

NEW URBAN GOTHIC

Gaiman, as previously noted, is but one of the writers continuing the urban Gothic tradition into the twentieth and twenty-first centuries, drawing on the city's history as a foundation for anxiety.[10] Some writers invoke the ghost of Victoria's London by writing historical Gothics, novels set during the Victorian era. Prominent among these is the recent *The Crimson Petal and the White* (2002) by Michel Faber, an 800-plus-page updating of the Victorian novel—a sort of Dickens for the twenty-first century that explores gender issues and the plight of the poor in the 1870s. Faber's work is a painstakingly researched and well-written pastiche that uses its subject matter to highlight contemporary concerns. Lee Jackson's 2003 novel *London Dust* is a more traditional Gothic, a murder mystery set in 1861. More modest in size and scope than Faber's book, *London Dust* is a modern penny dreadful, drawing on common tropes of the underside of Victorian life (seedy pubs, corrupt MPs, naughty music hall girls, the Holywell Street porn industry) and making narrative use of emerging technologies, particularly photography. Jackson has since published several more Victorian murder-mysteries, each one steeped in the reality of the nineteenth-century city.

Although Sarah Waters's first three novels, *Tipping the Velvet* (1998), *Affinity* (1999), and *Fingersmith* (2002) all evoke Victorian London to explore contemporary lesbian issues, the latter works best in the urban Gothic mode. *Fingersmith* is a reworking of Wilkie Collins's *The Woman in White*; it also contains self-conscious references to *Oliver Twist* in its protagonist, a female orphan who lives with a gang of child thieves in a Southwark rookery. At one point, protagonist Susan Trinder actually attends a performance of a stage adaptation of *Oliver Twist*, heavily underlining Waters's appropriation of urban Gothic tropes and narrative devices.

But the most prominent writers of modern urban Gothics, those most unswervingly interested in London as historical palimpsest, believe that the city's past continually influences its present, and thus find explicit connections between the nineteenth-century city and the contemporary one.

Self-proclaimed psychogeographer Iain Sinclair's poem cycles *Lud Heat* (1975) and *Suicide Bridge* (1979) attempt to trace ley-lines on the map of the city—Sinclair finds an unholy pentagram by connecting the sites of Nicholas Hawksmoor's seventeenth-century East London churches, for example. In *White Chapel, Scarlet Tracings* (1987), Sinclair juxtaposes the Jack the Ripper murders of 1888 with a quartet of modern-day booksellers and their quest to discover a coveted rare edition of *A Study in Scarlet* (1889), the first Sherlock Holmes story. The booksellers, an amalgamation of drug addicts and amoral outcasts, wander the same streets as the murderer of the late 1880s, and with similarly bloody and disturbing results. In the course of Sinclair's narrative, a defining list of Victorian grotesques is paraded for the reader, from the Ripper himself (Sinclair fingers royal surgeon Sir William Gull) to Elephant Man John Merrick.

Peter Ackroyd's considerable output encompasses postmodern historical novels such as *Dan Leno and the Limehouse Golem* (1994) and *The Clerkenwell Tales* (2003) as well as biographies of such figures as Charles Dickens, T. S. Eliot, William Blake, and Thomas More. The connecting thread in all of these disparate works is the city of London—no other writer has attempted to grapple with the mysteries and contradictions of London from as many different angles as Ackroyd. His 2001 "biography" of the city is the culmination of his lifetime obsession with the capital, but perhaps more germane to the Victorian urban Gothic would be Ackroyd's first novel, *The Great Fire of London* (1981).

In this book, filmmaker Spenser Spender attempts to adapt *Little Dorrit* for the screen and finds himself haunted not only by the London of Dickens but by the novel itself. Working in Southwark, a primary setting for *Little Dorrit* and one of the areas of modern London that most retains a Dickensian flavor, Spender becomes entwined with a host of grotesque characters, including an angry dwarf who runs a video arcade, and Audrey, an alienated young woman who becomes possessed by the spirit of Amy Dorrit.

What Ackroyd does in *Great Fire* is to create the vision of a city not only haunted by its past but by representations of that past. Audrey becomes possessed by a literary character, and historical sites repeatedly function in light of their literary pedigree, most notably the remains of the Marshalsea prison itself. One of the subtexts of Ackroyd's novel seems to be the recurrence of literary thematics—the pervasive imprisonment theme of *Little Dorrit* is resurrected and replicated in *The Great Fire of London*, and the speech of characters in Ackroyd's novel imitates the distinctive patterns of Dickens's denizens. Most strikingly, Spender has a meal at Cambridge, and one of the "black gowns" sitting next to him begins to talk in the unpunctuated and unending manner of Flora Finching from *Little Dorrit*. The dialogic style is unmistakable, as is the metonymic naming of the professors as "black gowns."

THE LODGER

All of these writers have found that the modern-day city is somehow unable to escape its Victorian pedigree. But it is not necessary to venture far into the twentieth century to find Victorian London already becoming a revenant for the city's modern citizens. We have already looked briefly at Chesterton's *The Man Who Was Thursday* and Conrad's *The Secret Agent* and seen how similar the Edwardian Gothic is to its Victorian predecessor. But only a few years later the Victorian city had become a separate entity in literary representations, forming in the general consciousness not part of a continuous historical spectrum but a distinct and self-contained piece of the past, an "elsewhere" perfectly capable of returning to plague the present. On the eve of the Great War we find one of the earliest examples of the Victorian city as a haunting presence in the modernist era: Marie Belloc Lowndes's *The Lodger* (1914).

In *The Lodger*, Mrs. Belloc Lowndes draws on the Whitechapel murders of twenty-five years earlier to craft a narrative of urban paranoia and crime. Mr. and Mrs. Bunting, owners of a lodging house in the Bayswater area of London, take in a lodger called Mr. Sleuth. All of London is in terror over a series of brutal murders performed by a man who kills women of questionable character and leaves calling cards on the bodies identifying himself as "The Avenger." Mrs. Bunting becomes suspicious of her new lodger, who only goes out at night and prefers to spend his days alone in his room reading the more misogynistic passages of the Bible. As the novel progresses, Mrs. Bunting's concerns grow until she is convinced of Mr. Sleuth's guilt, but her need for the lodger's rent money prevents her from going to the police. Indeed, Mrs. Bunting eventually begins lying to the police in an attempt to protect her lodger and her income.

Lowndes focuses on the psychology around the murders, in particular the savage delight ordinary citizens take in reading the lurid newspaper accounts of the crimes. After each murder, paperboys wind through the streets calling out headlines, and Mr. Bunting among many others eagerly rushes out to buy the earliest copy he can get, often reading the articles aloud to his horrified wife. Mrs. Bunting's complicity in the crimes is generally attributed to her need for money[11]—the Buntings come from middle-class stock but have reached a state of near destitution as the novel opens—and much of the tension in *The Lodger* is in the slowly mounting psychological strain that Mrs. Bunting's knowledge creates.

London figures significantly in *The Lodger*. The murders, originally occurring in Jack the Ripper territory in Whitechapel, slowly begin moving west through the city, until a death takes place just off the Marylebone Road near the Buntings' house. The public in the novel expresses outrage at this shift in geography, feeling that such happenings are more fitting in the East End.

The London fogs play a role in the novel as well, not only through atmospheric cloaking of the murders á la *Jekyll and Hyde*, but also as indicators of character and plot. Fog in *The Lodger* indicates terror and anxiety—Mrs. Bunting's fear that Mr. Sleuth will be out and at work on a particular night always dovetails with the descent of a fog, and the release of that fear after Mr. Sleuth's safe return (Mrs. Bunting fears not the murders but the arrest of her lodger) is physically manifested in the clearing of the weather. "It's a fine day," Mr. Sleuth tells Mrs. Bunting on the morning after one of the murders. "The fog has cleared. I don't know if you will agree with me, Mrs. Bunting, but I always feel brighter when the sun is shining."[12] There is even a scene of Gothic *flânerie* as Mr. Bunting walks home in the wee hours of the morning and encounters his lodger coming home at the same time:

> The lodger stopped and turned around.
>
> He had been walking so quickly, and he was in so poor a physical condition, that the sweat was pouring down his face.
>
> "Ah! So it's you, Mr. Bunting? I heard footsteps behind me, and I hurried on. I wish I'd known it was you; there are so many queer characters about at night in London."
>
> "Not on a night like this, sir. Only honest folk who have business out of doors would be out on such a night as this. It *is* cold, sir!"
>
> And then into Bunting's slow and honest mind there suddenly crept the query as to what on earth Mr. Sleuth's own business could be on this bitter night.[13]

But London is most present in Mrs. Belloc Lowndes's novel in the way the city's past underlines the savagery of Mr. Sleuth's crimes. The murders themselves are obviously modeled on the Jack the Ripper murders of 1888.

As discussed above, these killings encapsulated for many the dark side of the Victorian era. Although Lowndes's novel is set contemporaneously—there are references to motor-cars, for instance—Mr. Sleuth is a particularly Victorian character with his air of gentility and his "old-fashioned" clothing, including the Victorian gentleman's ubiquitous silk hat. Mrs. Bunting frequently comments on Mr. Sleuth's "gentlemanly" demeanor and sense of propriety. That the lodger's "propriety" takes the form of evangelically zealous religion and teetotaling evokes another Victorian figure—the abstinence preacher or Salvation Army devotee.

Most striking, however, are the two sites of the preserved past visited by characters in Belloc Lowndes's novel. Both Scotland Yard's Black Museum and Madame Tussaud's Wax Museum serve as repositories of municipal memory in *The Lodger*, and the memory held under glass in those places is decidedly savage and brutal. Mr. Bunting and his daughter Daisy are taken on a tour of the Black Museum by Joe Chandler, who is Daisy's suitor and the detective in charge of the Avenger investigation. The museum, housed in an interior room at New Scotland Yard and not generally open to the public, contains items connected with various crimes throughout the history of the Metropolitan Police Force, including murder weapons and the death-masks of criminals hanged at the Old Bailey. This is an actual museum that Belloc Lowndes appropriates for her narrative. Now officially called the Crime Museum, the Metropolitan Police's collection of ephemera from 150 years of violent crime is used for instruction within the department and is not accessible by members of the general public. Germane to *The Lodger* is the fact that the Crime Museum contained at the time of the novel's composition all the archival material relating to the Jack the Ripper case, including over two hundred letters purporting to be from the killer. The case files on the Ripper murders were moved to the Office of Public Records in 1992 and are available now to anyone who cares to view them.

In the novel, the Black Museum has a distinctly Victorian feel, due primarily to the Metropolitan Police being formed less than ten years before Victoria's ascension. Most of Scotland Yard's history up to the time of *The Lodger* occurred during Queen Victoria's reign; the majority of the criminals and crimes documented in the Black Museum are thus Victorian. The past on display here is a particularly violent one, but on first seeing the room displaying these horrors, Daisy Bunting is not impressed. The room feels to Daisy like "the Science Room in the Public Library" in the provincial town where she was raised:[14]

> She walked forward and peered into the case nearest the door. The exhibits shown there were mostly small, shabby-looking little things, the sort of things one might turn out of an old rubbish cupboard in an untidy house—old medi-

> cine bottles, a soiled neckerchief, what looked like a child's broken lantern, even a box of pills. . . .
> As for the walls, they were covered with the queerest-looking objects; bits of old iron, odd-looking things made of wood and leather, and so on.
> It really was rather disappointing.[15]

What Daisy sees appears to be historical trash, the sloughed-off detritus of an earlier time. It is only after being in the museum for some time, having the contents of the cases explained to her, and, especially, noticing the death-masks that she begins to realize that the history laid out before her is much darker than it at first appears:

> Daisy had gone a little pale. The sinister, breathless atmosphere of the place was beginning to tell on her. She now began to understand that the shabby little objects lying there in the glass case close to her were each and all links in the chain of evidence which, in almost every case, had brought some guilty man or woman to the gallows.[16]

The curator of the Black Museum tells the visitors of an Indian gentleman—"one of those Brahmins"—who had visited recently and declared that the objects in the room "exuded evil,"[17] and that the man had to leave the room in order to feel at ease. After a few more explanations of the exhibits, Daisy feels the same thing: "'I considers your museum's a very horrid place!' said Daisy pettishly, turning away. She longed to be out in the passage again, away from this brightly lighted, cheerful-looking, sinister room."[18] The Black Museum's dichotomous aspect—"cheerful-looking" but "sinister"—serves as a pithy description of the Victorian city's split personality, even as it neatly summarizes the appearance and character of Mr. Sleuth himself. What Daisy is feeling is Gothic tension—the fear of the violent past's intrusion into the here-and-now.

While at the Black Museum, Daisy complains that she has always wanted to visit the Chamber of Horrors at Madame Tussaud's, but that her aunt won't let her go because it isn't proper for a young woman to see such things. Late in the novel, however, her stepmother promises to fulfill Daisy's wish, both women being invited to visit Tussaud's by Mr. Sleuth and Mrs. Bunting, being too afraid to refuse. Madame Tussaud's Waxworks Exhibition is a Victorian institution, having opened in 1835 and been frequented by such luminaries of the day as the Duke of Wellington, himself an aficionado of the Chamber of Horrors. Although focusing on all aspects of British life and celebrity, one of the museum's major draws has always been the Chamber of Horrors, described by Baedeker's in 1900 as "containing the guillotine that decapitated Louis XVI and Marie Antoinette, and other articles of a ghastly nature."[19]

It should be noted that Jack the Ripper himself wasn't represented in the Chamber of Horrors until April 1980. Tussaud's had been reticent to put the Ripper into its galleries because he had never been identified and thus the museum could not sculpt an actual face for him. Complaints that the Chamber of Horrors was not scary or bloody enough led to the change of policy. Interestingly, Tussaud's chose to call the new exhibit "The Street of the Ripper," showing victim Mary Jane Kelly, the tenement housing and Whitechapel neighborhoods where the murders took place, and the butchered body of Catherine Eddowes. The Ripper himself is represented as a "disappearing shadow."[20] Atmosphere is evoked through fog and cobblestones, gaslight and reproductions of handbills sensationally trumpeting the murders. So Victorian London itself is used to represent the Ripper, who has for so long himself served as a symbol of the Gothic city.

Although they tour most of Madame Tussaud's, it is the Chamber of Horrors that both Daisy and Mr. Sleuth are most interested in seeing. Mrs. Bunting and her two companions move toward "the curious, vault-like chamber,"[21] but are stopped by the attendant, who is a friend of Mrs. Bunting's. The Chamber is being seen by a private party, consisting of Sir John Burney and his entourage, and the three visitors will have to wait until the way is clear. Burney is the Commissioner of Police, a man personally invested in bringing the Avenger to justice, who had in fact confined Mr. Sleuth to a lunatic asylum in the past. The present series of murders began soon after Sleuth's escape from that institution. As Burney's party leaves, the reader is allowed to eavesdrop on their conversation to learn this information.

Readers of *The Lodger* do not experience this site of the savage past as they did the Black Museum—Mrs. Bunting and Daisy do not enter the Chamber of Horrors. But the proximity of the Chamber and the knowledge of its contents play an important role in the complexity of Mr. Sleuth's final threat and unmasking. As the Bunting party wait at the entrance, they are poised on the brink of London's violent past, prepared to plunge out of the world of the modern city and into savage history. The living Victorian figure, Mr. Sleuth, waits with them, his brutality thinly veiled—Mrs. Bunting still only suspects him, and she has carefully avoided any true knowledge of her lodger's nocturnal activities. And at the moment the three are about to enter the Chamber, Mrs. Bunting is indeed suddenly confronted with London's savagery. Burney and his party come out of the Chamber of Horrors and pass the three waiting in the outer room. The Commissioner does not recognize the lodger, but Sleuth knows Burney by sight and assumes Mrs. Bunting has attempted to betray him. He tells the landlady that she will pay for her treachery, that her "end will be as bitter as wormwood and sharp as a two-edged sword,"[22] and then he disappears through the emergency exit. Thus Sleuth is confirmed as the Avenger, and Mrs. Bunting knows for certain that beneath the cultured veneer of her lodger lies the savage face of Victorian

London. After Mr. Sleuth's disappearance, the women decline to visit Madame Tussaud's Chamber of Horrors—they've just seen the real thing.

Mrs. Bunting would be perfectly happy to put the past firmly behind her, to move confidently through her enlightened world untroubled by the possibility of encountering the sort of savagery Mr. Sleuth embodies. But, as the urban Gothic novel reminds us, it is difficult to move confidently through the temporal labyrinth of London. The way is occluded by the unmappable topography, and the past keeps moving, showing up in the least likely places.

The industrial and cultural forces of the nineteenth century transformed London into an unprecedented phenomenon—both object and subject, cause and effect. The physical and societal extremes within the megalopolis, and the experiences of the people who lived in those extremes, were the beginnings of the modern condition. And the modern is always haunted by what came before; the past, whether cultural, municipal, or evolutionary, is always there, a threat to the progress which modernity trumpets. The anxiety that results from this threat is taken by authors writing in the Gothic mode and transformed into monsters, supernatural villains, and mass murderers, savage hunters with the potential to overthrow the unstable teleological height reached by progressive civilization. During the Victorian era, London became a focus for much of this anxiety, and it has remained so to the present day.

While in London doing research for this project, I found myself late one evening descending "Nancy's Steps," the last remnant of the old London Bridge and the site of Nancy's betrayal in *Oliver Twist*. If there are pieces of the Victorian city still floating around twenty-first century London, the space at the foot of Nancy's Steps is one of them. From the traffic crossing London Bridge above, the steps lead down around a 180-degree turn at midpoint, through darkness to the alley beneath. The alleyway is cobbled, passing beneath the Borough High Street through a brick archway. The place is most likely not the safest of venues for walking. The passage beneath the arch was shrouded in darkness as I stepped onto the cobblestones after midnight, and a lone figure slouched against the bricks, his face illumined fitfully by the orange tip of his cigarette. My middle-class sensibilities instinctively stiffened, not quite in fear but at least in a heightened awareness of my situation. As I moved to pass under the archway, I saw, standing in the center of the cobbled street, a fox.

It was, to my mind, the most incongruous thing possible. The fox stood in the street, looking through the archway beneath London Bridge. It was dirty and thin, a scraggly specimen, but it seemed comfortable on the street, completely at home. The man leaning against the wall was watching the animal as well. I looked at him and then looked back at the fox. I said, "Is that a fox?" The man barked a laugh and said, "Yep. That's central London, innit?"

I later learned that foxes are commonplace in London, nocturnal scavengers akin to the American raccoon in their urban habits. I had initially interpreted the man's comment to mean "Don't amazing things happen in this city?" What he had actually meant, most likely, was "Yeah, aren't we overrun with vermin like that?" The foxes are hidden from the casual glance, only roaming at night, and keeping out of main thoroughfares and populated areas. I encountered this little scavenger only because I was in an empty, darkened street at midnight. Perhaps the foxes sense how fitting their residence there is—primitive hunters lurking in the heart of the modern city.

NOTES

1. Roger Luckhurst, "The Contemporary London Gothic and the Limits of the Spectral Turn," *Textual Practice* 16 no. 3 (2002): 531.
2. Peter Ackroyd, *London: The Biography* (New York: Nan A. Talese, 2001), 2.
3. Neil Gaiman, *Neverwhere* (1996; London: Headline/Feature, 2000), 9–10.
4. Gaiman, *Neverwhere*, 127.
5. Gaiman, *Neverwhere*, 321.
6. Gaiman, *Neverwhere*, 103.
7. Gaiman, *Neverwhere*, 317.
8. Gaiman, *Neverwhere*, 235–36.
9. Gaiman, *Neverwhere*, 318–19.
10. The authors referred to in the following paragraphs do not include the equally numerous twentieth- and twenty-first-century writers who work within a London setting to explore the past of their own characters. Iris Murdoch, Martin Amis, Will Self, Zadie Smith, Monica Ali, Geoff Nicholson, and a host of others produce novels that are undeniably London Gothics in the sense that they feature London as a palpable presence and are fueled by the threat of the past erupting into the present. I am only considering at this point works which draw on London's own history as the source of their Gothic mode.
11. A significant side issue is brought out, however, when Mrs. Bunting reflects that her gender is responsible for her continued harboring of a serial killer: "So far, perhaps because she is subject rather than citizen, her duty as a component part of civilised society weighs but lightly on a woman's shoulders" (Marie Belloc Lowndes, *The Lodger* [1913; Chicago: Academy, 1988], 109). This tantalizing thought is not pursued in depth, but remains a pointed comment on Lowndes's self-perception of gender.
12. Belloc Lowndes, *The Lodger*, 130.
13. Belloc Lowndes, *The Lodger*, 179.
14. Belloc Lowndes, *The Lodger*, 72.
15. Belloc Lowndes, *The Lodger*, 73.
16. Belloc Lowndes, *The Lodger*, 74.
17. Belloc Lowndes, *The Lodger*, 74.
18. Belloc Lowndes, *The Lodger*, 76.
19. Belloc Lowndes, *The Lodger*, 68.
20. Judith Walkowitz, *City of Dreadful Delight: Narratives of Sexual Danger in Late-Victorian London*, Women in Culture and Society series (Chicago: University of Chicago Press, 1992), 1.
21. Belloc Lowndes, *The Lodger*, 212.
22. Belloc Lowndes, *The Lodger*, 216.

Works Cited

Ackroyd, Peter. *The Great Fire of London*. 1982. London: Penguin, 1993.

Ackroyd, Peter. *London: The Biography*. New York: Nan A. Talese, 2001.

Acton, William. "Prostitution, Considered in its Moral, Social, and Sanitary Aspects." 1870. In *Victorian Prose: An Anthology,* edited by Rosemary J. Mundhenk and LuAnn McCracken Fletcher, 222–27. New York: Columbia University Press, 1999.

Alighieri, Dante. *Inferno*. Translated by Allen Mandelbaum. *The Divine Comedy,* vol. 1. 1322. New York: Bantam, 1982.

Altick, Richard. *Victorian People and Ideas: A Companion for the Modern Reader of Victorian Literature.* New York: Norton, 1973.

Anderson, Howard. Introduction to *The Monk,* by Matthew Lewis. Oxford: Oxford University Press, 1980.

Baedeker, Karl. *London and Its Environs: A Handbook for Travellers*. 1900. Facsimile edition. Moretonhampstead, Devon: Old House Books, 2002.

Bakhtin, Mikhail. "Discourse in the Novel." In *The Dialogic Imagination,* edited by Michael Holquist, 259–422. Austin: University of Texas Press, 1981.

Baudelaire, Charles. "The Painter of Modern Life." 1863. *JahSonic: Sharing Tastes* (website) http://www.jahsonic.com/PoML.html.

Belford, Barbara. *Bram Stoker and the Man Who Was Dracula*. Cambridge, MA: De Capo Press, 2002.

Benjamin, Walter. *Charles Baudelaire: A Lyric Poet in the Era of High Capitalism*. London: NLB, 1973.

Besant, Walter. *All Sorts and Conditions of Men*. 1882. Oxford: Oxford University Press, 1997.

Blanchard, Marc Eli. *In Search of the City: Engels, Baudelaire, Rimbaud.* Saratoga, CA: Anma Libri, 1985.

Bond, Erik. "Flights of Madness: Self-Knowledge and Topography in the Cities of Burney and Dickens." *Literary London: Interdisciplinary Studies in the Representation of London* 1, no.1 (April 10, 2003). http://homepages.gold.ac.uk/london-journal/bond.html.

Briggs, Asa. "The Human Aggregate." *Dyos* 1: 83–104.

Brontë, Charlotte. *Jane Eyre*. 1847. Norton Critical Edition, edited by Richard Dunn. New York: Norton, 2001.

Burgan, Mary. "Mapping Contagion in Victorian London: Disease in the East End." In *Victorian Urban Settings: Essays on the Nineteenth-Century City and Its Contexts,* edited by Debra N. Mancoff and D. J. Trela, 43–56. New York: Garland, 1996.

Calvino, Italo. "Charles Dickens, *Our Mutual Friend*." In *Why Read The Classics?* translated by Martin McLaughlin, 145–50. New York: Vintage, 2000.

Carter, Lin. "About *The Three Impostors* and Arthur Machen: Baghdad-on-the-Thames." Introduction to *The Three Impostors,* by Arthur Machen, edited by Lin Carter, vii. New York: Ballantine, 1972.

Certeau, Michel de. "Walking in the City." In *The Practice of Everyday Life*, 91–110. Berkeley: University of California Press, 1984.

Chesterton, G. K. *The Man Who Was Thursday*. New York: Boni and Liveright, 1908.

Choi, Tina Young. "Writing the Victorian City: Discourses of Risk, Connection, and Inevitability." *Victorian Studies* 43, no. 4 (Summer 2001): 561–89.

Collins, Philip, ed. *Dickens: Interviews and Recollections*. 2 vols. Totowa, NJ: Barnes and Noble, 1981.

Conrad, Joseph. *The Secret Agent: A Simple Tale*. 1907. New York: Penguin, 1990.

Cotsell, Michael. "Mr Venus Rises from the Counter: Dickens's Taxidermist and his Contribution to *Our Mutual Friend*." *The Dickensian* 80, no. 2 (403) (Summer 1984): 105–13.

Danahay, Martin. Introduction to *The Strange Case of Dr. Jekyll and Mr. Hyde,* by Robert Louis Stevenson, 11–25. Ed. Martin A. Danahay. 1886. Peterborough: Broadview, 1995.

Danahay, Martin A., and Alex Chisholm. *Jekyll and Hyde Dramatized: The 1887 Richard Mansfield Script and the Evolution of the Story on Stage*. Jefferson, NC: McFarland, 2005.

Davies, Gill. "London in *Dracula*: Dracula in London." *Literary London: Interdisciplinary Studies in the Representation of London* 1, no. 3 (March 2004). http://homepages.gold.ac.uk/london-journal/davies.html.

Davis, Richard Harding. "The West and East Ends of London." *Harper's New Monthly Magazine,* January 1894. *The Victorian Dictionary* (website). http://www.victorianlondon.org/population/londoners.htm#East%20End.

De Quincey, Thomas. *Confessions of an English Opium-Eater and Other Writings*. 1821. Oxford World Classics. Oxford: Oxford University Press, 1985.

Dickens, Charles. "A Flight." *Household Words,* August 30, 1852, 530–33.

Dickens, Charles. *Bleak House*. 1853. Norton Critical Edition, edited by George Ford and Sylvère Monod. New York: Norton, 1977.

Dickens, Charles. *Dombey and Son*. 1848. Oxford World's Classics, edited by Alan Horsman. Oxford: Oxford University Press, 2001.

Dickens, Charles. *Little Dorrit*. 1857. Edited by John Holloway. Harmondsworth, England: Penguin, 1967.

Dickens, Charles. *Oliver Twist*. 1838. Norton Critical Edition, edited by Fred Kaplan. New York: Norton, 1993.

Dickens, Charles. *Our Mutual Friend*. 1865. New York: Bantam, 1990.

Dickens, Charles, Jr. "Opium Smoking Dens." *Dickens's Dictionary of London*. 1879. *The Victorian Dictionary* (website). http://www.victorianlondon.org/entertainment/opiumsmokingdens.htm.

Doré, Gustave, and Blanchard Jerrold. *London: A Pilgrimage*. 1872. New York: Dover, 1970.

Dyos, H. J., and Michael Wolff, eds. *The Victorian City: Images and Realities*. 2 vols. London: Routledge & Kegan Paul, 1973.

"East End Tragedies. A Seventh Murder. Another Case of Horrible Mutilation." *Daily Telegraph,* November 10, 1888. *Casebook: Jack the Ripper* (website). http://www.casebook.org/press_reports/daily_telegraph/dt881110.html.

Eco, Umberto. "Postscript." *The Name of the Rose,* translated by William Weaver, 503–36. San Diego: Harcourt, 1994.

Ellis, Markham. *The History of Gothic Fiction*. Edinburgh: Edinburgh University Press, 2000.

Engels, Frederick. *The Condition of the Working Class in England: From Personal Observation and Authentic Sources*. 1845. Chicago: Academy, 1984.

Faber, Michel. *The Crimson Petal and the White*. Edinburgh: Cannongate, 2002.

Gaiman, Neil. *Neverwhere*. 1996. London: Headline/Feature, 2000.

Gilbert, Pamela K. *Mapping the Victorian Social Body*. Albany: SUNY Press, 2004.

Gilloch, Graeme. *Myth and Metropolis: Walter Benjamin and the City*. Cambridge: Polity, 1996.

Greenwood, James. *The Seven Curses of London*. 1869. *The Victorian Dictionary* (website). http://www.victorianlondon.org/publications/seven6.htm.

Hogle, Jerrold E, ed. *The Cambridge Companion to Gothic Fiction*. Cambridge: Cambridge University Press, 2002.

Howard, Jaqueline. *Reading Gothic Fiction: A Bakhtinian Approach*. Oxford: Clarendon Press, 1994.

Humpherys, Anne. "Knowing the Victorian City: Writing and Representation." *Victorian Literature and Culture* (2002): 601–12.

Hyde, Ralph, ed. *The A to Z of Victorian London*. London: London Topographical Society, 1987.

James, Henry. "Review of *Our Mutual Friend*." 1865. In *Charles Dickens*, edited by Jorgen Riber Christensen. CD-ROM. Systime Publishing, 2000.

Jarret, David. "The Fall of the House of Clennam: Gothic Conventions in *Little Dorrit*." *The Dickensian* 73 (1977): 155–61.

Joyce, Simon. *Capital Offenses: Geographies of Class and Crime in Victorian London*. Charlottesville: University of Virginia Press, 2003.

Krasner, James. "Crime and Street Lighting in Jekyll and Hyde." *Perspectives on Jekyll and Hyde* (website). http://mural.uv.es/blasis/crime.html.

Krout, Mary H. *A Looker-On in London*. 1899. *The Victorian Dictionary* (website). http://www.victorianlondon.org/publications2/lookeron-1.htm.

Kucich, John. "Repression and Representation: Dickens's General Economy." In *Charles Dickens*, edited by Steven Connor, 197–210. London: Longman, 1996.

Lehan, Richard. *The City in Literature: An Intellectual and Cultural History*. Berkeley: University of California Press, 1998.

Levy, Amy. "James Thomson: A Minor Poet." In *The Broadview Anthology of Victorian Poetry and Poetic Theory*, edited by Thomas J. Collins and Vivienne J. Rundle, 1358–63. Petersborough, ON: Broadview, 1999.

Lodge, David. *The Art of Fiction*. New York: Viking, 1992.

London, Jack. *The People of the Abyss*. New York: Macmillan, 1903.

Lovecraft, H. P. *Supernatural Horror in Literature*. 1939. New York: Dover, 1973.

Lowndes, Marie Belloc. *The Lodger*. 1913. Chicago: Academy, 1988.

Luckhurst, Roger. "The Contemporary London Gothic and the Limits of the Spectral Turn." *Textual Practice* 16, no. 3 (2002): 527–46.

Machen, Arthur. *The Three Impostors*. 1895. New York: Knopf, 1923.

Mancoff, Debra N., and D. J. Trela, eds. *Victorian Urban Settings: Essays on the Nineteenth-Century City and Its Contexts*. New York: Garland, 1996.

Marsh, Richard. *The Beetle*. 1897. Edited by Julian Wolfreys. Peterborough: Broadview, 2004.

Masson, David. *British Novelists and Their Styles: Being a Critical Sketch of the History of British Prose Fiction*. Boston: Gould and Lincoln, 1859.

Mayhew, Henry. Article on Ballooning in *Illustrated London News*. *The Victorian Dictionary* (website). http://www.victorianlondon.org/entertainment/ballooning.htm.

Mayhew, Henry. *London Labour and the London Poor*. New York: Dover, 1983.

Metz, Nancy Aycock. "*Little Dorrit*'s London: Babylon Revisited." *Victorian Studies* 33, no. 3 (Spring 1990): 465–86.

Mighall, Robert. *A Geography of Victorian Gothic Fiction: Mapping History's Nightmares*. Oxford: Oxford University Press, 1999.

Mogg's New Picture of London and Visitor's Guide to its Sights. 1844. *The Victorian Dictionary* (website). http://www.victorianlondon.org/entertainment/sightseeing.htm.

Moorcock, Michael. "Lost London Writers." In *London Bone*. London: Scribner, 2002.

"More Murders at the East End." *Times* (London), October 1, 1888, 6.

Moretti, Franco. *Atlas of the European Novel, 1800–1900*. London: Verso, 1998.

Nead, Lynda. *Victorian Babylon: People, Streets, and Images in Nineteenth-Century London*. New Haven: Yale University Press, 2000.

Newsome, Robert. "Style of Dickens." In *The Oxford Reader's Companion to Dickens*, edited by Paul Schlicke. Oxford: Oxford University Press, 1994.

Nord, Deborah Epstein. *Walking the Victorian Streets: Women, Representation, and the City*. Ithaca: Cornell University Press, 1995.

Pariossien, David. "Characterization." In *The Oxford Reader's Companion to Dickens,* edited by Paul Schlicke. Oxford: Oxford University Press, 1994.

Poe, Edgar Allan. "The Man of the Crowd." In *Great Works of Edgar Allan Poe,* 240–45. New York: Chatham River Press, 1987.

Porter, Roy. *London: A Social History*. Cambridge, MA: Harvard University Press, 1994.

Pritchard, Allan. "The Urban Gothic of *Bleak House*." *Nineteenth Century Literature* 45, no. 4 (1991): 432–52.

Punter, David, ed. *A Companion to the Gothic*. Oxford: Blackwell, 2000.

Quincey, Thomas de. *Confessions of an English Opium-Eater*. 1821. Edited by Grevel Lindop. Oxford: Oxford University Press, 1985.

Reynolds, G. W. M. *The Mysteries of London*. 1844–56. Edited by Trefor Thomas. Keele, Staffordshire, UK: Keele University Press, 1996.

Rice, Thomas J. "Mapping Complexity in the Fiction of Umberto Eco." *Critique* 44, no. 4 (Summer 2003): 349–68.

Robbins, Ruth, and Julian Wolfreys, eds. *Victorian Gothic: Literary and Cultural Manifestations in the Nineteenth Century*. New York: Palgrave, 2000.

Rumbelow, Donald. *The Complete Jack the Ripper*. London: Penguin, 1988.

Ryder, Stephen P., ed. "Introduction to the Case." *Casebook: Jack the Ripper* (website). http://www.casebook.org/intro.html.

Sala, George Augustus. *London Up to Date*. 1895. *The Victorian Dictionary* (website). http://www.victorianlondon.org/ publications/uptodate-7.htm.

Sala, George Augustus. "Perfidious Patmos." In *Gaslight and Daylight with Some London Scenes They Shine Upon*. London: Chapman & Hall, 1872. Reprinted in *The Victorian Dictionary* (website).http://www.victorianlondon.org/publications2/gaslight-15.htm.

Schlesinger, Max. *Saunterings In and Around London*. 1858. *The Victorian Dictionary* (website). http://www.victorianlondon.org/weather/fog.htm.

Schlicke, Paul. "*Oliver Twist*." In *The Oxford Reader's Companion to Dickens,* 437–41. Oxford: Oxford University Press, 2000.

Schlicke, Paul. "*Our Mutual Friend*." In *The Oxford Reader's Companion to Dickens,* 442–46. Oxford: Oxford University Press, 2000.

Schmitt, Cannon. "The Gothic Romance in the Victorian Period." In *The Blackwell Companion to the Victorian Novel,* edited by Patrick Brantlinger and William Thesing, 302–17. Villston, VT: Blackwell, 2002.

Schwarzbach, F. S. *Dickens and the City*. London: Athlone Press, 1979.

Scoggin, Daniel. "A Speculative Resurrection: Death, Money, and the Vampiric Economy of *Our Mutual Friend*." *Victorian Literature and Culture* (2002): 99–125.

Sedgwick, Eve Kosofsky. "Homophobia, Misogyny, and Capital: The Example of *Our Mutual Friend*." In *Charles Dickens,* edited by Steven Connor, 178–96. London: Longman, 1996.

Sinclair, Catherine. *London Homes: Including The Murder Hole; The Drowning Dragoon; The Priest and the Curate; Lady Mary Pierrepoint; & Frank Vansittart*. London: Richard Bentley, 1853.

Sedgwick, Eve Kosofsky. *The Coherence of Gothic Conventions*. New York: Methuen, 1986.

Stevenson, Robert Louis. *The Strange Case of Dr. Jekyll and Mr. Hyde*. 1886. Edited by Martin A. Danahay. Peterborough: Broadview, 1995.

Stoker, Bram. *Dracula*. 1897. Norton Critical Edition, edited by Nina Auerbach and David J. Skal. New York: Norton, 1997.

"Talk, The: Iain Sinclair Answers Your Questions." *The Guardian,* April 23, 2004. http://talk.guardian.co.uk/WebX?14@175.fP1naprBgOb.0@.685f3e6d/0.

Taylor, W. Cooke. *Notes of a Tour in the Manufacturing Districts of Lancashire*. 1842. Reprints of Economic Classics. New York: Augustus M. Kelley, 1968.

Thesing, William. *The London Muse: Victorian Poetic Responses to the City*. Athens: University of Georgia Press, 1982.

"Thirst for Blood, A." *East London Advertiser*. October 6, 1888. *Casebook: Jack the Ripper* (website). http://casebook.org/press_reports/ east_london_advertiser/ela881006.html#.

Thomas, Trefor. Introduction to *The Mysteries of London,* by G. W. M. Reynolds, edited by Trefor Thomas, vii–xxiv. Keele, Staffordshire, UK: Keele University Press, 1996.

Thomson, James. *The City of Dreadful Night*. In *Broadview Anthology of Victorian Poetry,* edited by Thomas J. Collins and Vivienne J. Rundle, 896–914. Peterborough: Broadview, 1999.

"Vampyre, The." *Punch,* July-December 1847, 134.

Walkowitz, Judith R. *City of Dreadful Delight: Narratives of Sexual Danger in Late-Victorian London*. Women in Culture and Society series. Chicago: University of Chicago Press, 1992.

Walpole, Horace. *The Castle of Otranto*. 1764. New York: Collier Books, 1963.

"Whitechapel Startled by a Fourth Murder." *New York Times,* September 9, 1888. *Casebook: Jack the Ripper* (website). http://www.casebook.org/press_reports/new_york_times/nyt880909.html.

Whitfield, Peter. *London: A Life in Maps*. London: The British Library, 2006.

Wilde, Oscar. *The Picture of Dorian Gray*. 1891. Norton Critical Edition, edited by Donald L. Lawler. New York: Norton, 1988.

Weinreb, Ben, and Christopher Hibbert. *The London Encyclopaedia*. London: Macmillan, 1993.

Wolfreys, Julian. Introduction to *The Beetle,* by Richard Marsh, 1897. Edited by Julian Wolfreys, 9–34. Peterborough: Broadview, 2004.

"Worst Street in London: Where Our Criminals Are Trained." *Daily Mail,* July 16, 1901.

Index

About the Author

Jamieson Ridenhour is associate professor of English at the University of Mary in Bismarck, North Dakota. He is the editor of the Valancourt edition of Sheridan Le Fanu's *Carmilla* and has published essays on Iris Murdoch, Charles Dickens, the Swedish vampire film *Let the Right One In*, and steampunk rapper Professor Elemental. His novel *Barking Mad* was published in 2011.

www.ingramcontent.com/pod-product-compliance
Ingram Content Group UK Ltd.
Pitfield, Milton Keynes, MK11 3LW, UK
UKHW041835180126
467099UK00001B/1

9 780810 887770